Joseph's Life Story

Seeking Justice

Second Edition

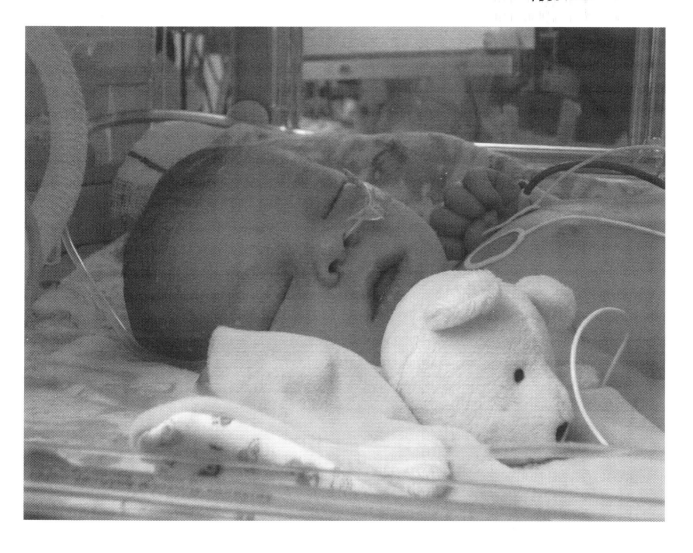

Darren Cunningham

AuthorHouse™ UK Ltd.
500 Avebury Boulevard
Central Milton Keynes, MK9 2BE
www.authorhouse.co.uk
Phone: 08001974150

First published by AuthorHouse 9/29/2011

ISBN: 978-1-4389-7486-6 (sc)

This book is printed on acid-free paper.

authorHOUSE®

Contents

Forward

As the solicitor who represented Darren and Charlotte Cunningham when they sought justice following the death of their son, Joseph, I was very moved to read the account of Joseph's life.

Unfortunately the death of a baby, either during or shortly after birth, is not as uncommon as one would hope. There is no doubt that these are amongst the saddest cases that a solicitor, like myself, will encounter and they require great sensitivity and understanding of the issues confronting the parents.

In the 16 years that I have been in practice I am concerned that so little progress appears to have been made in the way NHS Trusts deal with these incidents. They are rare, but nonetheless procedures should be in place to offer parents an open and honest explanation for what has happened from the outset. All efforts should be geared towards providing an early resolution. The explanation could be given either in person or in writing and the parents should be entitled to have a representative at a meeting and to help decipher the correspondence and documents, whether that is a legal representative or someone from the Patient Advisory Liaison Service, (PALS) or the Independent Advocacy Services (ICAS)

Once the explanation has been given the Trust would be able to offer condolences, an apology and an offer of compensation if appropriate. All of this should happen without the need for long and protracted correspondence, investigation and independent analysis by an outside expert.

I believe that the above procedure could be adopted by Trusts across the country, with a time limit of 3 months from the time the incident occurs until resolution, and this would be a huge benefit firstly to the parents and their feelings about the tragedy leaving them able to complete the grief cycle and move on as best they can and would be a huge saving in cost and time to the NHS.

I very much hope that the publication of this book will help to bring forward the time when cases involving the death of a baby can be dealt with openly, honestly and quickly.

May Joseph rest in peace.

Rosamund Rhodes-Kemp

I took responsibility for this claim at a quite advanced stage, in June 2008. It quickly became apparent to me that Mr Cunningham is a successful and intelligent man, who had suffered deep sorrow over the loss of his little boy.

The NHS Litigation Authority had just admitted liability for negligence and had made the offer to settle the claim. On face value, it was low considering the tragic circumstances of Joseph's death. However, I knew that in fact, it was relatively high considering the legal limits of compensation for fatalities.

It is always a difficult task to explain to the parents of a baby who has died due to negligence that, despite this, the compensation for this type of claim is very limited. I hoped that the admission of liability would show that the NHS were taking responsibility for the negligence that had occurred, but knew that the offer of money would seem low. Their admission also meant that no court hearing would take place to test the evidence on the events leading up to Joseph's death, and I knew that this would be disappointing.

Given the rules on formal offers to settle claims, Mr Cunningham was under pressure to respond to the offer quickly. Having had the claim continue for so long until that time, it was understandably difficult to come to terms with the fact that there was no further scope for continuing with the claim, and that the offer should be accepted.

I arranged for a meeting with an experienced barrister, so that we could discuss the options. It became clear to Mr Cunningham that no benefit would be found in continuing with the claim, and he decided to accept the offer.

I know that he is now looking into other possibilities, to include campaigning on the issue.

Unfortunately, there are many families in a similar position, and it may be that a co-ordinated campaign can lead to changes, both in the law relating to compensation, and also within hospitals to reduce the possibility of tragedies being repeated.

I would like to express my best wishes to Mr Cunningham and his family for the future.

Suzanne Trask

Preface to the Second Edition

The first edition of this book was released on the 10th April 2009 and was available for sale on Amazon.com website and could be ordered direct from the publisher or ordered from all high street book stores. However on the 13th May 2009, the Barking, Havering and Redbridge National Health Trust felt it was necessary to place an injunction on the 1st edition of the book 'Joseph's Life Story' for the publisher not to produce any further copies of the book, to prevent a local newspaper writing a story about the book, and for all copies that had been printed to be destroyed. As a result of the Injunction, an agreement was reached with the author (Darren Cunningham) to allow a revised version to be published providing Darren would comply with the following:

a) Remove, 'black out' or replace with job titles all the names of Barking, Havering and Redbridge National Health Trust staff in the book.

   In order to comply with this request the author had to make over a 100 changes to Text and images removing the names of NHS staff and hopes that the amendments will not affect the reading of the book.

b) Remove a 12 page report written by the Risk Management Midwife that was completed as part of an internal investigation which became the source for an action plan report listing recommendations and actions to improve the staff standards to help prevent injuries that occurred to Joseph occurring to other babies in the future.

   The 12 page report written by the Risk Management Midwife on behalf of the NHS has been removed from the book. To substitute the omission of the Report, the author received permission to include the Action Plan which was the outcome of the 12 page report. The Action plan highlights what the Risk manager found and also goes some way to highlight what was overlooked.

c) Allow the Barking, Havering and Redbridge National Health Trust to review and consent to the revised version of the book 'Josephs life Story' before it went to print.

   The author complied with this request and sent a copy of the revised manuscript for their review. After a number of minor revisions, the changes eventually met the NHS Legal Departments satisfaction.

Introduction

This book is an account complied by the parents of the life of Joseph L Cunningham, a baby boy born on the 22nd December 2006, weighing 8 pounds and measuring 20 inches long. It also includes the struggle to learn the truth of what happened during labour and their effort to seek justice.

The following chapters give the parents account of the events during labour, the days after while Joseph was in hospital until he died 38 days later, the effort to seek an explanation as to why Joseph suffered injuries during birth and to admit liability from the NHS.

The purpose of this document is to raise awareness on the difficulties that can arise during labour and the need for the correct decisions to be taken at the time. This is to also highlight the effort that was required by the grieving parents in order to learn why such a tragedy occurred, what could have been done to prevent it and to have someone admit fault.

All correspondence has been scanned to authenticate their originality and none of the letters documents or e-mails have been altered to change their meaning other than to protect the privacy of the sender and recipient.

Darren's statement – Part one

IN THE   **CLAIM NO.**

QUEEN'S BENCH DIVISION

B E T W E E N :

DARREN CUNNINGHAM

<u>Claimant</u>

-and-

BARKING HAVERING AND REDBRIDGE NHS TRUST

<u>Defendant</u>

FIRST WITNESS STATEMENT OF DARREN CUNNINGHAM

I, Darren Cunningham shall state as follows:

1. I am married to Charlotte Cunningham. Formerly a PA administrator/assistant to the head of operations for a Leukaemia charity.

2. Joseph was our first child. He was a planned pregnancy. We started trying for a baby in September 2005 after my wife came off the pill. She had a positive pregnancy test on 1 April 2006 and she made the appointment with her GP to get it confirmed. The appointment was cancelled because the GP was ill and apparently there was no-one else who could help her. Then there were the Easter holidays and so the next appointment was after the Easter holidays and therefore my wife did not get confirmation that she was pregnant from the GP surgery for several more weeks, when it was confirmed at eight weeks by a midwife.

3. Charlotte was keen to have the first scan – the nucal scan – but the midwife how visited our house on the 3rd June said that there had been a baby boom and so many women were not getting that first scan. This upset my wife a lot because her sister's first baby had died at 20 weeks gestation. My wife had called the antenatal department at King George hospital a week later, explained her circumstances but was refused an appointment and was told she would have to wait until her 20 week scan. We therefore decided to pay for a private scan at Harley Street and the earliest appointment we could get was on the 14th June when my wife was 15 weeks pregnant. It was by then too late to do the nucal scan but we did have a Fetal Wellbeing Scan. The results of the scan that we paid for was very good. The equipment that they use in the private sector is excellent and the scan was very detailed. We were told that all was well and that it was a boy. Rather ironically because my wife had previously complained about the lack of a nucal scan to the NHS she was given an appointment by King George hospital for a wellbeing scan on the NHS in addition to the one we paid for on the 21st June.

4. Everything about the pregnancy was perfect. My wife did not even suffer morning sickness. She was absolutely blooming. At 21 weeks we had a second NHS scan (fetal anomaly scan). We were told at this point that my wife had a low lying placenta and therefore she would be re-scanned before she gave birth to make sure that the placenta had moved and was given another appointment for a 34 week scan on 27th October. Since we were more confident with the results from the Harley Street clinic, we decided to get a second opinion and decided to pay for another private scan on the 11th October at 31 weeks. They said that everything was fine and that the placenta was no longer lying low and that the baby would be at least 8 pounds in weight, so quite large for a first baby.

5. My wife finished work on 17 November 2006. She was not going to go back because she wanted to be a full time mum. The baby, who we had called Joseph, was due to be born on 9 December 2006. We attended the 3 hour antenatal NHS course at King George Hospital on the 11ᵗʰ November which we felt was inadequate and left us with more questions than answers. We prepared for his arrival by going to private antenatal classes on the weekend on the 25ᵗʰ/26ᵗʰ November where we discussed the various options for delivery and the labour.

6. My wife was regularly attending her GP. Unfortunately Joseph was late and in the end the midwife decided to book my wife into King George Hospital for induction of labour on 19 December 2006. Then two weeks before this date my mother-in-law died 7ᵗʰ December. Due to the suddenness of her death and the lack of a cause, a post-mortem had to be carried out and the funeral postponed. She was suffering from bronchopneumonia. She had had a stroke ten years before and had been quite debilitated ever since. She was looked after by my Father-in-law. My in-laws live in North Wales and when my Mother-in-law died, because of the delays due to the post-mortem her funeral was arranged for 19 December 2006. My wife was not going to attend because of her condition and the fact that the baby's birth was imminent. I actually telephoned the labour ward on the morning of the 19ᵗʰ December, explained to the staff what had happened to my Mother-in-Law and if it remained at the 19ᵗʰ of December 2006 my wife would link the baby's birth with the funeral of her Mother and all through the labour she would be thinking about the funeral and how her Father was coping.

I asked if the date for the induction could be changed to the following day and if it was safe to do so. The midwife said that it was no problem and that the induction could take place on 21 December 2006, which co-incidentally was my parents-in-law wedding anniversary.

7.   Interestingly enough on 20 December 2006 I went to my annual evening Christmas do for a couple of hours just to say hello to people and during that day and evening my wife began to experience twinges. They were like contractions. I got back at 11pm but apart from the twinges my wife was well so we retired for the night. However Charlotte could not sleep due to the discomfort and by 1 o'clock in the morning she got up because she was too uncomfortable and left me asleep.

8.   She waited until 4am to wake me and said that the contractions were now regular. Between 4am and 9am Charlotte was wearing her Tens machine and I assisted Charlotte to help her through the contractions. By 9am the contractions were lasting 90 seconds and were taking place every 5 minutes. We decided to go to the hospital and we got a taxi to take us to King George Hospital. The traffic was light and we were there within minutes.

9.   On arrival Charlotte and I was taken to the delivery suite where my wife was examined by the midwife in charge and was told that she was 3cms dilated. She was recorded as being low risk, even though this was her first baby, he was large and he was late. I was also conscious that Charlotte had not slept for 24 hours. I was also tired but she must have been exhausted. We requested for the midwife to read our birthing plan and she confirmed that she understood it and would comply with the plan.

10. Charlotte removed her Tens machine and continued to manage her pain relief with gas and air. A midwife introduced herself and asked to look at our requests in the labour plan. The gas and air was noted and it was noted that my wife wanted a natural birth but that if there was any risk she would consent to a caesarean section. The midwife was very reassuring and said that this was fine and that there were no problems. She carried out the examination and confirmed that my wife was still 3cms dilated.

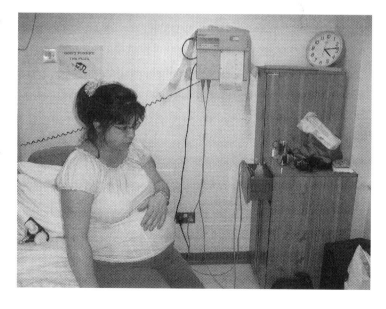

11. Nothing much happened then until a lady came in and did another assessment at about 14h00. She was a midwife but a temp. Her belief was that Charlotte was by now 4cms dilated and it seemed to me that there had been little progress in five hours. We had both been told that progress would be approximately 1cm per hour.

12. During this time Charlotte's contractions slowed down. She did not really think anything of it. She was reading the newspaper. I was recording the contractions and recorded that they were now occurring every 9 minutes instead of 5. At 5pm the midwife suggested that Charlotte went on her back. This was yet another midwife and was the third midwife we had seen since Charlotte was admitted. She said that Charlotte was still 3cms dilated and asked whether Charlotte wanted her waters broken. She explained that if her waters were broken then the contractions would be more painful because Joseph would be bearing down in preparation for delivery. I asked Charlotte if she wanted to sleep because I knew that she had now not slept for 36 hours but she decided not to and that she would be alright.

13. At 17h00 the midwife broke my wife's waters and discoloured water poured out. The midwife told us this was "common for late babies". We were also told that the midwifery staff had brought in a resuscitation trolley and that the paediatric staff had been bleeped so that they were ready for the delivery but these were precautionary measures for safety only. It was explained that Joseph may have difficulty breathing to begin with if he had swallowed or breathed in the water but was in no danger.

14. A CTG was supposed to be in place but it was a joke because it just kept slipping off her tummy.

15. I had in mind what we had been told when we were in the private parenting class. It is like an antenatal group and the midwife there had explained that if the waters were stained it was an indication of fetal distress but not necessarily meaning that the baby was in fact in fetal distress, it was just an indication that it might be. We were also told that this was more common in late babies because they were more likely to have their bowels open when they were being born. Therefore the stained fluid was of slight concern but we had sort of expected it. We assumed that the people looking after Charlotte knew what they were doing.

16. Even though Charlotte's waters were broken and she was on Syntocinon there was little progress between approximately 9am when we got to the hospital and 18h00. Despite Charlotte's waters having been broken, a Syntocinon drip being put up, a late and large baby, she also had Saline via a drip but the lines kept getting blocked – so did the Syntocinon. The lines were flushed during the course of the labour at least a dozen times but never refitted.

17. As far as I can recall, Charlotte was visited by a doctor before her waters were broken. From about 18h00 two doctors, a Southern European who looked like she was in her mid 40s accompanied with a young student who looked of Asian origin and wore a scarf. And an Asian doctor who looked like she was in her mid 30s popped in and out. They would look at the CTG which suggested the need for monitoring and some concern. The Asian doctor insisted that Charlotte lay on her back and to her left hand side and not to take up any other position even though she complained of low back ache. She mentioned this was to allow more oxygen to get to Joseph but offered no other explanation as to why. One of the doctors decided that they wanted to attach a probe to Joseph's head for the purposes of Fetal Scalp Monitoring but there were no leads to the device so for an hour or so they tried to find the right leads for the equipment that they had. The doctor who was Southern European started to demonstrate the procedure to fit the probe to the student but it was obvious that's the student had no previous experience with fitting a probe. I politely asked the student if she had ever attached a fetal scalp monitor before and the student replied 'no'. I thought that I did not want Charlotte being experimented on at this stage so I requested to the doctor if she would fit the probe and she happily agreed to do it. Unfortunately however

she did not get the probe to attach to the scalp and she requested a second probe but apparently there were no more in stock so she said lets carry on using external monitors.

18. The trouble was that the external monitors, i.e. the CTGs were frequently falling off Charlotte's stomach during her contractions so I am not sure that they were really much use at all. This is because underneath the pads which were attached to the leads which were in turn attached to the monitor had jelly underneath them so they were just slipping all over the place.

19. Charlotte was by now trying to rest but I was watching the CTG and I noticed that sometimes it showed a higher fetal heart rate and sometimes a lower one. I had no idea what was an acceptable heartbeat range and was not conscious that this was a cause for concern.

20. The next stage was that the Asian doctor suggested that some blood was obtained from Joseph's scalp to check that he was okay. I was not happy about this at all but eventually I gave in.

21. The Asian doctor discussed the procedure with the student doctor and allowed her to insert a steel cylindrical tube into Charlotte. The student doctor failed to get it into position and after the second attempt the Asian doctor lost patience with the student doctor and took over. Unfortunately the doctor failed to insert the probe after trying two or three times so with the help of a large midwife, they put my wife up into stirrups and inserted the probe. It took ten to fifteen minutes, every attempt was excruciating for Charlotte and as far as I was concerned it was all very barbaric. They took a reasonable amount of blood and sent this off for analysis. The midwife noticed the CTG reading go up and commented, 'that woke him up' and laughed. The steel cylinder was removed and Charlotte's legs were taken out of the stirrups. The Asian doctor then said she would need to take more blood samples in 45 minutes time and I protested against it. The doctor explained it was procedure but said that if the first sample was fine then there would not be any need. We agreed that if there was any concern with the first sample then a second sample would be taken.

22. When we later had the results of the MRI scan, it seemed to show bleeding across Joseph's scalp and there is evidence of several cuts in his scalp but I believe that this was due to the way in which the fetal blood sample was taken and I think unnecessary force was used and it may have caused some of the injuries shown on the scan.

23. About ten minutes later the doctor came back and said that the results were alright. Therefore there did not appear to be anything immediately wrong and no need to take a second sample.

24. By this stage at 22h00 we had another midwife with us. She had been transferred from Old

Church Hospital and had a lot of experience claiming to have delivered babies in the 10s of thousands. She also boasted on the low rate of caesarean births at King George's hospital. In different circumstances I dare say I would have trusted her implicitly but by now I was a bit reluctant to trust anyone.

25.   The Midwifery Sister carried out an internal examination at 22h00 and said that my wife was 7cms dilated.

26.   Then at 23h45 we were told by the Asian doctor that Charlotte was fully dilated and that she was ready to push but we were also advised that the baby was in the wrong position so his shoulders were coming out sideways. I implied that the her earlier decision to prevent Charlotte from not being able to take up other positions and move around had not helped and asked if Charlotte could be allowed to try altering her position to being on all fours to help turn Joseph. The doctor and the midwife had no objections providing monitoring Joseph's heart rate would not be compromised and assisted Charlotte into position.

27.   Charlotte remained on all fours for an hour and was quite anxious and often said 'I want this baby out now'. The Asian doctor returned to the room asked Charlotte to turn back onto her back and examined Charlotte. The doctor confirmed Joseph had still not turned.

28.   Charlotte went on to push for twenty minutes until the doctor returned then confirmed again that Joseph had still not turned and she asked the Midwifery Sister to get my wife to push more.

29.   For the next hour and a half Charlotte pushed whilst lying on her back. The midwife instructed Charlotte to put aside the gas and air to allow her to concentrate on pushing. Charlotte was unhappy about this but did as requested. Charlotte tried her best to push but had no strength left but no-one seemed to notice. They were asking her to push but she had no energy and nor did she always have a contraction to push against. It was awful for her.

30.   Towards the very end the baby's head started crowning and the next second the Midwifery Sister pressed the emergency bleep and a whole team of people came in immediately. There must have been eight of them in the room. Four or Five midwives, three paediatricians and the Asian doctor, so possibly nine.

31.   The events of the next few minutes left me feeling absolutely devastated and I shall never, ever forget what happened.

32.   It seemed to take ages for Joseph's head to crown. The Midwifery Sister told Charlotte that she

had to cut her to help Joseph come out and that during the next contraction she would cut her and that she must continue to push. Charlotte was cut and continued to push, Joseph's head simply popped out and he was stuck. There was no way around it. His head had come out but he could not get his shoulders out. There was no way that he was coming out on his own.

33. At this stage the women in the room started to panic. There really is no other word for it. The Midwifery Sister clamped her hands around Josephs head and pulled very hard. I honestly thought she was going to pull his head off and his neck was stretched. Since this had no effect she told the other midwives assist pushing Joseph.

A midwife got on either side and they slammed down the back of the bed so that my wife was flat on her back and that is why she could not see anything or push. One of the midwives was shrieking at my wife to push and Charlotte was saying that she simply did not have a contraction or the energy but she was told to push anyway because she had to. At this stage I was very concerned for Joseph and encouraged Charlotte to push. Charlotte was not in a position that she could push down from but tried. The Midwifery Sister was now panicking and I will remember for the rest of my life her putting her hands underneath Joseph's chin. She had quite long nails and she pulled so hard that her nails cut into his chin to get his head out. It must have been awful for him. His neck was elongated and at the same time the other two midwives were pushing on Charlotte's abdomen to push the baby out. It was a violent, traumatic delivery and not one that I would want anyone else to have to go through. The Midwifery Sister continued to pull on Joseph while the midwives on each side of Charlotte pushed her abdomen with absolutely full force and they effectively pushed Joseph out. Once he was out there was a sense of relief from the midwives.

34. As Joseph came out there was, what I can only describe as a tidal wave of meconium and blood. In the middle of it all Joseph was there blue and motionless. He was held suspended while the Midwifery Sister cut the cord. A Chinese lady assisted at the resuscitation trolley with an Asian man both in plain clothes. At this stage a white woman also in plain clothes stood by my side and watched over the Midwifery Sister to continue working on my wife. I cannot recall any of them having introduced themselves at this stage.

35. Joseph was born at 2h45 in these awful circumstances. I could read from the clock on the resuscitation trolley that it was five minutes and thirty four seconds after he was born before he took his first breath.

36. I could see the desperate attempts to resuscitate him and the silence from him was deafening. I knew that babies were supposed to cry when they were born. They were supposed to be able to move their arms but whenever anyone lifted Joseph's arm it just fell back down again.

He looked ill. Fortunately Charlotte could not see him but she was aware that something was terribly wrong.

37. I decided to leave the room for a moment to call my mother and give her the news. I very briefly explained that Joseph had been born and at what time but that he was not well and would explain later and headed back to the ward. While returning I heard a baby cry and felt a sense of relief but when I got outside the door to Charlotte's room I realised that the crying was from another room nearby. I was devastated.

38. Moments later a portable incubator arrived and Joseph was taken to the Special Care Baby Unit.

39. To make matters worse the placenta would not come away despite Charlotte receiving the injection to help speed things up after Joseph was delivered. There was a lot of worry about that as well. The Syntocinon drip was re-started to try and expedite the delivery of the placenta. Eventually the placenta was delivered after nearly 2 hours by being pulled out with great force by the Asian doctor in order to avoid having to operate on Charlotte.

40. The Chinese woman returned to inform us that Joseph had experienced oxygen starvation and may have brain damage. She was unable to tell us to what extent and if his injuries were permanent. She would not comment on what his outcome would be.

41. To my mind there were so many warning signs. This was a late and large baby. It was Charlotte's first baby, she is a petite woman with a small shoe size. There was a lack of progress with dilatation taking ages longer than normal. There were signs of meconium and the baby was in a mal condition. Surely someone could have put these pieces together and realised that our baby son needed help getting out.

Charlotte's Birthing Plan

Charlotte had been advised that it was good practice to write a Birthing plan and discuss it with the midwives on arrival. Weeks before the birth Charlotte thought carefully on how she wanted the birth to go and aimed at covering as many appropriate circumstances as she could think of.

Below is a copy of her birthing plan that she typed up and enclosed within her notes. As advised she shared the plan with the midwife in charge and they reviewed it together. The midwife confirmed that the plan was sound and would be followed as best they could. During the labour Charlotte and Darren made a point of each new midwife that took over to also read the plan and confirm the plan was acceptable. The Doctors that attended to Charlotte failed to take the time to read or acknowledge the plan.

The Birth Plan

PREFERRED PLACE OF BIRTH

King George Hospital as it is the nearest hospital to our home and is therefore more convenient for us both as we do not possess a car and will have to travel either via taxi or bus.

WHO WILL BE WITH ME

My husband Darren, who is my primary birthing partner, I may also wish for a friend to be there as well, but Darren will contact them if/when the need may arise.

PAIN RELIEF

We wish the birth to be as natural as possible, I plan to use my TENS machine and use Gas/Air as primary sources of pain relief, together with breathing techniques with the assistance of Darren.

We do not wish to receive Pethidine, as we are concerned regarding the effects that the drug may have on me and Joseph, with slowing down of the labour and problems with successful breast feeding after birth.

We will only wish for an assisted delivery (ventouse/forceps) in the event that Joseph is in distress and delivery needs to be swift.

We will only consider an epidural in the circumstances that a C section is required.

If a C section is required then it must be because there is risk to Joseph and he needs to be delivered quickly.

BIRTH

I wish to be in an upright position using gravity as an aid to delivery. We may wish to see/help Joseph being born after his head has crowned.

I do not want to be cut to assist delivery unless there is a high risk of a serious tears occurring.

If I am unable to offer skin-skin contact immediately after birth then I would like Darren to be able to do this.

At the moment I believe that I wish to receive the injection in order to speed up the delivery of the placenta, but would prefer to make the decision for this directly after birth.

In the event of a "normal" C section I would like to have a running commentary as to what is happening, I would like to see Joseph being born, so for the removal of the screen once he is about to emerge from my abdomen and for skin-skin contact as soon as is practical providing Joseph is ok and does not need medical intervention.

In the event of a crash C section, I would like Darren to be kept informed as much as possible as to the events of the birth and for him to see Joseph as soon as practical, whilst I am in recovery Darren can move between us both. I will want to see him as soon as I am able to and to kept informed.

FEEDING AFTER BIRTH

I wish Joseph and I to try to initiate breast feeding as soon as practically possible after the birth.

In the event of any circumstances happening that are not covered above, we will be happy to listen to the advice of the health care professionals, however we reserve the right to come to an informed decision together, which we believe will meet my needs and the needs of our baby..

MEDICAL INTERVENTION.

All medical intervention and examinations must be explained and consented to before taking place.

Josephs life in photo and Charlottes hospital diary

Day One – December 22nd 2006

Soon after Joseph was born, he was taken out of the delivery room in a portable incubator and taken to the hospitals Special Care Baby Unit to allow the paediatricians to care for him. Two hours later Charlotte was being stitched up by the midwife after a painful struggle to pull out the placenta by the doctor. Once the stitches were in place and Charlotte had been cleaned up, all the doctors and midwives left Darren and Charlotte alone in the delivery room exhausted and confused. Darren was aware that all the signs did not look good at all but tried to keep it together to save panicking Charlotte. Darren believed that Charlotte was quite unaware how serious Joseph's condition was and they waited for an explanation. However Charlotte much later confided to Darren that as she lay there listening to the paediatricians working on her baby boy and hearing just silence instead of the usual cry of a new born she felt so utterly low that she didn't care whether she lived or died because she knew in her heart of hearts that Joseph was desperately poorly and did not expect him to live.

Several minutes passed before an oriental doctor in plain clothes who assisted with Joseph on the resuscitation trolley earlier returned to the room. She explained that Joseph was not well and had suffered from oxygen starvation. When asked if Joseph had suffered brain damage she replied that it was possible and continued to explain the levels of severity which was far too medically technical for either Darren or Charlotte to understand.

Once the doctor left they comforted each other. Charlotte wanted to take a shower so Darren helped her up. Just outside each delivery room was a toilet/shower room. There was no hot water and the basin was still full of vomit from whoever had been ill before Charlotte had arrived at the hospital. Although the midwives were aware of this they had made no attempt to clean it or make arrangements to get it cleaned. Charlotte herself tried to clean the wash basin but without proper cleaning materials was only able to make it slightly more bearable. Once Charlotte had taken a cold shower, Darren pushed her in a wheelchair onto the ward where Joseph was being monitored. They were assured by the doctor supervising that Joseph was doing fine and believed he would make a full recovery and be home within 2 weeks. Darren requested for updates on Joseph's progress every day and was assured this would happen. The notes written that day recorded mentioning to the parents of Joseph's condition and that an EEG (Electroencephalogram is the measurement of electrical activity produced by the brain recorded from electrodes placed on the scalp) would be arranged although neither Darren nor Charlotte could recall the conversation.

A Polaroid picture of Joseph was taken and given to the parents to look upon while they were apart from Joseph, which was greatly appreciated.

Arrangements were then made to transfer Joseph onto the Sister hospital 'The Queens' located in Romford. This was because the facilities Joseph required were not available in King George Hospital. Darren took Charlotte back to the delivery room where the bed had been cleaned and re-made for her to sleep for a few hours before travelling to The Queens Hospital with Joseph. Darren made sure she was comfortable, turned the light out and left the door ajar so she was not left in total darkness. Darren left the hospital, caught a bus back home, and only managed a few steps into the house before breaking down in a flood of tears devastated that his Son was not well and may never come home. As promised he called Charlotte's elder sister and broke the news of what had happened.

Neither Darren nor Charlotte managed to sleep for long and Darren visited Charlotte and Joseph in the Queens Hospital that afternoon. Once Charlotte woke up, she learned that Joseph had already been transferred and she would follow once transport could be arranged. Charlotte remembers the journey there, the patient transfer vehicle had its radio playing and she recalls it playing Christmas songs. The staff and other patients being transferred were in a jovial mood with it being so close to Christmas, but Charlotte remembers crying silently all the way to the hospital. It didn't seem right to her that everyone was so happy and celebrating when her whole world had literally fallen apart.

Once Darren arrived at the post-natal ward where Charlotte was admitted, they were led by one of the midwives to the NICU, (Neonatal Intensive Care Unit) to see Joseph. During the afternoon two plain clothed men came onto the ward. They were pushing a trolley carrying a suitcase and a laptop. The nurse greeted them and directed them to Joseph and the two men commenced to unpack the suitcase containing a vast amount of cables and wires. Darren and Charlotte were asked to leave the ward while the men performed an EEG test to test for brain wave activity. An hour had passed before the test was over and the men had left. Darren stayed with Charlotte at Joseph's side until late into the evening before walking Charlotte back to her room in time for her dinner. After an emotional goodbye Darren left the hospital to catch the bus home.

Day Two – December 23rd 2006

Darren returned to the hospital the following morning, met Charlotte in her room and then walked onto the NICU ward where Joseph was being looked after. By lunch time Charlotte's sister and husband (Louisa and Gareth) had arrived from Southampton to visit. The four of them met at the hospital entrance then went to the hospital cafe for a drink and to allow Charlotte and Darren to explain all that had happened before seeing Joseph. Once cups were empty, they walked to the NICU ward to take a look on Joseph. Darren had brought his camera and took some photos.

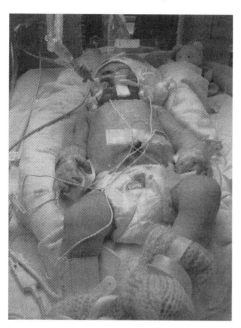 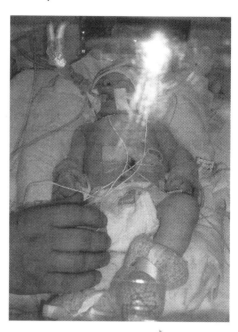

The NICU consultant assigned to watch over Joseph explained that Joseph had not passed water yet and was having trouble controlling his body temperature. He was also heavily sedated and on anti-convulsion medication because he had previously been fitting. The intention was to let him rest and wait for the swelling on his brain to go down. Charlotte was convinced by the assurance being given from the nurses and consultant that Joseph was set to recover and it would only be a matter of time before Charlotte would be taking her baby boy home. Darren was not so convinced knowing that brain damage was destructive and irreversible but chose not to speak out until he learnt more of the facts and to see what would happen over the coming weeks.

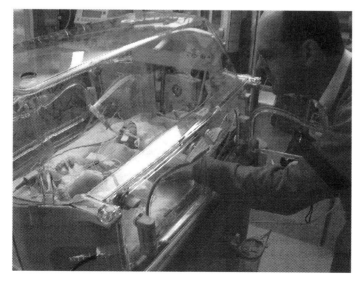

Day Three – December 24th 2006

On arriving at the NICU ward where Joseph was being looked after Darren and Charlotte were met by the NICU consultant who had just finished his morning rounds to give an update on Joseph's progress. There was positive news in that Joseph had passed water and his organs had recovered from the shock of his birth.

Darren asked if Joseph was likely to come off the ventilator soon and was assured that Joseph's progress was being closely monitored and hoped that it would be soon if he continued to improve. This news was well received and was the best Christmas present Darren and Charlotte could have hoped for under the circumstances.

At lunch time Darren got a call from his Mother letting him know that his sisters Heather and Janine were on the train from North Wales to spend Christmas with Darren, Charlotte and Joseph.

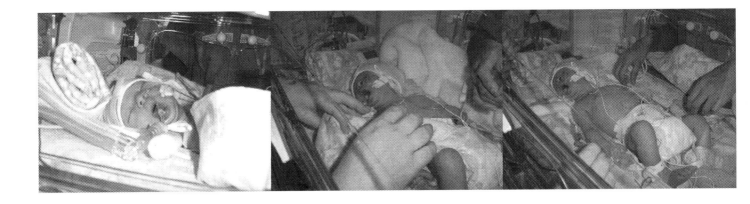

Charlotte was permitted to remain in the hospital in order to have access to visit Joseph over Christmas but was informed that she would have to give up her room come Boxing Day (26th December). Darren made arrangements with a local taxi firm to be able to get to the hospital on Christmas Day, since he did not own a car and the public transport was not running.

As the day came to a close once again Darren left, leaving his son and wife behind in the hospital.

Day Four – December 25th 2006 Christmas Day

Christmas was put on hold this year and was agreed it would be celebrated once Joseph came home no matter how long it would take. Darren was up early and prepared a meal for his sisters to enjoy while they were away from their partners and children. Darren sent a text to Charlotte that read 'Merry xmas my dear wife I will aim to be with you by 1pm'. Charlotte still has the text to this day on her mobile phone.

The taxi arrived at 12:30 as ordered and took Darren, Heather and Janine to the hospital. Heather and Janine were looking forward to meeting their nephew but also uneasy on what to expect after never seeing a baby being looked after in hospital and on a ventilator. When the three of them arrived, they first made their way up to the post-natal ward where Charlotte was on and then onto the NICU ward where Joseph was being looked after.

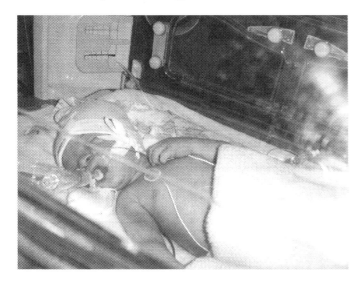 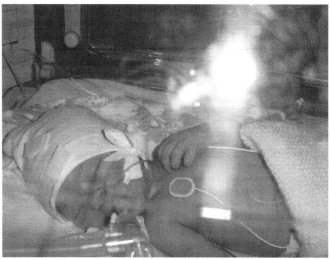

Due to regulations only two adults were permitted on the NICU ward at one time so for most of the day Heather and Janine stayed in the waiting room and took it in turns to pop in and see Joseph often only a few minutes at a time.

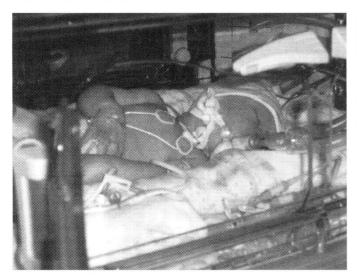 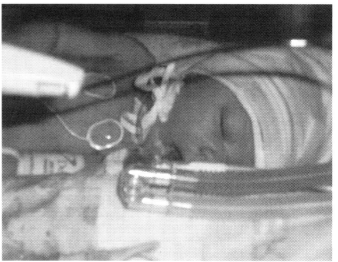

Once Darren and his sisters returned home, the kettle was put on and they reflected over the day and tried to remain positive and hopeful for Joseph's outcome. Even though all were tired no one slept soundly that night. This was not a Christmas day as ever experienced before and would not be quickly forgotten.

Day Five – December 26th 2006 Boxing Day

All were up bright an early and arrived at the hospital while Charlotte was still having breakfast. Once Charlotte had finished eating, all four headed back to NICU to be by Joseph's side. As they arrived at the ward they were met with the consultant and was delighted to be told that Joseph was going to be taken off the ventilator this morning but they would have to stay in the waiting room until he was satisfied that Joseph was stable before they could go into see him.

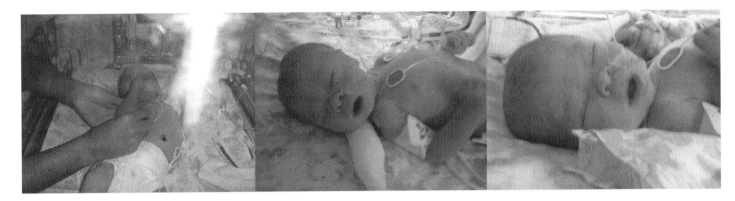

Darren and Charlotte were taken in onto the NICU ward to see Joseph's face unobstructed for the first time. His blood pressure was taken and was satisfactory and was finally breathing unsupported.

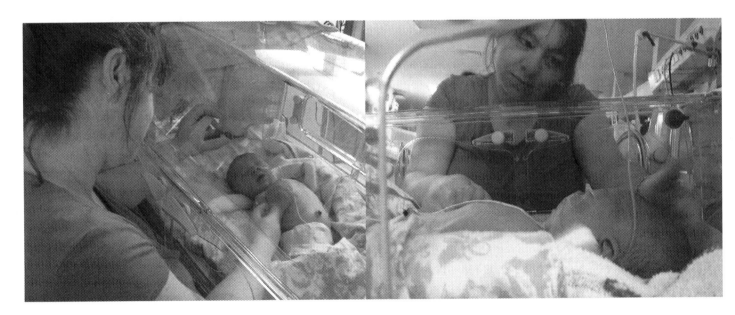

That morning Joseph was closely monitored in case of any relapse. By the afternoon the nurse in charge asked if Charlotte wanted to hold her baby boy for the first time while they changed his bedding. This was a long awaited moment for Charlotte.

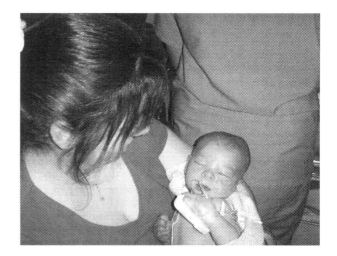
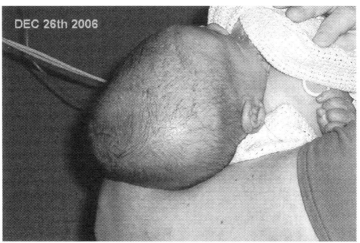

DEC 26th 2006

Darren noticed the cuts on Joseph's head caused by taking a blood sample and discussed this with the nurse and NICU consultant. They felt unable to comment regarding this as they were not present at the birth and such matters were best taken up with the Obstetrician. Darren counted six cuts all, each at least 1 inch long on Joseph's head.

That evening, Charlotte was discharged from the post-natal ward and was relieved that she was able to return home. Thankfully the midwives on the post-natal ward had been sympathetic to Charlotte's plight and had allowed her to have had a private room, meaning that she didn't have to sleep in a bay full of mothers and babies. However despite their consideration, throughout the ward was the unavoidable sounds of newborns and that had been deeply distressing to her. She had spent each night alone, away from the familiar surroundings of her home and her husband, in a strange environment and had cried herself to sleep each night feeling so utterly helpless. In the space of a couple of weeks she had lost her Mum and now it looked like she might also lose her beloved baby boy.

During her short stay other new mums had left the ward and each time Charlotte felt envy and resentment. She had also seen new Fathers come onto the ward carrying empty car seats in order to take their babies home. It didn't seem fair to her that they could be so happy. Couldn't they see the pain that she felt? However, Charlotte reasoned with her emotions that they couldn't possibly understand the pain that she suffered because they simply didn't know.

She was extremely upset to be leaving her baby boy behind as she walked out of the hospital.

Day Six – December 27th 2006

Darren's sisters Janine and Heather got up early and made their way to Euston station to get the next train back to North Wales. They were concerned about Joseph but pleased with his progress and like Darren and Charlotte hoping that it would not be long before Joseph would be well enough to leave hospital. Darren and Charlotte caught the bus at the top of their street and made their way back to the hospital arriving just after the NICU consultants had done their morning ward rounds.

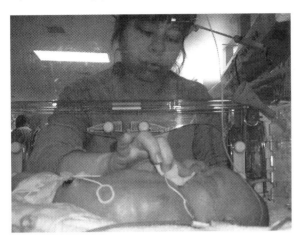 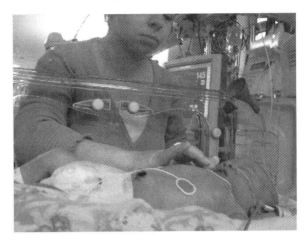

Charlotte was encouraged to clean and change Joseph to help the nurses to look after him and to help Charlotte bond. Once he was clean Charlotte was able to give him another cuddle.

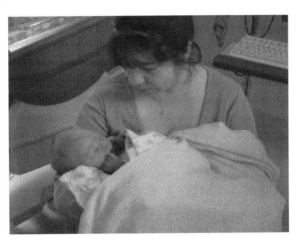 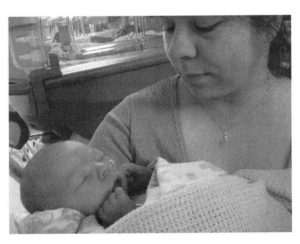

After lunch in the hospital canteen, Darren and Charlotte returned to Joseph's side and Darren got his first cuddle with his new born son.

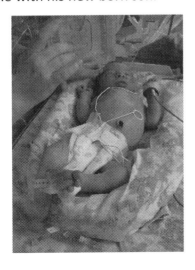 

Day Seven – December 28th 2006

Darren was now worried about Charlotte's state of mind. She was beginning to question the fact that Joseph's condition was due to something she may or may not have done during pregnancy or during the labour and not the fact that the midwives and doctors present at birth failed to take the necessary precautions to prevent such injuries. Darren urged her to speak to someone, a professional, but she was reluctant and Darren didn't feel that he could push her too much.

The NICU consultant explained that in order to understand the severity of Joseph's injuries they needed to perform a second EEG and an MRI scan and since he was now no longer on the ventilator they planned to arrange for the scan in the afternoon.

The EEG was carried out in the morning and by 14:30 a portable incubator arrived on the NICU ward and Joseph was carefully placed inside it. Charlotte accompanied Joseph and the nurse assigned to look after Joseph to the MRI department.

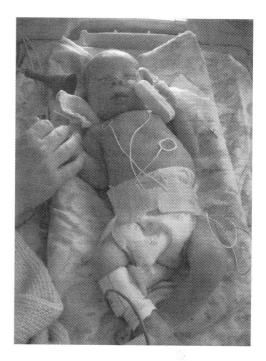

It was close to 2 hours before they returned onto the NICU ward and the NICU consultant gave his assurance that the images were taken successfully but it may be as long as a week before they got the results due to the seasonal holidays and the limited specialists that were available capable to analyse infant MRI brain scans.

The NICU consultant informed Darren and Charlotte that Joseph's medication was being reduced since he was now stable without the ventilator and was expecting him to be conscious once the medication within his system wore off over the next few days.

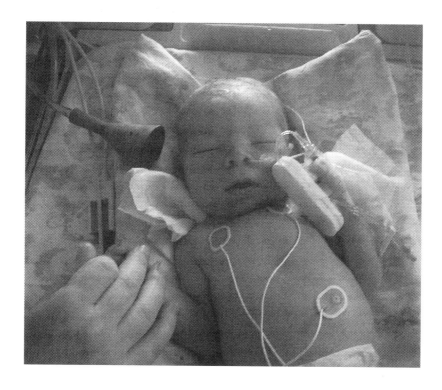

Day Eight – December 29th 2006

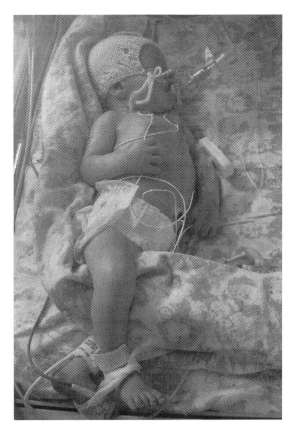

The nurse in charge came to meet Darren and Charlotte as soon as they were let onto the NICU ward via the security door. The nurse explained that Joseph did not have a good night and that he became uncomfortable which affected his breathing. As a means of precaution, the decision was made to put him back on the ventilator and re-administer his medication.

Seeing Joseph back on the ventilator was a heavy blow not only for Darren and Charlotte but also for friends and family who were praying and hoping the best for him.

The results of the EEG taken the week before had been given to the NICU consultant along with the initial analysis of the MRI scan. Unfortunately the consultant was reluctant to give any details or to speculate what the results meant. Darren found the conversation with the consultant worrying and frustrating but did not want to alarm or distress Charlotte so chose not to probe or demand to see the results.

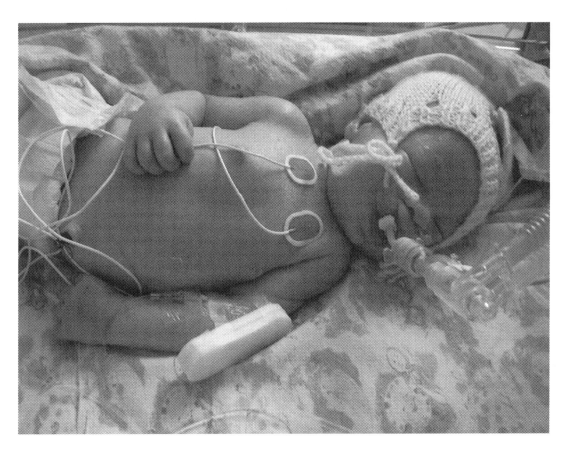

Day Nine – December 30th 2006

Darren and Charlotte had their fingers crossed as they travelled to the hospital hoping to see Joseph off the ventilator again and back on the road to recovery. Once they arrived at his side their hearts sank again. They requested for an update on his progress during the night but apart from the fact he was stable there was no further improvement.

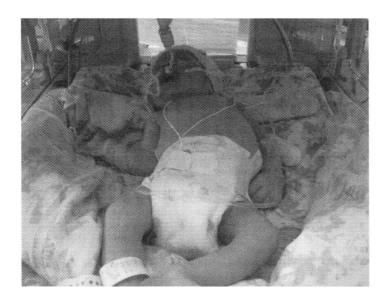

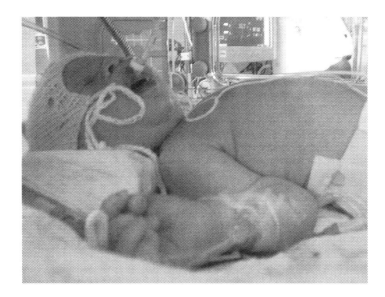

The nurse on duty assigned to look after Joseph mentioned that the NICU consultant was not on the ward today but was expected tomorrow. Darren asked the nurse to pass on a message to the NICU consultant to request for an update on what steps would be taken to help Joseph's condition improve.

Charlotte attended to Joseph's needs keeping him clean and fed until it was time to return home late in the evening.

Day Ten – December 31st 2006

With only one more day of 2006 to go, Darren and Charlotte secretly hoped that 2007 would be a good year and were keen to put 2006 behind them. Knowing that the NICU consultant would be back on the ward today they were eager to ask what was the hospitals next move to help Joseph onto the road to recovery.

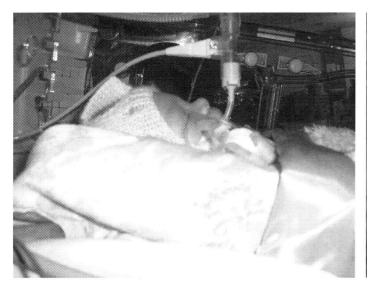 

The update from the consultant was more of a wait and see and trial and error rather than a calculated plan. The unusual decision had been taken to give Joseph another injection of vitamin K of the same dosage he had received soon after birth.

Charlotte had brought in a blue blanket that she had received as a gift for Joseph. Once she had carefully washed, changed and fed him she wrapped him up in his new blue blanket to keep him safe and warm.

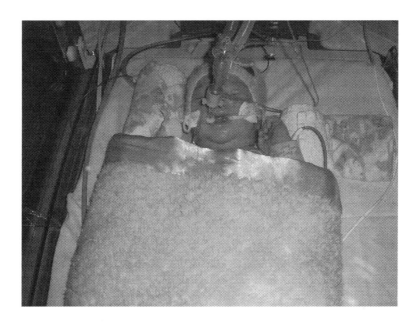

Once again it was dark by the time Darren and Charlotte left the hospital to travel home together.

Day Eleven – January 1st 2007

Today started off very quietly in the Cunningham household even though the TV was celebrating the New Year all over the world as back ground noise during breakfast. As Big Ben rang, the TV replayed the bells to herald in the New Year at Midnight. Charlotte was already taking the Christmas decorations down. To her Christmas was over, she didn't want to be surrounded by festive baubles and tinsel, to see Joseph's Christmas presents still unwrapped under the tree was a stark reminder that they were so far apart from him and completely powerless to help him.

Darren and Charlotte were now practically on auto pilot when it came to getting up and ready to head to the hospital each morning. However today Darren phoned for a taxi and once it arrived they were off to spend another day alongside Joseph.

There was no update or significant progress and Joseph remained stable on the ventilator and seemed to have had a peaceful night.

The nurse noted that Josephs feeds were still every other hour via a NGT (Nasal Gastric Tube) but were now increased from 5 up to 6 Mils per feed of Charlottes expressed milk. Charlotte had always wanted to breast feed from day one but since Joseph was so ill it was not possible. The NICU consultant and nurses had frequently encouraged Charlotte to express milk for Joseph as they believed it was far better for him than manufactured milk.

For the first time since Joseph was in hospital Darren had mistakenly left the camera at home. Joseph did not look any different from the day he had been put back on the ventilator on the 29th December.

Day Twelve – January 2nd 2007

Again without fail Darren and Charlotte made their way to the hospital to spend the day at Joseph's bedside to take care of him as best they could. While Charlotte and Darren stood at his side a Consultant Paediatrician they have not met before came over, he introduced himself and invited them to talk about Joseph in private. Even though the NICU consultant had read the reports, he requested to learn the events of labour especially the details leading up to the deliver and soon after to try and assess the situation. He asked if we smoked, if we were genetically related, suffered any illnesses, were on any medication and a variety of other questions. The NICU consultant admitted that Joseph was not well and when asked he did not think Joseph would die from his injuries, he was concerned that Joseph's injuries may leave him permanently disabled. He confirmed that the MRI scan came back clear but was seeking a second opinion and may have to perform a second MRI scan.

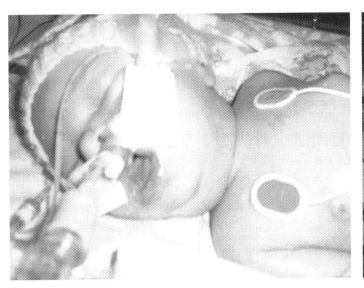 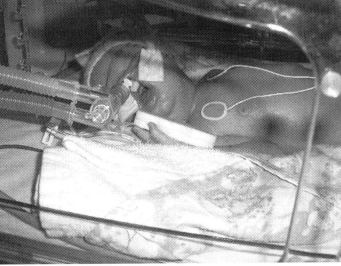

The meeting with the Consultant Paediatrician was not what they wanted to hear and even though it brought Charlotte to tears it gave them hope that one day soon they could be taking Joseph home and no matter how disabled he may turn out to be they would care and love him as best they could.

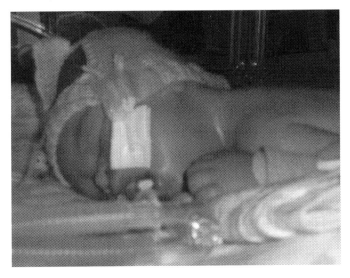

Once the night drew in and it was time to leave, they gave Joseph a kiss good night and left the ward and waited at the main entrance for the taxi to arrive and take them back home.

Day Thirteen – January 3rd 2007

The day at Joseph's side today was uneventful except for the decision to stop administering Clonazepam. The reason given to Darren and Charlotte for wanting to stop the drug was that the NICU consultant wanted Joseph to regain consciousness so they could get a better understanding of his condition. While Joseph was heavily sedated it was too difficult to determine the severity of his condition and the best course of action.

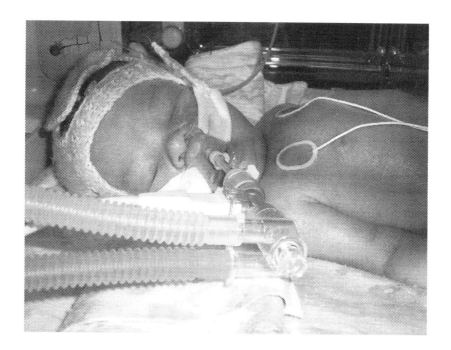

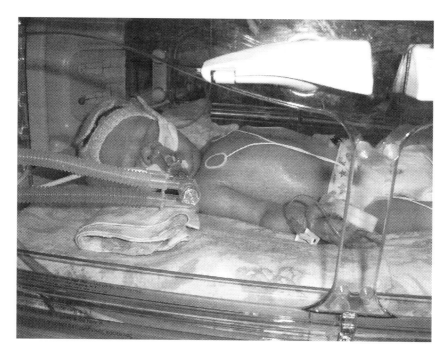

When the day came to an end Darren and Charlotte were eager to return the next day hoping that Joseph would wake for the first time.

Day Fourteen – January 4th 2007

During the night the nurses had increased Joseph's feed to what they called a full feed for his age (10 mils every 2 hours). It was satisfying to learn Joseph was eating and growing well all be it via a tube. During the night he had his bonnet changed from the green bonnet a light blue. What Darren found surprising was that once used the bonnets were thrown away and not washed and re-used. The nurse said that the bonnets were knitted by a local charity group at no cost to the hospital.

Once Joseph was washed and changed by Charlotte she was permitted to give him a cuddle even though he was still on the ventilator, providing she was careful and constantly monitored by the nurse assigned to look after Joseph.

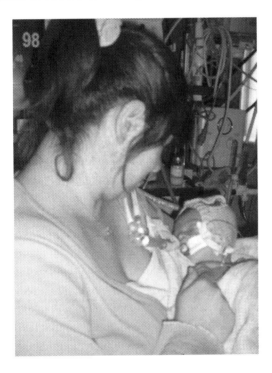
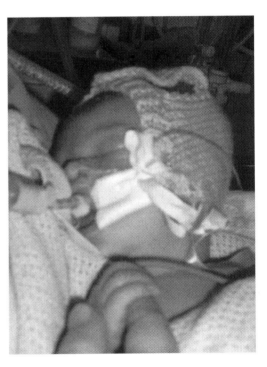

While cuddling Joseph, Charlotte noticed that he had made an attempt to open his eyes, but before a photo could be taken they were closed again. It was now just a matter of time before Joseph would come to and let the world know what colour his eyes were.

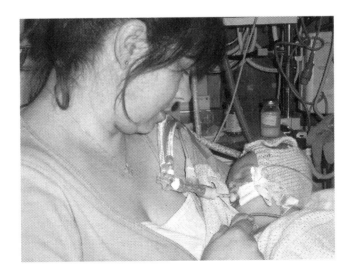

Day Fifteen – January 5th 2007

By the time Darren and Charlotte had arrived back on the NICU ward the NICU consultant had completed his ward round and come to decision that Joseph was again well enough to come off the vent by the afternoon.

At 13:15 the ventilator was removed and much to everyone's relief Joseph was once again breathing unaided. Darren took a picture, a picture that now hangs in their living room.

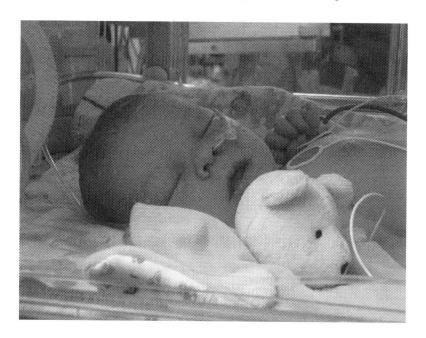

The news that Joseph was once again off the ventilator was well received by all friends and family. Everyone sent their best wishes for Joseph to recover and to be leaving hospital soon.

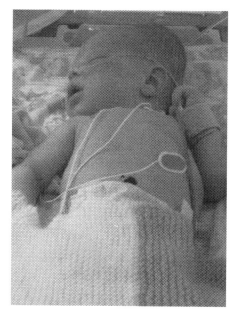

In the evening Darren and Charlotte spoke with the NICU consultant and it was the hospitals view that all were satisfied with Josephs progress and that it was now a case of 'when' rather than 'maybe' Joseph would recover and eventually leave hospital.

Day Sixteen – January 6th 2007

Charlotte decided to start a diary on Joseph's progress to compliment the photos Darren had been taking each day.

Charlotte's Diary: Still off vent, jerking of arms/legs much more alert, eyes open.

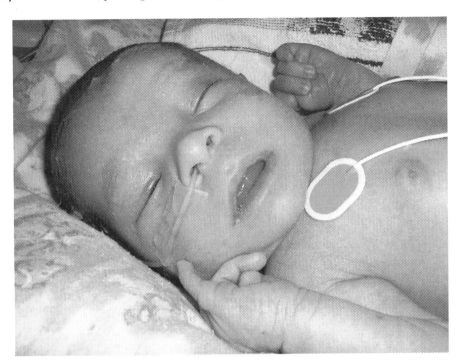

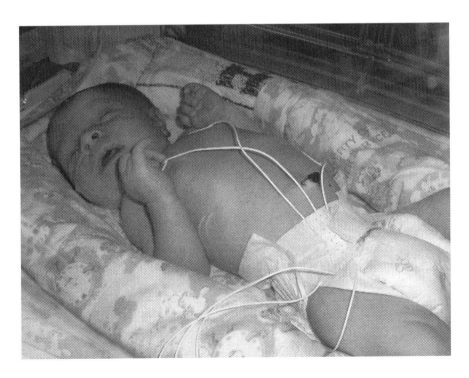

Darren's mother called to say she was travelling down to London from Rhyl. She was looking forward to the opportunity to meet Joseph for the first time and give her grandson a cuddle.

Day Seventeen – January 7th 2007

Charlotte's Diary: All lines have now been removed apart from NGT. Joseph had his first bath today. Feeds are now 2 hourly and are starting to introduce the bottle. Medication is now administered orally.

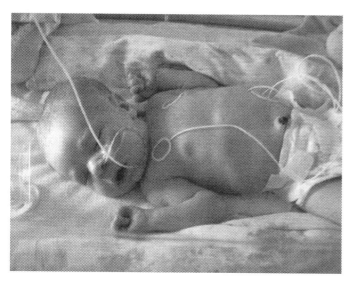 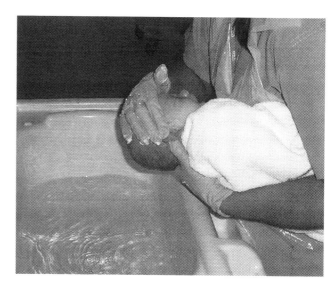

The nurse explained the process of bathing Joseph, brought over a bath mounted on a trolley, filled with water and took Joseph wrapped in a towel. She carefully washed his head and all was well.

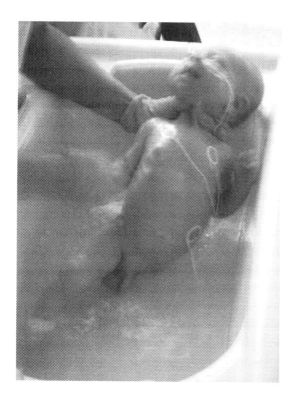 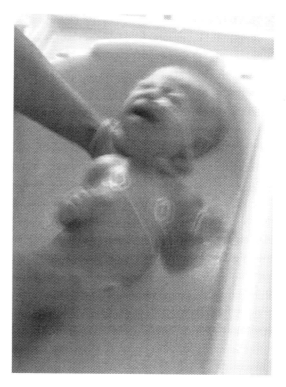

When it came to washing Joseph's body, the parents were concerned in the way he was being held considering his condition and existing head injuries. The nurse supported and washed Joseph by her hand around his throat and once washed, even lifted him out of the bath the same way before wrapping him in a towel.

Once Joseph was dry, he was handed to Charlotte to try and attempt to bottle feed him but unfortunately his ability to suck was not sufficient for him to move onto bottle feeding and to stop feeding by NGT. This was a concern as it would complicate matters about deciding when Joseph could eventually leave hospital with Darren and Charlotte.

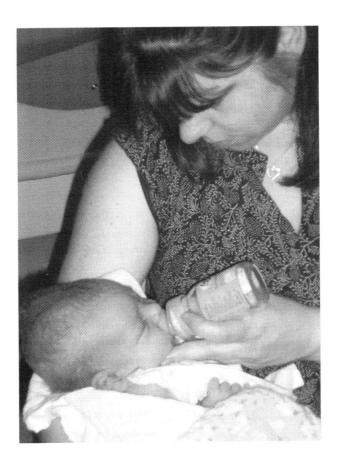

Charlotte gave Joseph a cuddle and smiled as she looked into his eyes before placing him back in his incubator for the night.

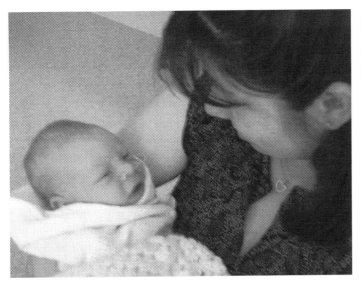
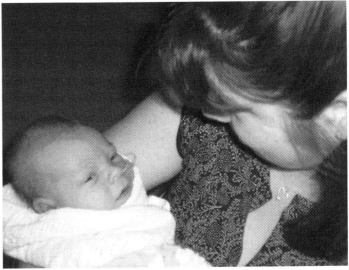

Day Eighteen – January 8th 2007

Charlotte's Diary: Joseph still remains unventilated. His oxygen (O2) stats were slightly low during the night and the nurse on duty decided he required minimal O2 in his incubator. Joseph went for an EMG (ElectroMyoGraphy is a technique for evaluating and recording the activation signal of muscles). in the neurophysiology department. A needle was inserted into the muscle of his right thigh and the muscle tone checked by testing his kicking reflexes. The NICU consultant is waiting for a written report; however the consultant performing the test believes Joseph shows no sign of any muscle wasting disease. Clonazepam still being administered orally.

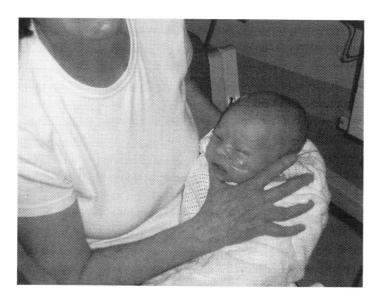

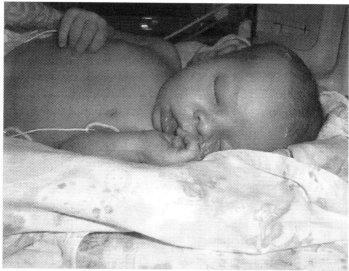

Today it was Grandmothers turn for a cuddle with Joseph and much to her delight he was awake and alert.

The NICU consultant had arranged for an EMG/Nerve Conduction Study to be carried out in the afternoon to assess Joseph. Charlotte was present while the test was done. A test by which an electrode (needle) is inserted into the muscle and the electrical activity is measured. The results of the test proved that there was nothing wrong with Josephs muscle tissue. With the exception of his brain injuries he was physically fine.

Day Nineteen – January 9th 2007

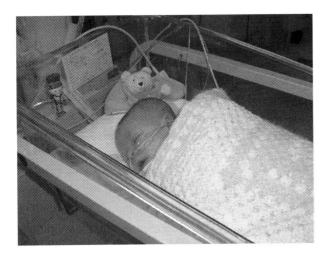

Charlotte's Diary: Joseph was transferred to a cot from his incubator. O2 stats were low briefly so nasal O2 was administered. Joseph is to be referred to a physiotherapist and speech therapist before trying again with bottle feeding. The plan is to stop Clorazepan and record seizure activity. Joseph is still written up for Phenobarbitone and Phenytoyn.

When the parents walked on to the ward to find his incubator empty they initially thought the worst had happened during the night and the staff had failed to contact them. Charlotte asked the nearest nurse and was taken to Joseph where he lay sound asleep in a cot. Both parents were overjoyed.

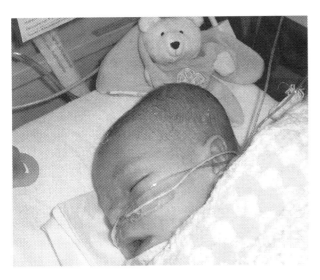

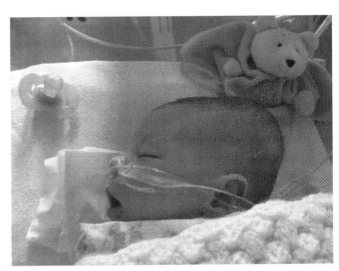

The nurse appointed to watching over Joseph came over to check on him and explained that they were pleased with his progress and felt that he was no longer in need of being in an incubator as he was able to regulate his temperature and no longer needed the ventilator equipment to hand. However it had been noticed during the night that his O2 stats were slightly low so as a precaution he had been given O2 to help him.

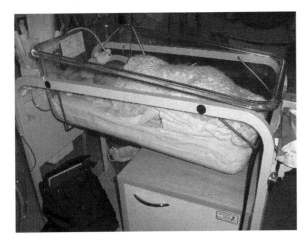

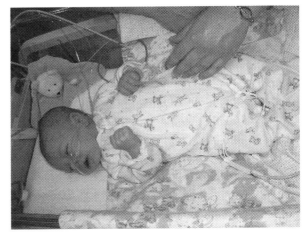

Day Twenty – January 10th 2007

Charlotte's Diary: No significant change. He has had a chest x-ray preformed but no reason given. Was approached regarding hearing test, consent form signed and the test will be performed in due course.

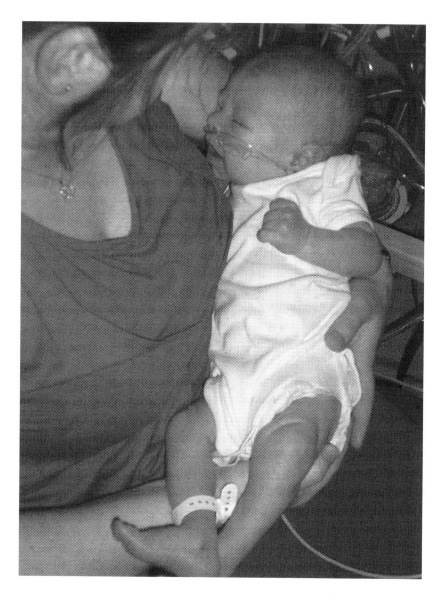

Darren was in high spirits believing that there was real hope that Joseph could be home in time for Charlotte's birthday. Staying on the side of caution Darren kept this thought to himself not wanting to build up Charlottes hopes but he was sure that she was thinking along the same lines.

Joseph continued to receive O2 (0.03 L/F O2) via a nasal prong through the night and day. The nurse had recorded that Joseph was experiencing the occasional jerky movement He also had one episode of a high temperature of 38.5c so was stripped of his clothing which helped bring his temperature back down. His feeds remained the same at 10mils every other hour and no further changes were made to his medication today.

Charlotte continued to be by his side caring to his needs throughout the day and took every opportunity to give him a cuddle when the nurses permitted her to do so.

Day Twenty One – January 11th 2007

Charlotte's Diary: Joseph has been re-commenced on Clorazepan given orally. The chest x-ray performed yesterday showed the results were fine. The reason given for the x-ray is that the hospital likes to check that no milk has been aspirated onto lungs because Joseph is on NGT for feeds. He may be moved onto the lower dependency area shortly and there is the possibility that he may be moved back to King George in order for his Physio and speech therapy appointment to be fulfilled. Hearing test will be performed tomorrow and eye sight may also be done at the same time.

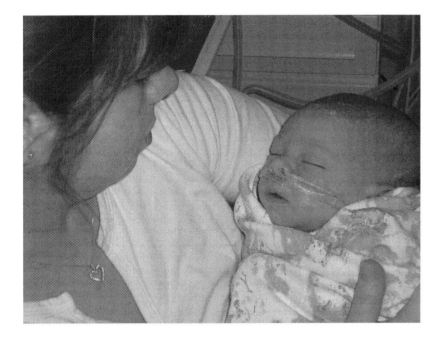 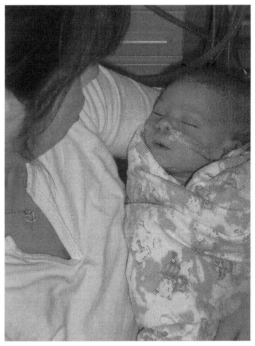

Charlotte had brought Joseph a selection of clothes from home to wear today and decided to change him into his red sleep suit.

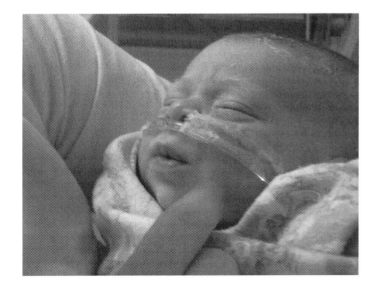 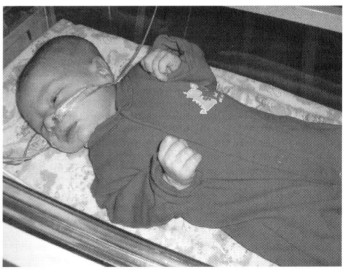

Day Twenty Two – January 12th 2007

Charlotte's Diary: No significant change since yesterday. Joseph was assessed by a physiotherapist who suggested various position changes to prevent Joseph becoming stiff from staying in the same position for too long. Since the physiotherapist was not a neonatal expert, she would speak with specialists to see if anything else needs to be recommended.

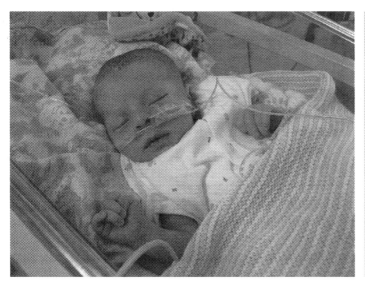 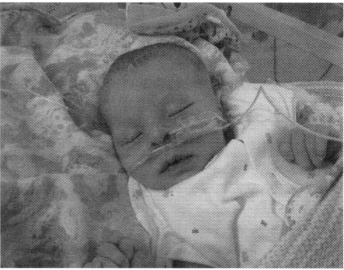

Joseph had a peaceful day and when it came time for the parents to leave, Joseph was made comfortable and given a kiss goodnight.

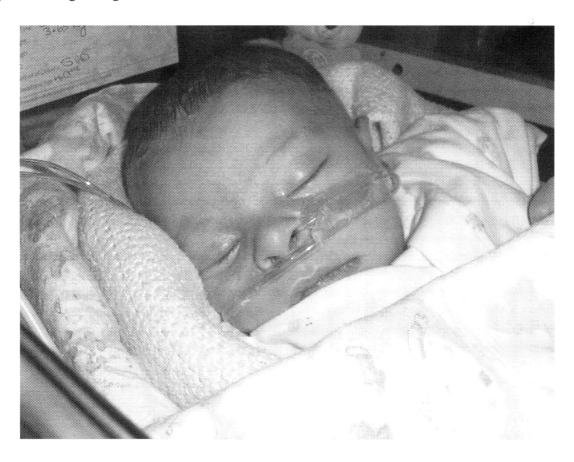

Day Twenty Three – January 13th 2007

Charlotte's Diary: Joseph had a slight rise in temperature, so his baby-gro was removed. It was then noticed that he appeared to be having difficulties breathing – very laboured. Registrar was called to take a look. It was viewed that Joseph may have reflex problems which was thought to be common in babies on some much medication, so Joseph was to be nursed on an incline and not laid flat. It was suggested that the nerves and muscles of the voice box may also be weakened making his breathing sound worse than it is. Having been ventilated for so many days may have also caused complications. An ENT specialist will be called for a consult and a bronchoscopy may be required.

The nappy rash on Joseph's bottom (noticed by the night staff during the previous night) has got worse. Barrier cream has been applied and exposure to air.

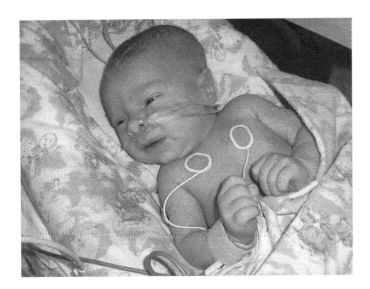 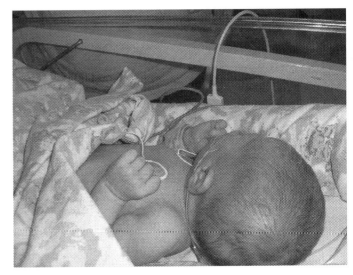

The scars on the back of Joseph's head were healing and not so noticeable any more. The fact that they could still be made out after 22 days was evidence that they had been deep cuts. Darren was concerned that these cuts may have contributed to Joseph's condition and trauma. Only the MRI scan would reveal any clues if this were true or not.

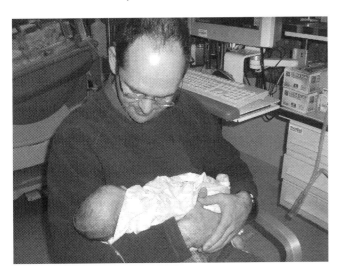 

Darren took the opportunity to give Joseph a cuddle and give his feed before it was once again time to leave Joseph in the care of the night staff.

Day Twenty Four – January 14th 2007

Charlotte's Diary: On arrival Joseph's temperature was still a little high so he was still not wearing any clothes. It was noted on his medical records that he had been given Paracetamol to try and help bring down his temperature. Joseph required a new NGT today and a trainee under supervision passed a new tube. Although it appeared to be sited correctly we have our doubts because when he was having his next feed he brought up a load of milk, went gray, his vital statistics plummeted, he passed out and stopped breathing. Nurses administered 02 via a face mask and aspirated milk from the NGT. Within seconds his colour returned to a more acceptable shade and breathing and heart rate returned to normal. The registrar was bleeped and was at Joseph's bedside very quickly to ascertain what had been going on. He quickly re-assured that everything was now ok and that the plan was to keep a close eye on him, keep his position elevated and the ENT team to be contacted. A new NGT was re-sited by the nurse who supervised the trainee and the remainder of his feed was given without incident, left alone to settle down. After returning from visiting the canteen for a drink, Joseph was much calmer and had a lovely cuddle with Dad and promptly fell asleep in his arms. The remainder of the visit was thankfully uneventful with Joseph showing no ill effects despite the course of the afternoon.

MRI scans are hopefully being sent to GOSH tomorrow to make an assessment by a child specialist.

 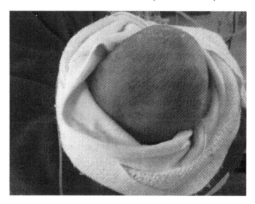

As usual Darren and Charlotte arrived at the hospital in the morning and learnt how Joseph had been during the night. Darren was still concerned about the effects of the blood sample that was taken from Joseph during labour and with Charlottes assistance took a further photo for their records and evidence of his injury to be used to raise questions at a later date. Charlotte left Darren holding Joseph while she went to express milk as Joseph was soon to have his next feed. No sooner had she left when a nurse and trainee nurse came to see Joseph. They checked his notes together and said it was time for Joseph to have his Nasal Gastric Tube (NGT) replaced and this was a standard practice. The nurse asked Darren if it was ok for the trainee to refit the tube while under her supervision. Darren agreed and watched. From the outset it was obvious that the trainee had no idea what to do and was guided by the nurse that grew impatiently in her advice and instructions with every breath. The first two attempts resulted in the tube being coughed up by Joseph and brought up into his mouth. On the third attempt it seemed to be in place. The trainee was having difficulty extracting a sample of fluid from Joseph's stomach in order to test the acidity (PH test) to ensure the tube was in the stomach and not elsewhere such as the lung. The nurse eventually lost her patience with the trainee and took over. The nurse managed to withdraw a small amount of clear fluid, tested it and it failed to register as acidic. The nurse casually said that Joseph had no feed left to digest which is why the test failed but was confident the tube was in place. Darren was not so convinced after having seen the test being done so many times with Joseph before but reluctantly accepted the fact because the nurse was experienced and Joseph was due a feed. Charlotte returned and gave her milk to the nurse to the nurse to place in a syringe. Charlotte was permitted to hold Joseph while he was being fed.

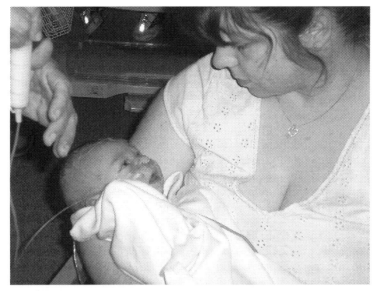

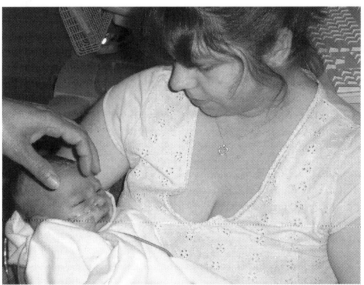

Joseph was given his feed and almost immediately he started to change colour and began to cough up his milk. It was obvious something was wrong and Joseph was not breathing. His colour turned grey and he was motionless and had passed out. The nurse took Joseph from Charlotte and laid him back in the incubator, disconnected his feed and gave him oxygen using a cone over his face. It had little effect and his stats were now dropping rapidly. Darren watched as his heart rate dropped from 90, 75, 60, 50, 40. At this point a second nurse came over and was instructed to get an empty syringe and extract the milk he had been fed. The stats continued to fall 35, 30, 25, 20, 15, 6. At this point the milk had been extracted and Joseph responded instantly. He started to breath, his colour came back, his stats rose and he awoke seconds later. The nurse removed the NGT. By this time the trainee was nearly in tears fearing that it was her fault for putting Joseph's life in danger but Darren knew she was not to blame and assured her she was not at fault. Darren thanked the nurses for their quick thinking which had obviously saved Josephs life but questioned what the cause was. The nurse put it down to Joseph having a fit but Darren openly said that he believed it was due to the NGT being replaced and that it was now positioned in one of Joseph's lungs. The registrar was bleeped to assess the situation and came onto the ward very shortly, within minutes. The event was explained to the registrar who then examined Joseph and then called the parents to a private room and explained to the parents that from now on a close eye would be kept on Joseph when being fed and that he would also be elevated and not left to lie flat from now on.

He would also arrange for an ENT specialist to examine Joseph that could help to understand what could have caused the episode. On returning to Joseph, the NGT had been removed and replaced and had been given the remainder of his feed.

Thankfully the rest of the day was uneventful.

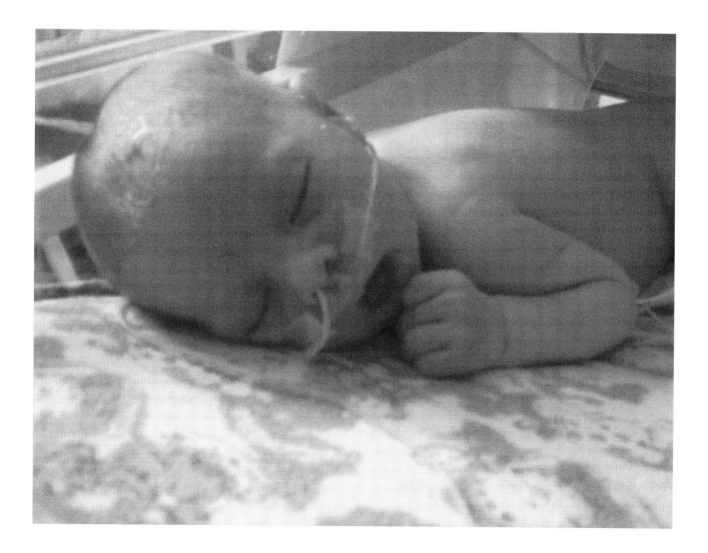

Day Twenty Five – January 15th 2007

Charlotte's Diary: Still showing signs of laboured breathing when in an agitated state. An Asian Consultant Paediatrician contacted GOSH for their opinion and has asked for an ENT specialist to have a look at Joseph ASAP – will hopefully be carried out this week. Had a lovely bath and a change of bed linen – next time mummy will bathe him! Bottom still quite sore but better than previously.

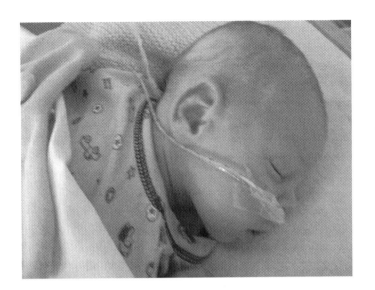
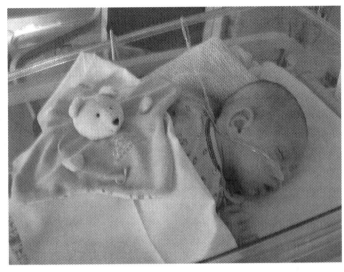
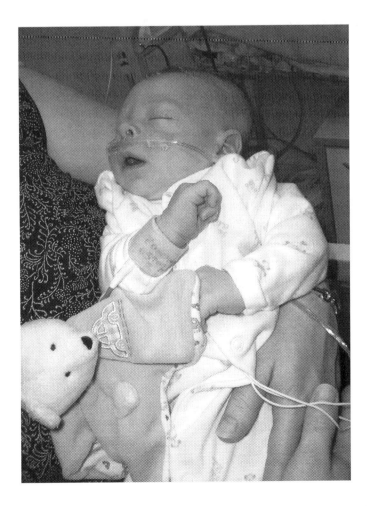
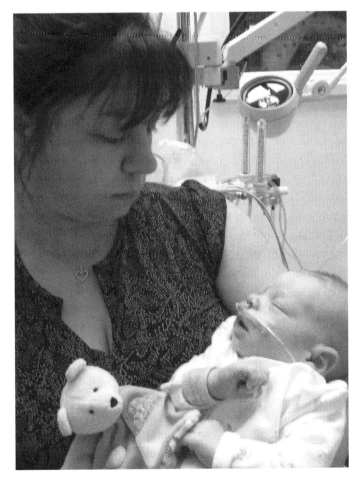

Day Twenty Six – January 16th 2007

Charlotte's Diary: Promoted yet again – Joseph has been moved back to the nursery. NGT feeds lowered from 52mils down to 49mils, reason being previously miscalculated on the wrong amount. Joseph is now on the correct amount for his weight. Asked regarding his hearing test, audiologist had been but it was too noisy for the test to be completed, they will come again. His bottom is looking extremely better now.

Joseph had a funny turn after 7pm feed, 02 statistics fell, he required more oxygen and had some milk removed then Joseph quickly recovered.

Telephoned at 22:30 and was informed that Joseph was more settled and had no further episodes.

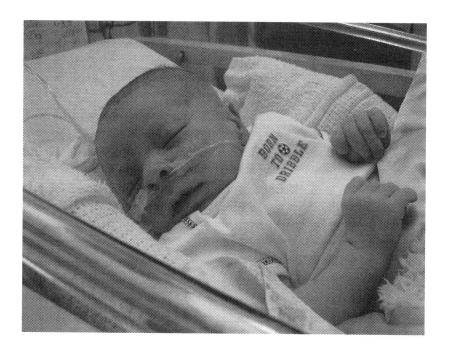

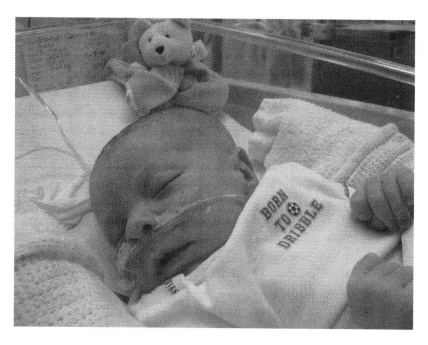

Day Twenty Seven – January 17th 2007

Charlotte's Diary: Telephoned first thing in the morning and learnt that Joseph has a high temp and had been commenced on a broad spectrum of anti-biotics even though he shows no sign of a bacterial infection. An x-ray had been taken due to the event on the 14th Jan and was reported as clear and showing no signs of milk. A new NGT passed. Met with the Asian Consultant Paediatrician, the MRI scan is at GOSH and has been seen by one consultant and awaiting a second opinion. Blood tests etc are still waiting to come back for signs of infection. Appointment at GOSH regarding Joseph's throat issues are not classed as urgent, so not considered a priority at present. Both to see the Asian Consultant Paediatrician again on Friday as Darren is unavailable to see him today because he is now back in work. Mum to see the Clinical Psychologist next Wednesday at 14:00.

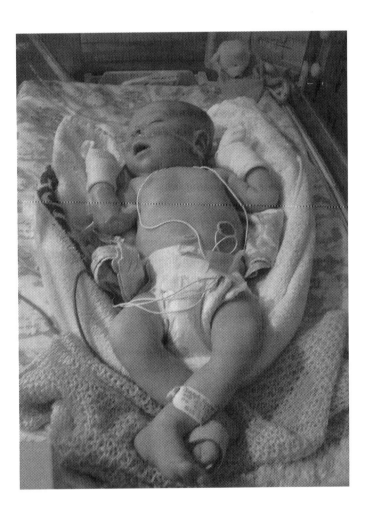
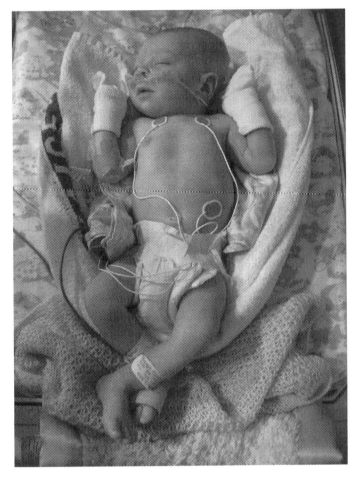

Day Twenty Eight – January 18th 2007

Charlotte's Diary: Still suffering from an infection, temperature had been as high as 39c, but has steadily been coming down. Paracetamol was given and sponging at regular intervals. Sister in charge believes that the appointment at GOSH will be next Thursday, so will require transferring the day before.

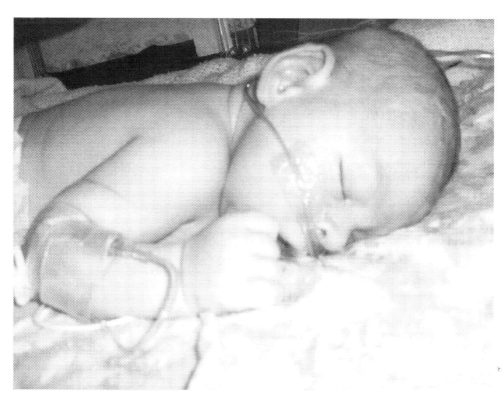

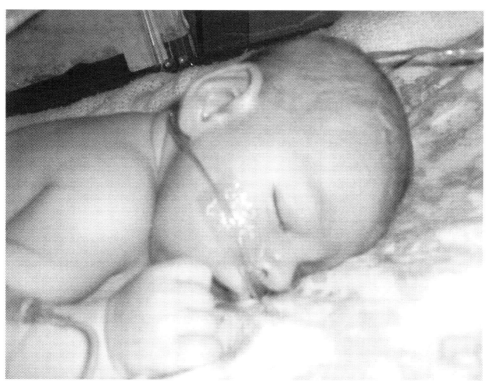

Day Twenty Nine – January 19th 2007

Charlotte's Diary: Had a meeting today with the Asian Consultant Paediatrician. The plan is to send Joseph to GOSH possibly earlier than previously thought; still awaiting results of MRI, reduction of anti-convulsants Joseph will require long term after care, physiotherapy, speech and language therapy etc. Tremors may lessen as he gets older and he may possibly be prescribed a mild sedative to aid muscle relaxation. Nasal secretions sent off to the lab to ascertain if infection is viral or bacterial, but still commences on antibiotics in case of bacterial infection. A routine blood sample was taken. He has also been prescribed an anti-reflex drug to help guard against aspiration. They may also wish to perform a spinal tap to rule out meningitis. Hearing test will hopefully be performed on Sunday.

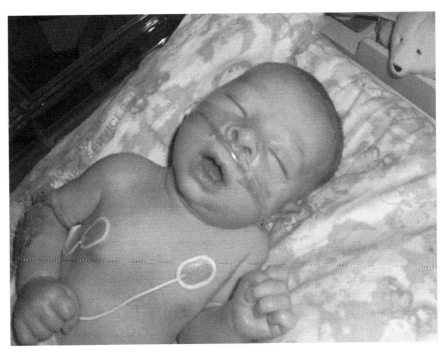

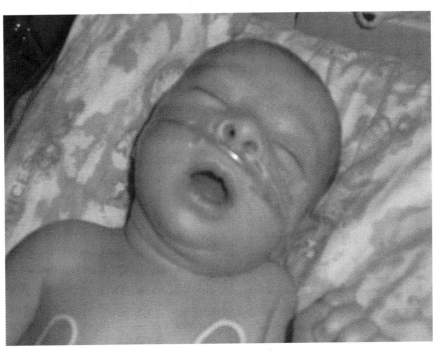

Day Thirty – January 20th 2007

Charlotte's Diary: Temperature high again during the night, Paracetamol given and tepid sponging applied. Temperature came down again during the afternoon to normal limits. Repeat blood cultures taken again to check if a bacterial infection is present. Joseph slept a great deal this afternoon, physiotherapy to arms and legs performed which Joseph seemed to enjoy and was very alert when awake. He remained quite calm and no evidence of strider despite being awake – a very good day for everyone!

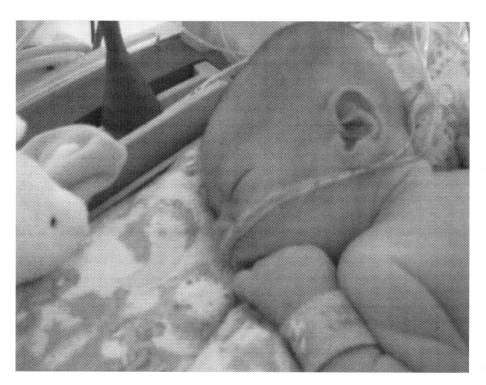

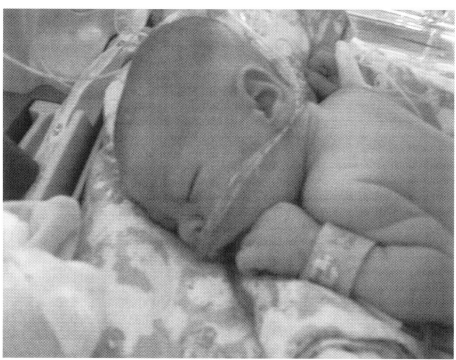

Day Thirty One – January 21st 2007

Charlotte's Diary: Not as good a day as yesterday, temperature still remains quite high and continues to fluctuate. Chest x-ray performed again and secretions increased – needing suctioning at times. Josephs 02 statistics are fluctuating when being administered to and requires high flow of 02. Doctors feel that he is tired and needs additional help so the plan is to ventilate him again until he is stronger.

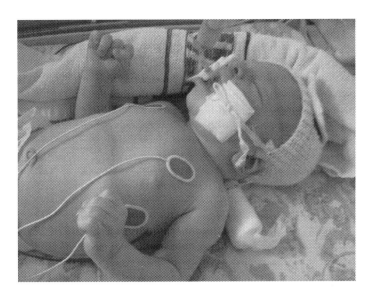 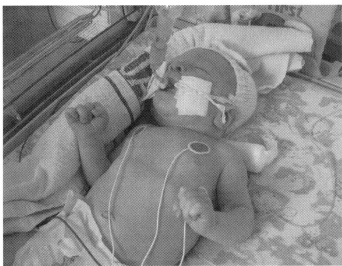

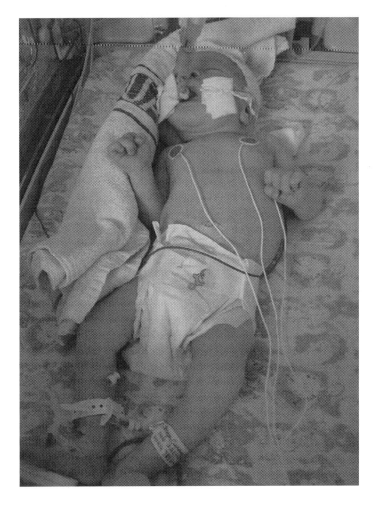

Day Thirty Two – January 22nd 2007

Charlotte's Diary: Still ventilated but appears more aware of surroundings than yesterday. Has required a blood transfusion today – 60 mils in total as haemoglobin levels have been quite low. Blood gases interestingly remain ok, temperature still fluctuating though. Secretions are quite yellow indicating that he may have an infection although all tests so far don't highlight anything in particular.

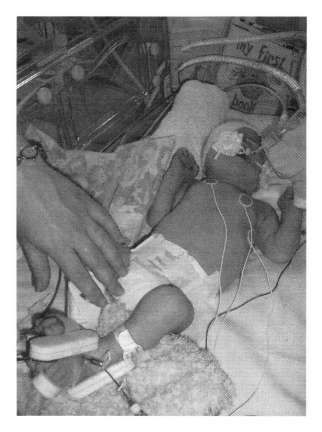

Today was Charlotte's birthday, she was thirty two. Darren managed to convince her to spend the day at a health spa to try and unwind a little. They enjoyed the use of a pool then had treatments. Charlotte had a facial and manicure while Darren had a massage. Although they both enjoyed the day they were missing Joseph and both eager to return to the hospital that evening to learn of his progress.

They arrived to see Joseph receiving a blood transfusion and were immediately concerned. The nurse calmly explained that the decision was due to the fact that his haemoglobin levels had been quite low and this can be the case for some babies when they have frequent blood samples taken from them.

Charlotte did all that she could to make Joseph as comfortable as she could but seeing Joseph as he was, was not the birthday present she had hoped for. She longed to be able to take her baby boy home.

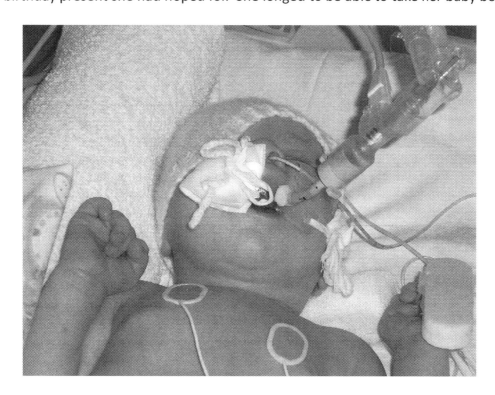

Day Thirty Three – January 23rd 2007

Charlotte's Diary: No significant changes as such, Joseph continues to be on the ventilator. No need for an additional transfusion today which is good. Urine and nasal secretions were taken and sent for analysis. Quite possible that Joseph may have a chest infection, he has been quite peaceful today – still continues on morphine infusion.

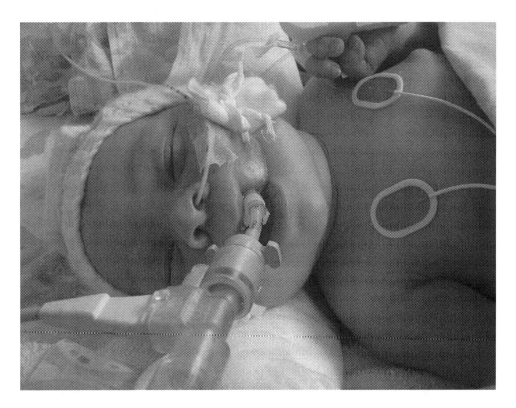

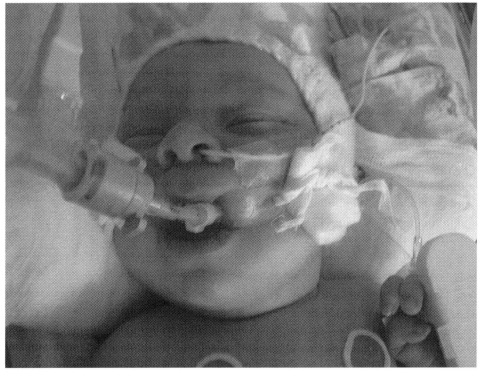

Day Thirty Four – January 24th 2007

Charlotte's Diary: Usual day spent at the hospital – Joseph was restless at times trying to remove tube but had periods of rest. His temperature remains normal and the plan is to transfer him to GOSH (Great Ormond Street Hospital) around 2pm if all goes to plan.

I saw the Clinical Psychologist this afternoon, I was initially reluctant to see her but I must admit that after speaking with her I did feel a little better. I was of the opinion that there was no point in talking to anyone professional, what difference would it make? We spoke at length, well mainly she asked the usual appropriate leading questions and I just prattled on and on once I got going. I spoke about my feelings of guilt and the fact that it must have been something that I did wrong that had caused Joseph to be in the current state that he was in, my theory being that millions of women have given birth to happy and healthy babies, so why shouldn't I have been able to have done the same? I also spoke about my underlying fear that Darren must blame me for what had happened to Joseph; and she has encouraged me to talk to him about my fears. I perhaps will once I have the courage to learn his answer, I don't think I'm emotionally strong enough yet, what will I do if he says yes? The nursing staff was aware that I had recently lost Mum and they must have informed her of this since I didn't bring the subject up. She encouraged me to talk about her and the additional strain that losing her had on me and the fact that I had probably not had chance to grieve for her before what with everything that had happened since Joseph's delivery.

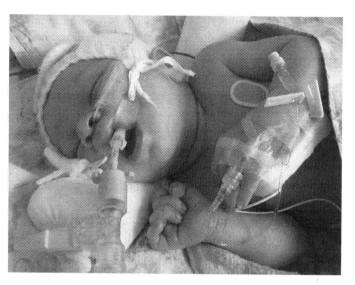

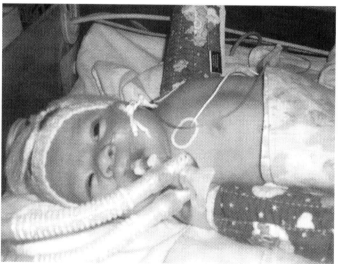

The transport team arrived at 5pm; there is a dextrose drip in situ as he needs to be NBM (Nil by Mouth) from 4pm to prevent aspiration during the journey across London. New cannula inserted as his previous line kept occluding. Joseph was placed in a portable ventilator and we all set off for GOSH around 6pm. I had planned to stay until Joseph left and then follow on the underground, but once the transport team learned that I didn't have my own transport, they very kindly offered me a lift providing I didn't interfere in any way if they had to stop for any reason. I was surprised by the fact that the blue lights were on all the way which made the journey that much quicker, but they explained that it was normal procedure with intensive care babies to get to their destination at speed.

Arrived at GOSH and transferred onto the NICU ward (Dolphin). Routine blood samples were taken. Arrangements made to meet with the ENT consultant at 8am to discuss the procedure and sign the consent form and once a theatre slot is free, Joseph will go down and have the bronchoscopy performed.

Day Thirty Five – January 25th 2007

Charlotte's Diary: The ENT consultant, anaesthetist, and physiotherapist have all been and seen Joseph in the morning. Joseph will go to theatre around midday. Joseph was taken down to theatre at about 12:35 and was back on the ward roughly an hour later. The consultant had nothing to report, Joseph's throat is absolutely fine, so has been extubated and was on an oxygen mask to begin with, but then saturated well for the rest of the afternoon with no additional aid. Joseph has been seen by the physiotherapist and gave him bandages to hold to prevent his hands from getting sore because he keeps clenching his fists. Hourly feeds have re-commenced. Since he no longer requires ventilation, he will be transferred to an ordinary paediatric ward – probably the parrot ward, and will be moved in the morning once a bed becomes free. It may be possible to sit in on a meeting with neurology dept and family liaison team to discuss future plans. Had a lovely cuddle with him for most of the evening.

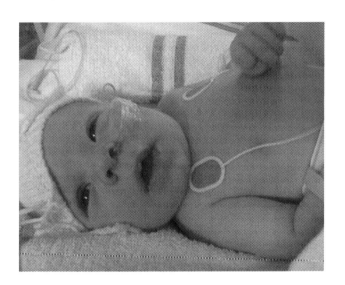
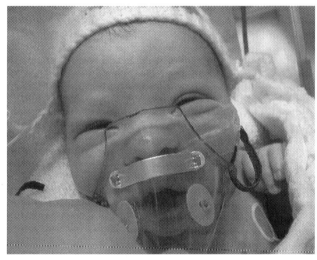
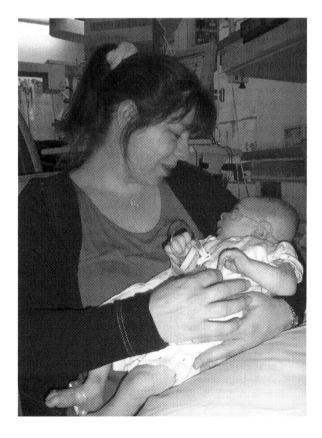
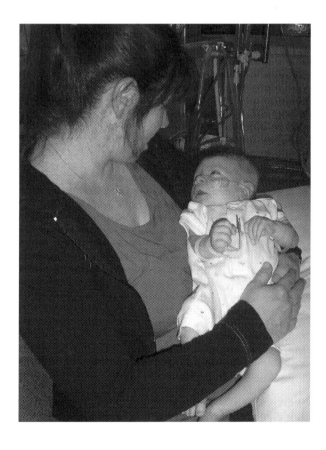

Day Thirty Six – January 26th 2007

Charlotte's Diary: Had a bit of a sleepless night, stats did drop on a couple of occasions and nasal 02 in situ to keep them maintained. Noticed about 8am that the chest recession issue has started again and stats dropped accordingly. Whilst waiting to see if he needed to be re-ventilated a nasal prong was inserted to see if any nasal blockages were the cause. At ward round it was decided to put Joseph back on the ventilator (nasal one this time) as they could not allow his sat levels to drop any further. The doctors plan to repeat the EEG today, x-ray this morning is clear. Around 12 noon Linda and Monica arrived to see our little man. Due to the strict visiting policy at Queen's hospital friends are not allowed, only family. So once we knew when he was going to be at GOSH, I invited them to come and see him as I knew they were desperate to see him in the flesh. About 1pm we were taken to a side room where unfortunately we were informed that the area of the brain that controls breathing had been irreparably damaged during delivery. We were informed that there was nothing that could be done and that once the ventilator is switched

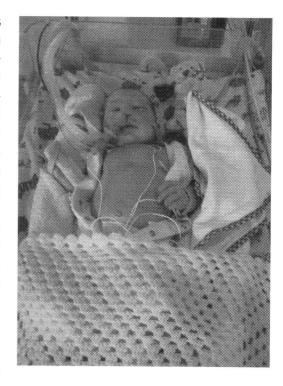

off – he would die. Obviously devastated by this heart breaking news, we informed Linda and Monica first simply because they happened to be there with us in the hospital, families were also informed. The GOSH family service team intervened and helped us in deciding where we would like Joseph to be extubated and what arrangements/details we would like to initiate.

We had the choice of staying in the hospital, transferring him to a hospice or to take him home. I couldn't bear the thought of taking him home knowing that he would never grow up there. I decided against the hospice simply because I had seen at first hand the lengths it took to transfer him would mean, so we decided to stay in the hospital. The staff very kindly offered us the use of a private room which we gratefully accepted. We have decided that we would very much like for Joseph to be baptised so a Chaplin was requested to visit also wanted keepsakes of hair, foot and hand prints, so we will do that in the morning. Chaplin visited and outlined the service which sounds simple but exactly what we would like and to tell the staff when we would like service to take place, it will be either James or Dorothy depending on who is on call. Both sides of the family invited down to see Joseph, but only Nanny Boo (Carolyne, Darren's mother) and Daniel (Darren's Son) will travel as everyone is too upset – they will remember him as he is.

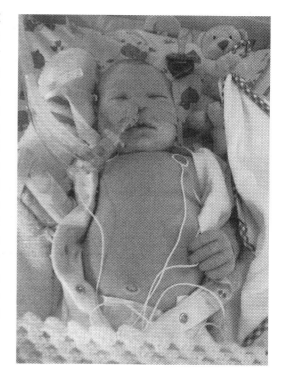

Darren had stayed overnight with Charlotte in the accommodation rooms across the road from the hospital provided by GOSH. They were both up and dressed early and headed over to look in on Joseph. He was asleep and had been given oxygen during the night to help keep his oxygen saturation levels at an acceptable level. By 7:30 Darren had planned to make his way to work and then onto Rhyl in the evening to see his daughter Rachael. It had been her 16th birthday only a few days ago and he wanted to spend the weekend with her, returning to London on the Sunday to be back with Joseph. Darren decided to join Charlotte for breakfast and then head to the tube station so as not to be late for work. At 8:00 they had quickly finished breakfast and Darren decided to pop in and give Joseph just one more kiss since it would be a few days before he would see him again.

They got to Josephs bed side and noticed that Joseph was restless; the nurse was tickling his feet to try and stimulate him to breath and help raise his oxygen saturation levels up. It seemed that disturbing him while he was asleep seemed to make matters worse. Darren recognised the exaggerated breaths and asked the nurse to open his sleep suit to look at his chest and sure enough with every breath his chest was sinking in deep. Within moments his levels started to drop so the oxygen was turned up even more. His airways were checked and confirmed as all clear. When the consultant was updated of the latest event the decision was taken to put him back on a ventilator.

Darren called the office and notified his manager that Joseph was not well and that he would not be in the office today. For the rest of the morning the parents remained by Joseph's bed side helplessly watching on. By lunch time Charlotte's manageress Linda from her previous job arrived to visit with her sister Monica. Shortly after they had arrived, Darren and Charlotte were led into a private room by a tall female doctor with long blond hair accompanied by a family liaison officer to be briefed on Joseph's condition. Darren and Charlotte were invited to take a seat and once seated the doctor placed her chair directly facing Charlotte. Without any signs of emotion she explained the damage that had been caused due to oxygen starvation during Joseph's birth. It was the hospitals conclusion that the damage was preventing Joseph to reliably control his breathing which is why he had needed to spend so much of his time on a ventilator, and when off the ventilator would struggle to maintain his oxygen levels. The damage to his brain was irreparable and inoperable; there was nothing they could do. Coldly the doctor looked at Charlotte and said 'Joseph is going to die'. Darren and Charlotte were stunned into silence. She repeated 'Joseph is going to die' and once again 'Joseph is going to Die'. On the third time Charlotte broke down and was inconsolable, it was obvious this is the reaction the doctor was seeking. Darren was outraged by the doctor's 'bedside manner' and asked her to leave. He also looked at the family liaison officer as if disappointed in her lack of support. The family liaison officer decided to leave the room while Darren and Charlotte came to terms with what they had been told.

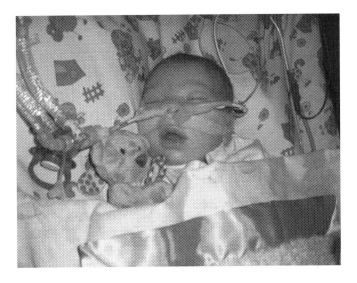

Linda and Monica were the first to learn of Joseph's fate and were also very upset. While they sat together in the room hours passed by for Darren and Charlotte as both found it very difficult to come to terms that Joseph would not be coming home with them. The family liaison officer eventually returned and was very sorry about Joseph's outcome and offered her support. The rest of the day was spent making decisions and notifying family and friends.

Day Thirty Seven – January 27th 2007

Charlotte's Diary: Awake extremely early unable to sleep, decided on some of the details we would like for when we need to prepare for his committal. It seems strange to be arranging these things while he is still with us, but I know that making decisions afterwards will be too difficult. We went into the city to buy a video camera, so that we may record the baptism. Returned and gave Joseph a nice wash before changing him into a little blue suit for his baptism.

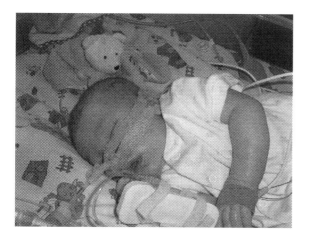 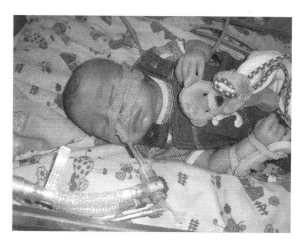

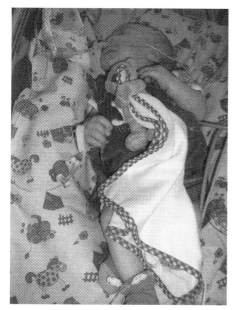

Prior to this, we had taken hand and foot prints as well as hair clippings. The baptism then took place which was understandably very moving and emotional – Dorothy's words were comforting and extremely appropriate. We were given a candle and a certificate of Holy Baptism and informed that Joseph's name will be entered into GOSH's book of Baptism.

Darren then left to collect family from Euston railway station. Visited by Carolyne, Daniel, Wayne, Teresa and Leon, others wanted to come down but were unable to due to work commitments or emotionally unable. As 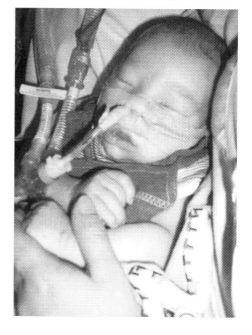 we were in a private room and due to the severity of Joseph's condition the usual two to a bed rule was ignored and everyone was invited to be at his bedside. Carolyne and Daniel are going to stay for a few days, but everyone else was only here for the day. In the evening Darren took his mum and Daniel back to our house and left me with my side of the family. Even though it was in sad circumstances that they were present it was good to see them and for a few minutes I quite forgot the reason that they were there, which was to say goodbye to Joseph. Around 18:50 they also had to leave in order to catch the train back to Rhyl, they had stayed for as long as they could for which I was extremely grateful for.

Once Darren had got back we left to get something to eat and with the help of alcohol, Nytol and sheer exhaustion we managed to sleep properly for the first time in days.

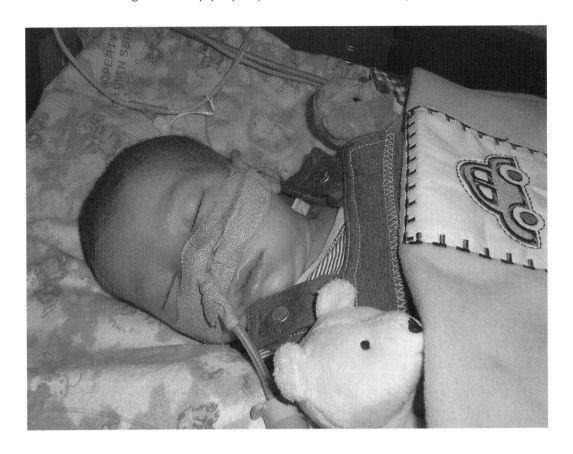

Day Thirty Eight – January 28th 2007

Charlotte's Diary: This had to have been the most difficult day we have ever had to face in our entire lives. We were at Joseph's bed side early before Carolyne and Daniel joined us. As Joseph looked so gorgeous in his little blue outfit that he wore for his baptism – we decided not to disturb him too much, so he just had a cat lick and a fresh nappy. I had remembered the day before that I had purchased a baby hand/foot casting kit a few months ago; Carolyne brought it back with her from the house and so we set about immortalising Joseph's hand and foot using the casting kit. What should have been a solemn occasion very quickly turned into one of the most funniest things you have ever seen. The first attempt did not work out at all; the mould had set even before Darren managed to put his foot in, so we had to start again. This time we were slightly more successful and by the time we got to cast his hand we were beginning to be like experts.

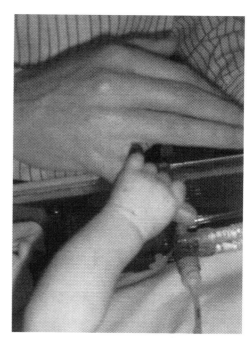

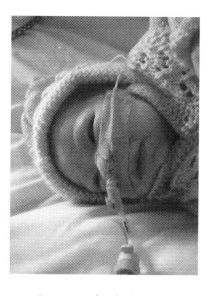 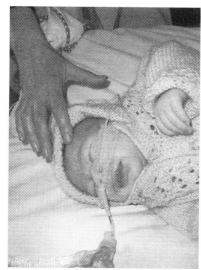 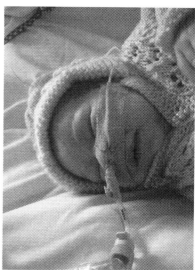

Once we had cleaned Joseph and tidied his room up a bit we all then had cuddles with photos and video imaging as well. After another nappy change it was time for me to have one last lovely cuddle before we took the tube out.

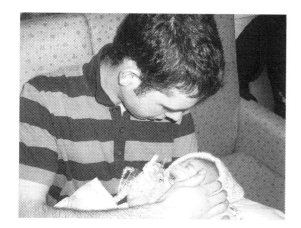 

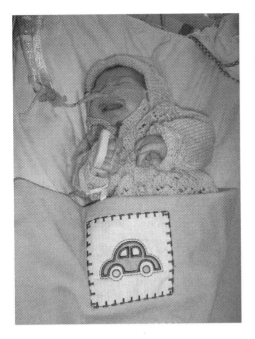

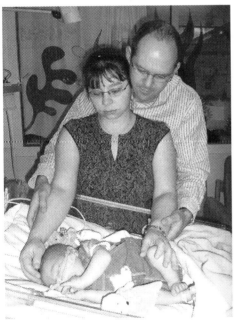

The Specialist Registrar very gently removed the tape that was keeping the tube in place and at 14:45 the breathing tube was removed and Joseph began breathing for himself without the aid of the ventilator. We thought that Joseph would pass away very quickly but after a couple of hours he was still with us so we asked Carolyne and Daniel if they wanted to come back in the room. At 20:30 they decided to make their way back home as we had intended to remain with our beautiful boy until the very end even if hours/days passed by. The PICU nurses very kindly offered us the use of the parents room on the unit or to snooze in Joseph's room should we need too. At 21:00 we thought he had passed on and when the nurse left the room to fetch the doctor we realised that he was in fact still breathing and obviously not ready to leave us just yet and we were not entirely ready to let him go either. We did realise though that Joseph could not carry on much longer and all we could do was hold him, be with him and try to make him as comfortable as we possibly could by increasing his morphine when we believed that he may have been in pain. We began reminiscing about when we got married and Wales in general when we suddenly looked down and noticed that our brave beautiful boy had gently slipped away without a fuss or a murmur at all. Joseph must have known somehow that we weren't ready for him to go at 21:00 and stayed with us a bit longer until he knew that we were ready for him to leave us. The nurse fetched the Doctor who confirmed that our brave little man had gone. Because this time we were ready for his departure – it was a relief for us to know that he was finally free of pain and no longer suffering. Once we were ready, we washed his hands and face and performed one last nappy change before the nurse wrapped him in a blanket and carried him downstairs to the Chapel of Rest. The offer of the Parents room was still available to us, but we decided that we would rather go home so we could break the news to family in the morning. I also couldn't bear being in the hospital knowing that Joseph was no longer with us.

At 23:40 and 23:41, Charlotte captured Joseph's image using Darren's mobile phone for the last time alive, moments before he slipped away.

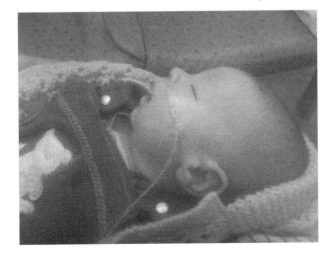

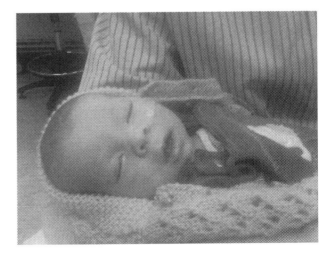

Time of death was recorded at 23:45.

The memory of Josephs last day is framed and on display in the parents living room as a reminder and tribute to their beautiful son who they will always love and never forget.

Darren's statement – Part two

42. As it turned out King George did not have the facilities for Joseph. He required controlled ventilation. The only place where a cot was available was Queen's Hospital so he was transferred hours after being born to Queen's Hospital and on January 24th 2007 moved from Queen's Hospital to Great Ormond Street. Charlotte was at Joseph's side every day of his life and when Charlotte had to return home we travelled by public transport and stayed with him for at least 6 hours each day. Charlotte actively cared for him whenever permitted by washing and cleaning him. During this time we had hope and had some happy moments. These moments have been lost and consumed by the overwhelming emotions of grief and loss.

43. In all the time that Joseph was in King George or Queen's Hospital no-one told us how serious his condition was. Yes we knew he was in the Special Care Baby Unit, that he had had convulsions and that he was requiring ventilation on times and we had put this together and thought that he may well have some handicap. We were prepared to take home a handicapped baby and love him and look after him as much as we possibly could. Unfortunately it was far worse than that.

44. As soon as Joseph was transferred to Great Ormond Street Hospital we started to learn the truth. A scan was interpreted there with us present and the specialist showed us how much of Joseph's brain had been damaged.   We had several discussions with medical staff and right from the outset they painted a very bleak picture. The only conversation that I have issue with there is when we were called in to a doctor's office and she started explaining what was wrong with Joseph and how he had excessive brain damage and then said very coldly while staring into my wife's eyes that he was going to die. Not just once, but three times.

45. The family liaison officer was present but she did nothing to stop this even though the distress to my wife was evident. After the doctor was finished, Charlotte broke down and was inconsolable for a long time.

46. However, in fairness to Great Ormond Street they told us the truth. For the first time we learnt that Joseph's condition was so bad he was going to die. There would be no taking home a baby, handicapped or not.

47. Eventually when we realised that there was absolutely no hope, we agreed to remove Joseph from the ventilator. We knew what the consequences would be and he died in our arms after nine hours following the removal of the ventilation on 28 January 2007. Joseph was in no discomfort while off the ventilator as he was receiving a large continuous dose of morphine which was

used to sedate him. We were told it would also suppress his breathing and this was a standard procedure in such circumstances. We were not given any choice or alternative. It was made clear to us that if we did not decide to take him off the ventilator then the hospital would take action and do it themselves. Even though we were told there was no rush to select the moment to remove Joseph from the ventilator it was evident from comments made by staff that we only had a few days to pick the moment. We used the time to invite friends and family to see him alive for the last time and also have him baptised.

48. During his short life Joseph suffered terribly. He had at least five needles inserted into him from the start and hardly a day went by without needles until he was dead.. He had a tube down his throat and he was fed intravenously. Always on my mind are these abrasions on his scalp. Tear like marks and the bleeding which I think was caused by the overzealous use of the foetal scalp probe for the foetal scalp sampling. That must have been agonisingly painful for Joseph.

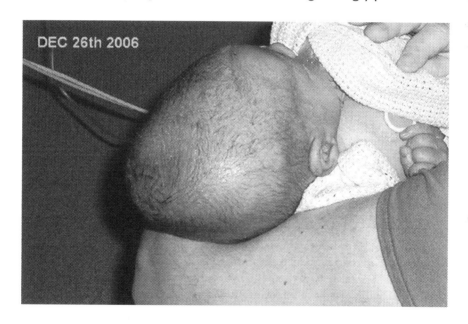

DEC 26th 2006

49. Since Joseph's delivery and death we have had no contact from King George's Hospital. No apology. No sign of remorse. No referral to bereavement counselling. We have had an invite from Romford and GOSH but they are not willing or able to comment about his birth only his condition while in their care. We have managed on our own but always we feel that Joseph's pain and suffering and his death were avoidable. He need never have suffered brain damage. This was due to a lack of observation, experience and competence on the part of the people looking after Joseph and my wife during his birth. Warning signs were ignored and communication was poor. The result is that our son is dead.

50. We would like the people concerned to have learned from this mistake, to prevent it happening to anyone else. We will do whatever it takes because we do not want to feel in ten years time that

we could and should have done more. We do not want to leave any stone unturned in our quest for accountability.

51. Whilst we would like compensation there is no amount of money that will pay us for Joseph's loss. The compensation would repay us for the expenditure that we paid out in anticipation of his birth, his cot and layette and his funeral expenses.

52. I would also like to know whether the extent of the damage that Joseph sustained during his foetal scalp sampling process was such that it could amount to unlawful assault or involuntary manslaughter. I am absolutely serious about this because I have seen the scan and the damage that was caused and there is no way that that should have happened to a baby.

53. Since all of this happened my wife and I have dealt with it in different ways. She finds it very difficult to itemise and set down what happened. That is one of the reasons for her not preparing the statement.

54. I have thought about preparing a Blog but my wife cannot participate. She finds it too painful.

55. My wife gave up work to look after her baby son. When Joseph died, her work contacted her and asked her to go back but she could not face it. The idea of going back to a place where she had been pregnant and where everyone would know she had been pregnant and would be asking about the baby possibly or trying to avoid the subject was just too much for her to cope with. There had also been a bit of a baby boom there and the others would all be returning from their maternity leave with happy discussions about their particular child. For that reason Charlotte has taken a much reduced role as a temporary secretary for the time being. She did not feel up to taking on a full time job. She did not have the commitment and she was worried that on really bad days she would not be able to cope. She was worried about coping at all but at least with temp work she could build up gradually and she would not have to work every day or every week. In the end she felt that she ought to do something because sitting at home all day was just making her far worse. She does whatever she can to stop intrusive thoughts about the life and death of our son Joseph.

56. I suppose I have channelled my grief into trying to make changes to prevent it happening to anyone else but it is not easy when the Trust consistently ignore us and do not seem to want to change.

57. It has impacted on us in other ways. We would still like a family and we need to get on with it because we always wanted more than one child but Charlotte would never dream of having a

baby by natural delivery anymore. If she has another baby it will be by elective caesarean section just to prevent any complication like this occurring again.

Statement of Truth

I make this statement to be best of my knowledge and belief.

Darren Cunningham

Dated this day of July 2007

Charlotte's diary and the days after Joseph

January 29th 2007

Today was the day when we had to start breaking the news to family and friends that our little man was no more. We tried to keep busy with trivial things but the thoughts kept coming back to haunt us. We travelled with Carolyne and Daniel to Euston and saw them onto the train before carrying on to GOSH to collect the medical certificate so that we could register Joseph's death.

We arranged to go to the chapel of rest so that we may see Joseph again and put him in his bear suit that was meant to have been his coming home suit. The viewing room was designed just like a child's bedroom and Joseph just looked like he was sleeping on the single bed with teddy bears around him to keep him company. He was so cold to the touch and so I was pleased to put him in his bear suit as it would keep him warm. After we had both had cuddles it was time to leave him again and so we put him back down on the bed and tucked him in. We left quietly with our documentation so that we were able to register the death. On our way home we had a meal in the local pub and called in at David and Sandra's (our neighbours) and informed them accordingly and asked that they take care of our cats while we are away.

January 30th 2007

Today was also another difficult day; we went to Camden to register Joseph's death and were given the paperwork which will mean the arrangements can start to be made for the service and burial. The green form was taken back to GOSH so that the funeral directors can transfer Joseph to North Wales (to be buried in the cemetery where Darren's relatives rest). We were given a white form to cancel his child benefit and also we requested two copies of his death certificate. On our return home I started returning people's phone calls and the sympathy cards have started to arrive.

In the afternoon we went shopping and bought clothing suitable for the funeral. The Reverend telephoned saying that the service will take place on the Thursday 8th Feb at 10:30. We chose St. Ann's as that was the church where we were married.

January 31st 2007

We didn't do an awful lot today. Just made more arrangements and started packing ready for going up to North Wales. Darren spoke to Auntie Susie who has helped us to decide on a suitable venue for refreshments after the burial. We plan to go and see her before the service. Also spoke to Uncle Dennis who will show us around the cemetery so we can see other members of the family who are also there. We have decided to travel up on Friday morning (2nd February) to finalise any arrangements still left outstanding.

February 1st 2007

Spent most of the day packing and tidying the house prior to us leaving for North Wales tomorrow. Sandra and David (who live at No.45) will pop in daily and take care of the cats for us, so that is one thing less to worry about.

February 2nd 2007

Travelled to Rhyl today and arrived at 12:15. As soon as we arrived we drove to Flint cemetery to have a look around. It seems to be a beautiful place very peaceful and I truly believe that we all will be very happy being laid to rest there as we have decided on a family plot. We then spent some time with Auntie Susie who has very kindly offered to cover the cost of the reception which is more than we could hope for. We will see Uncle Dennis tomorrow who will show us where the majority of the family are and we will then decide on Monday which plot to take. We also need to decide on flower arrangements etc, but will decide tomorrow.

February 3rd 2007

We met Uncle Dennis and Cousin Jacqueline (Dennis's daughter) at the cemetery today. Took some flowers and helped to arrange them on Aunt Sally's grave (Uncle Dennis's late wife). Dennis and family attend the graveyard every Saturday and have very kindly offered to look after Joseph for us and ensure that he will have fresh flowers each week which brings us great comfort to know that he will be so well looked after whilst we are not there.

Went into town to compare the cost of our flowers for Joseph, they are all much the same price so we have asked the funeral directors to arrange them for us. We have decided on 'LITTLE MAN' because to us that was him in a nut shell.

At 16:00 we went and saw the Reverend that will be performing the service for us and we discussed what arrangements we would like and how the service would proceed. It appears to be exactly what we want on the whole of it, simple but hopefully it will be effective.

February 4th 2007

A quiet day spent today, did not do an awful lot, just spent the day with family. Tomorrow we plan to meet with an official from the council to discuss the plot.

February 5th 2007

At 11:00 we met with Andy from the council and we decided where we would like Joseph to sleep and await us to join him.

We chose a really nice spot in the cemetery very near to the remains of Aunty Sally so that Joseph will be very well looked after until the time comes that Darren and I join him. Andy phoned soon after our meeting and confirmed that our preferred choice was available and would be dug soon after and be ready for Thursday.

In the afternoon we collected Nanny Boo and Granddad John (Darren's parents) and took them to the chapel of rest in order to see Joseph. He looked just as beautiful as he did when we last saw him, still in his little brown bear suit wrapped in his blue blanket. We chose a soft blue coffin for him and chose all the flower arrangements for him. I forgot to take his teddy bears today for him and so will take them tomorrow so that he is not on his own in the coffin. Tomorrow we will also ensure that all the arrangements are made and that instructions are carried out to the letter.

February 6th 2007

We went to the funeral directors this morning mainly because I had forgotten to take Joseph's teddy bears with me the day before. Whilst we were there we were able to check that all the flower arrangements have been ordered and we brought home some cards for the family to write if they wished. Before leaving, we went into Joseph's viewing room and spent some more time with him. We both had another cuddle, but finally decided to let him be and leave him alone, before leaving we made sure he was cosy, tucked in and put his bears with him to keep him company.

In the afternoon we spent some time with Heather, James and Lauren (my brother-in-law and sister-in-law, and niece) as we had not seen them since coming up and thought we should see them all before Thursday.

Tomorrow we are planning to settle the bill so everything is all square as we may feel it easier before the funeral as opposed to after when we will be feeling emotionally drained.

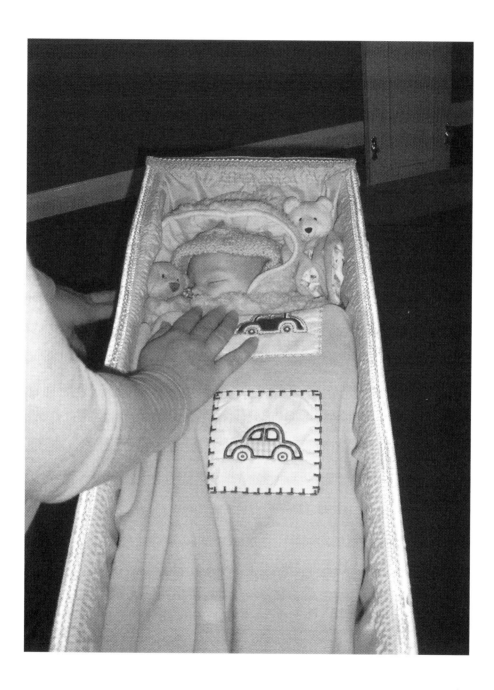

February 7th 2007

We went to the funeral directors once more and paid the invoice. Whilst there, I saw our little angel alone for the last time before the funeral tomorrow. He looked so beautiful and peaceful just like he was asleep; it was so hard to believe that he will never open his eyes again. We had a quiet afternoon and evening and had an early night in preparation for the hardest day of our lives tomorrow.

February 8th 2007

Today was the worst day of my life, today was the day that our sweet little boy was going to be taken away from us forever. There will be no more trips to the hospital and no more car journeys to Prestatyn to the chapel of rest in order to see him and have a nice cuddle.

The cars arrived exactly on time and drove us all to St. Ann's where the rest of the family were waiting for us watching over Joseph who had arrived before us. The hearse was completely surrounded by flowers. The Reverend came out of church and the undertakers took Joseph out of the hearse and handed him to Darren. Then with my arm linked with Darren's he carried Joseph into St. Ann's in order for the service to start. The service was very simple and went according to plan which was what we wanted.

Darren's Speech

Just over 10 years ago many of you joined us in this church to celebrate one of the happiest days of our lives. Today we have asked you all to join us on what is one of our saddest days and we are indebted to you all for your support and kind words.

On the morning of 1st April 2006 Charlotte got out of bed, went to the bathroom and carried out a pregnancy test. She returned to the bedroom waving a stick asking if I could see a pink dot. At first I thought I was being played for an April fool, but sure enough we learnt that day that Charlotte was pregnant and on the 14th June we learnt it was a boy and we named him Joseph Lloyd Cunningham. This had to be the happiest time of our lives and we could not wait to meet our little man.

Since we knew he was on the way into our lives he has been constantly in our thoughts and from the day he arrived he has touched the hearts of everyone who has met him and we are the ones who have been privileged to have known him.

Charlotte and I have learnt over the past weeks that life is not given for free and to be taken for granted, but every day is a gift. Joseph was kind enough to give us 38 gifts one after another wanting nothing more in return but our love.

On Sunday the 28th January we had to make the hardest decision of our lives and hope we never have to do it again. That was to take away our little boys life line and then patiently wait for him to die. He fought hard to survive to be with us but after 9 hours he gently slipped away while in his daddy's arms.

Joseph has passed on and today we will lay him to rest, but his memory will live on and our love for him will never falter and we will wait until such times we meet him again. Until then we are sure that family members who have passed before him will watch over him for us.

Joseph you're our comet Shining in the sky.

Joseph we've been watching you climbing up so high.

Joseph we now miss you as you've passed us by.

Joseph we will remember you, and pray for you each night.

Thank you.

After Darren's very moving speech we had prayers and our two songs were played that we had chosen specifically – 'Songbird' by the artists 'All Angels' and 'Days' by 'Kirsty MacColl'.

Once the service was over the cars then proceeded to Flint and onto the cemetery. More prayers were said over Joseph and all too soon he was lowered gently into the grave out of our reach until such time that we join him.

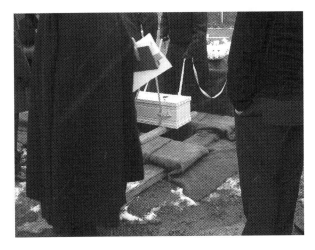

We threw red rose petals into the grave and then it was time to leave him and move onto the 'Coach and Horses' pub to raise a toast to our brave little man.

The afternoon sped by and all too soon people started to leave one by one until only a few of us remained. Eventually it was time to depart and we got taxis back from Auntie Susie's house at Rock Cottage. Although it was an extremely sad day for us, it was beautiful as well because it had snowed all day and everywhere looked so pretty and clean and fresh.

It also seemed poignant as well because I'm absolutely certain that Joseph would have loved the snow but perhaps Nain (my late Mother) arranged it especially for him on his special day – we will never know.

February 9th 2007

We spent the morning quietly, in the afternoon we travelled back to the cemetery. Obviously the grave had been filled in, but the staff had arranged the flowers really beautifully. What surprised us was that they had marked his grave with a simple cross which was very thoughtful. We had been meaning to ask if there was any possibility that the grave could be marked before a headstone was put in place so it was lovely to see that someone had already thought to do it on our behalf.

It was snowing still when we were there and it was such a shame that Joseph never saw snow, whilst we were there we went over to Auntie Sal's grave and asked that she look after our little man for us until such time that we are together again.

February 10th 2007

Walked into town in the morning and did a bit of shopping. Afternoon spent very quietly at home. Darren went out for a few drinks with Daniel in the evening.

February 11th 2007

Spent a quiet morning, after lunch took a drive with Dad to Llanddulas to where my grandfather and great grandparents are buried. Unfortunately although Dad knew the area where Granddad is buried – the family had never arranged to have a headstone erected, so the actual grave is unmarked. Once we are back from Ireland we can call the Reverend to see if it is possible to determine the grid reference of Dad's family. In the afternoon we drove to Flint to see Joseph again before we go to Dublin for a few days in the morning tomorrow. It was nice to be able to admire all of the flowers now that the snow had melted, even though the graveyard did look pretty with all the snow on the ground.

February 12th – 14th 2007

Spent an enjoyable couple of days in Southern Ireland's capital city, explored a bit more of Darren's family tree. Did a bit of sightseeing, but all too soon it was time to catch the ferry back to Holyhead and then the train back to Rhyl. Although it was nice to get away from all the stresses and strains that we have been under during the past few weeks, I did not enjoy the break as much as we would have done if things have turned out differently with Joseph. I did feel guilty as well.

February 15th – 28th 2007

Days spent with family.

March 1st 2007

Travelled back down to London today, the journey was very good which made a change – however I was very conscious of the fact that with each mile travelled was another mile away from my little mans resting place.

March 2nd 2007

A telephone call from the antenatal department at King George hospital called to confirm that my antenatal notes have been photocopied and are available for collection – will collect them on Monday.

March 5th 2007

Collected antenatal notes from the King George hospital.

March 8th 2007

A letter and form came in the post today from the Chaplain's office at GOSH asking if we wanted Joseph's name to be added into the book of remembrance which is on display in the Chapel. Form completed and will be posted tomorrow.

March 10th 2007

Darren made three extra copies of the antenatal notes so that we can send them off to people to see if a claim can be made.

March 11th – 14th 2007

SOUTHAMPTON
Spent a few days with my Sister Louisa and her family. Didn't do an awful lot but spent most of the time just talking about old times and just basically caught up with the goings on. We spoke a lot about Mum which we hadn't been able to do before what with everything that has been going on lately. Even though it was nice to see everyone else again under more normal circumstances – I was very pleased to come back home, back to Darren and the cats, I missed them a great deal.

March 18th 2007

It's a sad day today, firstly because it is the first Mother's day that I no longer have my mum with me and secondly because today should have been my first Mother's day. So today understandably I am not very happy at all – I should have been enjoying a lovely day of being pampered by my men, but it is just an ordinary day. Hopefully next year or the one after will be cause for celebration, but at the moment my heart is broken and my arms feel empty – they ache to hold a baby again. I wish I could turn the clock back to a time when I was holding my little Joseph – I miss holding him so much and I would never let him go.

Charlotte's diary ends here.

Joseph's Medication

During Joseph's time in hospital he was given a whole mixture of drugs those known to be CLONAZEPAM, LORAZEPAM, PHENOBARBITONE, PHENYTOIN, MORPHINE, PARACETAMOL, PYRIDOXINE, CEFOTAXIME, TEICOPLANIN, AUGMENTIN the trade name for CO-AMOXICLAV, FENTANYL, ATROPINE, VECURONIUM, DOMPERIDONE, TRICLOFOS , ALIMEMAZINE, and another drug that cannot be identified on Josephs drug chart.

Not all of the drugs given to Joseph were explained to the parents what was their purpose. The use of the drugs below is assumed by the parents from the conversations with the NHS staff and from reading the medical records they received.

CLONAZEPAM, LORAZEPAM, PHENOBARBITONE, PHENYTOIN

These drugs were given frequently to Joseph during his short life to control his seizures.

MORPHINE

Morphine is a highly potent drug used to relieve pain by acting directly on the central nervous system. Joseph received Morphine while in Great Ormond Street hospital to help relieve his suffering once he was taken off the ventilator.

PARACETAMOL

Paracetamol is commonly used for the relief of fever, headaches, and other minor aches and pains. It was prescribed to Joseph to help bring down his temperature.

PYRIDOXINE

Pyridoxine is vitamin B6 which assists red blood cell formation and the nervous system function.

CEFOTAXIME

Cefotaxime is a third-generation antibiotic and has broad spectrum activity against Gram positive and negative bacteria.

TEICOPLANIN

Teicoplanin is an antibiotic used in the treatment of serious infections caused by Gram positive bacteria including MRSA.

AUGMENTIN

Co-Amoxiclav is an antibiotic also known by its trade name AUGMENTIN. It has an increased spectrum of action used against amoxicillin-resistant bacteria.

FENTANYL

Fentanyl is a general anaesthetic which may have been given to Joseph which having the bronchoscopy at Great Ormond Street hospital.

ATROPINE

Atrophine has a number of uses but in Joseph's case it's believed it was used as a premedication before being given a general anaesthetic prior to having the bronchoscopy at Great Ormond Street hospital.

VECURONIUM

Vecuronium is a muscle relaxant and is believed to have been given to Joseph as part of his treatment during the bronchoscopy at Great Ormond Street hospital.

DOMPERIDONE

Domperidone can be used to help prevent vomiting and feeling nauseous. In Joseph's case it's believed it was given prior to having the bronchoscopy at Great Ormond Street hospital.

ALIMEMAZINE

Alimemazine is an antihistamine that may have been given to Joseph in order to prevent a reaction to his medication. If it was given to Joseph for another reason then it's not known by the parents.

TRICLOFOS

Triclofos is a sleeping drug, as to why it was given to Joseph is not known by the parents.

Unknown Drug

Joseph was given a drug that is listed on his drug chart on the 25th January 2007. Due to the poor writing it's not possible to recognise the name of the drug to understand what it was. It was also not explained to the parents that Joseph was given this drug and to what purpose.

GREAT ORMOND STREET HOSPITAL FOR CHILDREN NHS TRUST

INTENSIVE CARE UNIT DRUG PRESCRIPTION CHART

SURNAME	FIRST NAME		HOSPITAL NUMBER
CUNNINGHAM	JOSEPH		848 366
DATE OF BIRTH	WEIGHT	CONSULTANT	COST CODE
22/12/06	4.3 kg	M. Peters	ICSE

ONCE ONLY AND PREMEDICATION DRUGS

DATE	TIME	DRUG	DOSE	ROUTE	SIGNATURE	TIME GIVEN	GIVEN BY	PHARMACY USE
25/1/07		Atropine	0.1 mg	IV		1220	Duncan	
27/1/07	0830	Lorazepam	0.43mg	IV	WJB	08:20	KW/Y	

Requesting for Medical Notes

Darren took it upon himself to obtain the hospital records recorded during Joseph's labour and a copy of the MRI scans taken while he was in Queen's Hospital on the 28th December. This proved to be far more challenging than had initially been expected. Even with the fact that Darren and Charlotte were legally entitled to copies under the data protection act while Joseph was alive and under the Access to Health Records Act 1990 after his death.

What now follows are e-mail and letter exchanges in the quest to obtain the information. There were also a number of phone calls made chasing up requests but the conversations were not recorded and are not mentioned below. However no significant information was given or decisions made during the calls.

Darren began with contacting the hospital via the switchboard on Wednesday 3rd January 2007 and received a letter on the 10th January dated the 8th January 2008 with a yellow form to complete.

8th January 2007

Dear Mrs Cunningham

Re: Application for Health Records (Data Protection) Act 1998

Further to your letter requesting medical records. I would be grateful if you would complete the enclosed form and return it to me, on receipt I will process your application.

There is a charge for this service of:-

    30p per photocopied page
    Per x-ray – to be advised
    £10.00 handling charge, plus postage (if applicable)

Records applied for within 40 days of the last entry will not incur the handling charge.

Please note that by completing and signing this form you signing an agreement to pay the above charges.

Medical records requested in respect of deceased patients are applied for under Access to Health Records Act 1990 and as such will incur the standard copying charge, plus the handling charge. Signature of next-of-kin or the executor will be required when completing the form.

If you have any queries please do not hesitate to contact us.

Yours sincerely

Acting Medical Records Manager

The form was completed and returned by hand to the queen's Hospital. Weeks became months and there was no reply. So Darren chose to chase for updates and on the Friday 2nd March Charlotte answered the phone to learn that her antenatal notes were available for collection from King George.

Come Monday, Darren and Charlotte travelled on the bus the King George hospital paid for and collected the notes. Darren asked about the MRI scans and was told that there must have been a misunderstanding with the request as only the notes were copied. The advice given was to complete another yellow form asking for a copy of the MRI scans. The form was completed there and then and handed to the receptionist. Disappointingly the notes were not in any sensible order and the quality of the copying was poor especially the ECG graphs. As it turned out it was later learnt that the notes were also incomplete.

Again weeks became months and there was no reply. Darren decided to contact the Patient Advice and Liaison Service (PALS) for assistance who were based at Queen's hospital and explained the situation. Darren was informed that the delay was due to more than one hospital being involved with Joseph's care. However as a result of PALS assistance it became evident that the form completed in March for the MRI scans had gone missing. So on the 1st June 2007 Charlotte received a letter dated 24th May 2007 along with another yellow form to complete in order to request for copies of Joseph's MRI scans.

24 May 2007

Dear Mrs Cunningham

Re: Application for Health Records (Data Protection) Act 1998/Health Records Act 1990

Further to your telephone call/letter requesting medical records please find enclosed a form. I would be grateful if you would complete the form and return it to me. On its receipt I will process your application.

There is a charge for this service of:

Per photocopied page	30p
Per X-Ray film	To be advised
Handling charge	£10.00p, plus postage (if applicable)

Records applied for within 40 days of the last entry will not incur the handling charge.

Please note that by completing and signing this form you are also signing an agreement to pay the above charges.

Medical records requested in respect of deceased patients are applied for under the Access to Health Records Act 1990 and as such will incur the standard copying charges, plus the handling charge. Signature of the next of kin, or the Executor will be required when completing the form.

If you have any queries, please contact us on the above extension.

Yours sincerely

Medico-Legal Team Leader

The form was completed and posted by recorded delivery to the address on the letter.

Again weeks passed by but with the assistance of PALS the images were put onto CD and once the hospital had received payment from Charlotte by cheque, the CD was posted onto Darren and Charlotte with the following letter dated 17th July 2007.

17 July 2007

Dear Ms Cunningham

Re: Joseph Cunningham   dob 22.12.06

We enclose herewith copies of your son's MRI scan (disc) as requested under the Access to Health Records (Data Protection) Act 1990.

We would like to take this opportunity to thank you for your cheque in the sum of £11.14p in settlement of our charges,

Yours sincerely

Medico Legal Team Leader

Josephs MRI Scans

The CD containing the MRI images was labelled:

CUNNINGHAM/BABY 01538821 362846
D.O.B. 22/12/2006
28/12/2006 Consultant Paediatrician
MRHI Head
QRHNI QUEEN'S HOSPITAL

The report that came with the CD read:

362846 28/12/2006 MRI Head
This examination shows severe artefacts due to the patient movements.
There is a normal aeration of the paranasal sinuses. No pathology is seen
in the orbits. The differentiation of the grey and white matter is normal and no
pathological alterations in signal are present. The cortical structures and the
ventricular system are normal in its configuration and width. There is no midline
shift. The posterior fossa structures return a normal signal without any pathologic
changes. The brain vessels, as far as they are presented, show a normal signal of
flow. Conclusion
Normal cranial MRI related to the patients age group.
Dictated by Consultant Radiologist

The images that were provided were as follows:

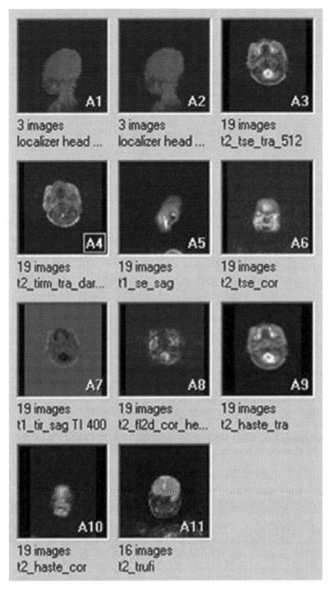

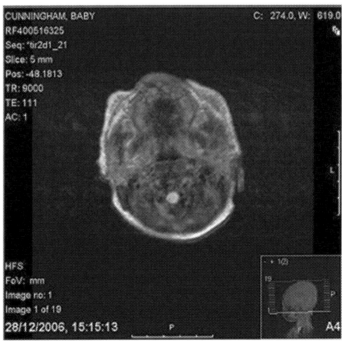

Darren noticed that the 2 images used to explain Joseph's serious condition by the Specialist Registrar at GOSH that had helped him agree with the doctors that Joseph's condition was so serious that he would not have any quality of life were missing and there was no mistake. None of the images on the CD were at eye level or revealed the blood clot between each hemisphere or the swelling at the rear of Joseph's head.

At this point Darren had no desire to wait months or even weeks to get a reply so called PALS located at the Queen's hospital for an update each week. His persistence paid off and the following letter dated the 27th July 2007 was received on Monday 30th July.

27 July 2007

Dear Mr Cunningham

Re: Joseph Cunningham dob 22.12.06

Further to our telephone conversation today, I have contacted the MRI Department who confirm that Joseph had two groups of MRI's taken. The first group consisted of one MRI image and the second group consisted of ten MRI images, making a total of eleven images.

I trust this information is of assistance to you. If I can be of further help, please do not hesitate to contact me on the above telephone number.

Yours sincerely

Medico Legal Team Leader

Darren wrote back on the 1st August returning a copy of the CD he had received so there would be no confusion on what he had received requesting to be sent the missing images.

1st August 2007

Dear Ms ████████,

In reply to your letter received on the 31st July which reads:

Further to our telephone conversation today, I have contacted the MRI Department who confirm that Joseph had two groups of MRI's taken. The first group consisted of one MRI image and the second group consisted of ten MRI images making a total of eleven images.

Please review the information in the table below taken from the 11 images as mentioned above:

Cunningham, Baby MRI Scans taken on 28/12/2006			
Ref	Time	Image	Slice
A1	15:07:18	1 of 3	8mm
A2	15:07:47	1 of 3	8mm
A3	15:13:16	1 of 19	5mm
A4	15:15:13	1 of 19	5mm
A5	15:20:32	1 of 19	5mm
A6	15:22:42	1 of 19	5mm
A7	15:26:20	1 of 19	5mm
A8	15:30:06	1 of 19	5mm
A9	15:32:23	1 of 19	5mm
A10	15:33:33	1 of 19	5mm
A11	15:38:32	1 of 16	4mm

The data in the column 'Image' implies there were 3 sets taken:
First set of 3 (which I have 2 of, please note the times taken), a second set of 19 (which I have 8 of), and a third set of 16 (which I only have 1 of).

I have also included a copy of the statement made by the GOSH Radiology Department on their findings of my sons condition once they received a set of MRI scans from Queens Hospital. If the MRI Department look at the scans given to me along with the report from GOSH, such findings cannot be made from the 11 images. I can only draw the conclusion that the MRI department are with holding scans taken of my son or that the 11 images are not of my son but another child.

I am confident in saying that there are at the very least 2 images missing that were used by the neurologist in GOSH to explain the findings made by the Radiologists in detail using the images as reference. I can confirm that those used to explain to me my sons condition are not on the CD I have received from you.

Yours Sincerely

Mr Darren Cunningham

ENCLOSED: 1 CD copy containing the 11 MRI images, 1 photo copy of the GOSH report following a review of the MRI scans sent to GOSH.

On the 7th August the NHS sent a reply which read:

7 August 2007

Dear Mr Cunningham

Re: Joseph Cunningham   dob 22.12.06

Thank you for your letter dated 1 August 2007 with enclosure of cd.

I note your comments in respect of the cd and will contact you shortly in respect of this matter.

Your sincerely

Medico Legal Team Leader

Requesting assistance from GOSH

While pursuing the MRI Scans from Queen's hospital, Darren had also been in contact with the Family Liaison Sisters for the PICU ward in Great Ormond Street Hospital (GOSH) by e-mail.

Below are the e-mails exchanged with the Family Liaison Sisters and Darren (on behalf of himself and Charlotte).

```
To - Family Liaison Nurse
From - Cunningham, Darren
Date - Tue 08/05/2007 12:21
Subject - Notes for Joseph Cunningham

Family Liaison Nurse,

We are still waiting to receive the medical notes taken for Joseph L
Cunningham during his short stay at GOSH.  Are you able to tell me when we
can expect to receive them by please?  As mentioned on the phone we would
also like copies of the MRI scans.



Thank you.


Darren Cunningham
```

```
To - Cunningham, Darren
From - Family Liaison Nurse
Date - Tue 08/05/2007 18:32
Subject - Re: Notes for Joseph Cunningham

Darren,

The notes were mailed to you on Thursday of last week. If they have not
arrived by the end of the week please email me again. I had put the CD with
the radiology records in to be posted this am. Again let me know if this
arrives safely.



Take care,

Family Liaison Nurse
```

To - Family Liaison Nurse
From - Cunningham, Darren
Date - Fri 11/05/2007 09:31
Subject - Re: Notes for Joseph Cunningham

Family Liaison Nurse,

We have received the medical records and a CD with an image of a chest x-ray.

Can we have a copy of the MRI scans please?

Darren Cunningham

To - Cunningham, Darren
From - Family Liaison Nurse
Date - Fri 11/05/2007 16:33
Subject - Re: Notes for Joseph Cunningham

Darren,

I'll check this out and will get back to you regarding it early next week.

Family Liaison Nurse

To - Cunningham, Darren
From - Family Liaison Nurse
Date - Mon 14/05/2007 16:50
Subject - Re: Notes for Joseph Cunningham

Darren,

I've looked into this today, basically Joseph's MRI, although reported on by Great Ormond Street was not loaded onto our system here. You will however be able to gain a copy from Queen's Hospital; I did try and ring them today to find out who you needed to talk to but without much success. The best thing is to contact the PALS dept or Patient and Staff safety there.

The report on the MRI was completed here and a copy of this is contained within the notes you received.

I'm in the office on Friday of this week if you need to discuss this further.

Hope that's helpful.

Family Liaison Nurse

```
To - Family Liaison Nurse
From - Cunningham, Darren
Date - Wed 27/06/2007 13:37
Subject - Joseph L Cunningham
```

Family Liaison Nurse,

Charlotte and I received your letter today with your invitation.

I plan to discuss with Charlotte and will get back to you in due course.

As for myself I would find value in an explanation of the events during Joseph's birth by those present or accountable for those present. I have not requested for such an account simply because I have decided to involve a third party (a medical solicitor) in the hope that we can learn who or what was responsible for Joseph's injuries.

To date, I have recently managed to get copies of the hospital notes taken but there is still no sign of the MRI scan. This I hope to receive very soon in order to then request for an independent review of all the decisions taken during Charlotte's and Joseph's care.

My objective is to try and provide proof to Charlotte that she was not accountable for Joseph's injuries. Charlotte will only release this guilt once she has a statement that will convince her otherwise and an explanation what was the reason. Sadly this may take another year to come to an end.

Charlotte was interested to learn if Joseph's name had been written into the book of remembrance. She has also decided to start a direct debit to GOSH as a way of saying thank you.

Regards

Darren Cunningham

To - Family Liaison Nurse
From - Cunningham, Darren
Date - Fri 27/07/2007 09:30
Subject - RE: Notes for Joseph Cunningham

Family Liaison Nurse,

I received the MRI scans from Romford hospital yesterday and they are not those that were shown to me while at GOSH. The scans I have received look fine although from the numbers it seems that there may be some images missing. What is more concerning is the report that comes with these scans implies there is nothing wrong which as we know that is far from true. Can you get a copy of the MRI scans that were sent to GOSH and shown to me please? As it was these scans and the explanation I was given while looking at the scans convinced me that letting Joseph die and not insisting on further care and treatment was the right decision. If the scans and the report that I have now been given are the correct information then I would never have allowed Joseph to have been taken off the vent without at least a second opinion and further scans.

This is very important to me and your assistance would be appreciated.

I can hand in the CD sent to me into GOSH for your attention today if it's of any use to you.

Please feel free to call me if you need any further information.

Regards

Darren Cunningham

```
To - Family Liaison Nurse
From - Cunningham, Darren
Date - Fri 27/07/2007 13:39
Subject - RE: Notes for Joseph Cunningham

Family Liaison Nurse,

Since writing to you this morning, I have spoken to the Medic-Legal Team
Leader who sent the CD on behalf of Queens Hospital based in Romford and
she plans to request for another CD specifically to contain all scans.  The
numbering on the images confirmed that there were 2 sets (a set of 3 and a
set of 19).  The CD I received only contained 16 images so I am missing
6.  Once I receive the new CD I would like to arrange a visit with the
Specialist Registrar who took the time to show me the scans of Joseph
while he was in GOSH to look at the images I hope to receive to confirm they
are of the same child and to point out again his injuries.



Respectfully



Darren Cunningham
```

```
To - Family Liaison Nurse
From - Cunningham, Darren
Date - Wed 01/08/2007 10:06
Subject - RE: Notes for Joseph Cunningham
```

Family Liaison Nurse,

Following our call yesterday I have received a letter from the Medic-Legal Team Leader which reads as follows:

> Dear Mr Cunningham
> Re: Joseph Cunningham dob 22.12.06
> Further to our telephone conversation today, I have contacted the MRI department who confirm that Joseph had two groups of MRI's taken. The first group consisted of one MRI image and the second group consisted of ten MRI images, making a total of eleven images.

Below are the details taken from the 11 images I have been sent and I can confirm none of these images where those that were shown to me by the Specialist Registrar in order to explain Joseph's injuries. The reply in my understanding simply does not match with the data recorded on the images and I am still adamant that vial images are being withheld.

Would you call me to help advise me on how I can obtain the images shown to me by the Specialist Registrar please. I am happy to bring in the CD that I have received for your reference if required.

Respectfully

Darren Cunningham

Cunningham, Baby MRI Scans taken on 28/12/2006			
Ref	Time	Image	Slice
A1	15:07:18	1 of 3	8mm
A2	15:07:47	1 of 3	8mm
A3	15:13:16	1 of 19	5mm
A4	15:15:13	1 of 19	5mm
A5	15:20:32	1 of 19	5mm
A6	15:22:42	1 of 19	5mm
A7	15:26:20	1 of 19	5mm
A8	15:30:06	1 of 19	5mm
A9	15:32:23	1 of 19	5mm
A10	15:33:33	1 of 19	5mm
A11	15:38:32	1 of 16	4mm

Can't help won't help

During August, Darren received a call from the Family Liaison Nurse stating that the Specialist Registrar did not recall the conversation he had with Darren when explaining the MRI images of Joseph's injuries and even could not recall treating Joseph. The Family Liaison Nurse also said that GOSH no longer had copies of the MRI images as they were returned to the Queen's Hospital on the 24th May. The Family Liaison Nurse found the information she had been given by the doctors are unusual and advised that Darren to speak with the PALS team located at GOSH.

Darren took her advice and attempts were made by the GOSH PALS team to understand why there appeared to be missing images and why GOSH had not kept the MRI Images for their own records as was the standard practice. Unfortunately before they could learn anything the NHS had received a letter from Darren's solicitors. The GOSH PALS team called Darren to explain they could no longer be involved and all further requests for information from the NHS would now have to be made via the solicitor.

```
To - Family Liaison Nurse
From - Cunningham, Darren
Date - Thu 30/08/2007 10:07
Subject - Joseph Cunningham
```

Family Liaison Nurse,

I just wanted to thank you for your recent assistance in an attempt to obtain the complete set of MRI scans for Joseph.
It was always my intention to have an independent person review the notes and images and to present the findings to the NHS and to request to meet and discuss rather than drag the whole process through a legal proceeding, which can often go on for years.
I had not envisioned that getting the notes would take so long and requesting for the scans to be so painful.

I have taken advice from a medical solicitor over the past months and I even prepared a statement with their assistance. I have now resigned myself to the fact that if I am going to learn what happened and what should have happened during Joseph's birth then the only route will have to be the legal route. The attitude and response from The Queens hospital made this very clear even though this all could have been avoided if we had received full co-operation right from the beginning. Would you also send my thanks to the GOSH PALS staff for their recent assistance and guidance?

Darren Cunningham

From: Family Liaison Nurse
Sent: 03 September 2007 11:25
To: Cunningham, Darren
Subject: Re: Joseph Cunningham

Dear Darren

Thank you very much for your email. Sadly it seems that you are going to have a long drawn out process and I am sorry we could not have been any more assistance to you. I hope it does get resolved for you, Charlotte and your family as quickly as possible. As always if we can be of any further assistance to you in anyway please do not hesitate to contact us.

Regards to you all

Family Liaison Sister PICU

Working with the Solicitor

Specialist Compensation Claim Solicitors
BOLT BURDON KEMP

Joseph's parents Darren and Charlotte had come to the decision that the NHS needed to answer for their actions of their staff both during labour and after. It was evident that they would not get answers to difficult questions that milled around their minds every waking hour without assistance.

Darren checked the internet in search for a solicitor that would be suitable to deal with his case against the NHS. After looking over the many options and finding Bolt Burdon Kemp website, Darren decided to pick up the phone to learn what they could do to help. He left his contact details and a brief description of the situation with a clerk and waited for his call to be returned by a solicitor.

Rosamund Rhodes-Kemp a renowned and well respected medical solicitor replied to Darren's call in writing dated 12th February 2007 giving an overview of what would be involved in making a claim for compensation against the NHS.

All letters and e-mail exchanges with the solicitor are as follows. The content has not been altered and although the content may seem excessive on times they are the words of grieving frustrated parents wanting answers and someone to blame for their loss and pain.

Specialist Compensation Claim Solicitors

BOLT BURDON KEMP

12th February 2007

Dear Mr Cunningham

RE: Clinical Negligence Claim

I apologise for the delay in getting back to you. I think you spoke to my colleague Claire Levene regarding the sad death of your son Joseph.

First of all please accept my condolences on your loss.

I am a partner and head of the clinical negligence department and I specialise in claims involving babies – mainly the birth of babies and problems arising when the birth goes wrong.

I am not exactly sure what has happened here but it looks as though the baby was either not in the correct position or possibly was too big. There was what is known as cephalic – pelvic disproportion – the head is too big to get through the pelvis.

Signs that there was a problem include slow progress, meconium and the fact that staff brought in a rescusitaire because that shows they were anticipating a problem.

You have asked whether the correct action was taken and to be able to answer that question we would have to get a copy of the medical records. This would cost money – about £50 from each source - and we would have to get the King George Hospital and the Great Ormond Street Hospital records as well as possibly the GP records.

If you were to get the records yourself it will cost less simply because the hospital would charge you less than they would have done the solicitors.

You might be eligible for public funding, i.e. legal aid but there are huge restraints on that funding now for political reasons and you have to be able to show not just that you are financially eligible but also that the case has merit and that it is worth enough to justify public money being spent on legal claims. Usually the amount is about £20,000.

Cases involving the death of a baby very sadly attract minimal compensation and that is because the law in relation to fatal accidents is based on legislation from the early 20th Century which was designed to recompense the widow and children of industrial workers such as miners and steel workers and is frankly not relevant to the sort of accidents that occur in our day or the various family set ups. Nonetheless we are stuck with it.

1

In your enquiry you raise the point about the impact on your career but at the same time it says you are not working and I think it will be difficult to show that there has therefore been an impact on any earnings. I guess you could say that you were going to take longer to get back to work because of the trauma of what has happened. A lot depends on your personal circumstances.

It is possible on occasion to enter into a no win no fee agreement on a case involving a baby that has died if public funding is refused, but to do that we would definitely need to obtain copies of your medical records first because you would not be able to get after the event insurance that you need to go with the no win no fee agreement without some evidence of negligence.

You need insurance because although a so called no win no fee agreement or a conditional fee agreement as it is commonly known is an agreement between you and Bolt Burdon Kemp to the effect that if you lose you do not have to pay Bolt Burdon Kemp's costs. There is a liability for the defendant's costs if you are unsuccessful and so you need insurance to cover those.

Financial eligibility for public funding is another difficult area because nowadays they take into account the value of your house if you own a property and any savings whatsoever and so it may be that you are not entitled to public funding but it is often refused in any event for a case involving the death of a baby because the LSC take the view that the claim may not be worth enough to justify public funding expense.

There are therefore lots of issues to consider before embarking on a legal claim and I wonder whether the best first step would be to request copies of your medical records. I would be quite happy to review these for you for free and then advise you on whether I think a legal claim is appropriate or whether you should make an NHS complaint, i.e. a formal complaint.

Have you spoken to anyone at the Trust about what happened and voiced your concerns?

The halfway mark might be to write a letter of complaint to the Chief Executive and at the same time request copies of your records so that you can got through them with a view perhaps to arranging a meeting at the Trust. That way you might flush out a response from them which would be helpful and obtain copies of the notes. You would need to check how much the copies are going to cost to go down that route if you would struggle to pay the £50 maximum that they can change.

Have a think about all of this and let me know what you intend to do, but my first suggestion would be that you obtain copies of the records and set out a formal complaint. As I say I am more than happy to review the records for you.

If it easier for you to contact me by email please feel free to do so when you have decided what you want to do.

Once again I am sorry about what has happened.

With best wishes and kind regards.

Yours sincerely

ROSAMUND RHODES-KEMP

2

Darren talked over the situation with Charlotte and they agreed it was the right course of action as they needed answers and to learn who was accountable for Joseph's death.

Darren replied to Rosamund via e-mail as she had suggested and the case commenced.

To: 'rosamund rhodes-kemp'

Date - Tue 20/02/2007 12:25

Subject - Clinical Negligence Claim - Mr Cunningham (Joseph Lloyd Cunningham)

Dear Rosamund,

I would like to thank you for your time in replying in detail giving your advice in connection with the death of my son.

My wife and I requested for a copy of the pre-natal records at the beginning of the year and received a confirmation on the 8th Jan but to date have not received a copy of the notes. It is my intention to pursue a copy of the notes and I will then contact you to take you up on your offer in reviewing them in order for you to advice me on what is the best way forward.

Respectfully

Darren Cunningham

09/03/07

Subject - RRK/New Enquiry/Clinical Negligence Claim ~ Joseph Lloyd Cunningham

Dear Ms Rhodes-Kemp
Thank you for your reply (dated 12/02/07) to my husband's query regarding the sad death of our little baby boy following what we believe may have resulted in a mismanaged second stage labour.

Following your advice we have now received copies of my ante-natal notes and I will send a copy via Royal Mail for your attention for you to review and see if you believe in your opinion that any negligence has occurred.

We look forward to hearing from you in due course.

With kind regards

Charlotte Cunningham

From: Charlotte Cunningham
Sent: 16 March 2007 04:08 PM
To: Rosamund Rhodes-Kemp
Subject: Joseph Lloyd Cunningham[Scanned]

Dear Rosamund,

I hope you have received a copy of Charlotte's Anti natal notes along with a few photos taken on the 26th December. I have attached another digital photo to this mail taken on the 14th Jan.

Can you give me your opinion if you think that there was a need to make at least 6 lacerations in order to take a single blood sample? I have requested for a copy of Josephs medial notes which includes an MRI scan. When I was shown the MRI, I didn't think to ask at the time if there was a connection to some of the injuries Joseph had received due to taking the blood sample.

Once I receive Joseph's notes I will of course send a copy onto you.

Respectfully

Darren Cunningham

RE: Joseph Lloyd Cunningham[Scanned]
From: **Rosamund Rhodes-Kemp**
Sent: 16 March 2007 16:16
To: Charlotte Cunningham

Hello I am looking at these over the weekend and will get back to you

ROSAMUND RHODES-KEMP

Support from a Friend

18th March 2007

Dear Darren & Charlotte,

As promised I have looked at the medical records you sent me with a midwifery colleague.

I think you are both wise to meet both with GOSH & midwifery consultants who cared for Joseph and Charlotte during her labour. I will post the photocopied notes back today with a summary of notes and questions we have put together for you to ask the teams you are due to meet with in due course. If they can give answers you might have a clearer understanding of what occurred. If they can't, it might indicate that the best care for both Charlotte and Joseph was not provided.

Whether it is worth having an appointment with the medical solicitor first or later is a decision for you both to make. However, if you have a meeting with the solicitor first they may be able to advice you about support person to attend meetings with the rest of the medical teams at the hospitals.
Also they should look at both Charlotte and Joseph's notes in detail. Then they will be able to reassure you that appropriate care was given in all circumstances or highlight any areas they believe had occurred that were lacking in a duty of care and advice you accordingly.

Unfortunately I do not know of anyone directly at present that could accompany you both to these meetings but I will continue to enquire for you. As I am not registered as a M/W in UK I am happy to advice but neither myself nor my colleague who helped to review your notes, are qualified enough to act as expert witnesses that would be appropriate in a court of law.

It seems that both the Neurologist and the pediatricians at GSOH have given you advice already though, so would they be willing to accompany you or act as specialist witness if required?
The other people that may be able to advice are the PALS department at your maternity hospital. I'm not sure if they have professional bodies but it is an independent organization there to support parents' rights so it might be worth approaching them.

Other professional bodies you might want to discuss this case with are;
NMC - Nursing and Midwifery Council
GMC - General Medical council
You could also mention to the teams (obstetric and paediatric) you are due to meet with that you would like the case to be reviewed by these independent bodies as well.

I wish you well and I hope your questions are thoroughly answered soon.

Fondest regards,

Andrea.

Can you have;
- Copy of drug kardex
- Copy of fluid balance
- Photocopied section of labour notes / partogram where midwives sign and note care

Notes documented on 21/12/06

Midwife noted baby not happy @ 19.25hrs – called Dr to review CTG (tracing) & PV bleed (blood loss per vagina).

Q; Can you remember how much blood loss there was? (answer might be provided on missing fluid balance chart)

Q; Was an estimated blood loss documented on fluid balance or partogram?

Q; Did the midwife believe Charlotte had possibly suffered a APH (ante partum haemorrhage?)

Q; LOC (loss of contact via CTG tracing) that occurred afterwards- was Charlotte moving or did the midwife appear concerned that the blood loss and being unable to obtain a clear tracing of a fetal heart rate might be related?

Q; Did the midwife show blood loss & clots to Dr?

Q; At 22.00hrs the Dr's have documented that obtaining a FSB was an uncomplicated procedure', do you agree with this statement? (This is when Dr's took blood sample from Joseph's scalp during labour).

Q; Photos that you have show Joseph's head suffered quite a lot of marks from this procedure, do the medical team think that this amount of scarring is appropriate?

Q; You have been told that Joseph's MRI results show a blood mass on the bump of his head and also between his brain and the skin where the sample as taken, do the team believe that this could have been a direct result of this procedure?

Q; Can you have a copy of any midwifery notes/ partogram / labour history for care administered during period 21.30hrs – 22.40hrs?

Q; Did a Dr review CTG tracings 94 & 95?

Q; Appear to be missing medical / midwifery notes & CTG tracings No 96 & 97 for period between 22.40hrs – 00.15hrs

Q; Appear to be missing CTG tracing 104?

Q; Need to obtain another copy of CTG tracing 105 as unable to see time line.

22/12/06 Notes documented on continuation sheets

Q; Was 2nd stage -with active pushing- commenced at 01.25hrs?

Q; Is there any other documentation of maternal pulse prior to 01.57hrs? If not why not given that Joseph's HR (heart rate) was documented at 100bpm. What was done to confirm that it was babies HR being monitored not maternal HR at this time?

Q; Who was 2nd midwife at this stage?

Q; Was the Dr called at 02.20hrs when FHR (fetal heart rate) dropped to 93bpm and the Syntocinon infusion was stopped?

Q; Is there a hospitals policy in place regarding Dr review after 1 hour of active pushing?

Q; If so was there a review by Dr @ 02.15hrs documented in the midwifery or medical notes?

Q; Who did midwife call to assist her between 02.20hrs to delivery at 02.41 and at what time were they called?

Q; At 02.35hrs when FHR rose to 165-170bp, who was called and at what time?

Q; It is documented by midwife that paediatrician was present in the delivery room – when were they called? Was it a 'crash call'? (emergency call that goes through he hospital switch and has priority over all other calls, ensuring that appropriate medical personnel attend immediately).

Q; Appears to be a discrepancy about crash call timing and arrival of SHO (Senior house officer) to delivery room.

Q; What position was Joseph's in at delivery?

Q; Can Joseph's notes be obtained to see what time the paediatrician documented they arrived in the delivery room.

Q; Does hospital switchboard keep a log of crash calls. Can this be obtained to answer above questions?

Q; Were cord gases done at time of delivery, are the results in Joseph's notes? Is there any thing to indicate that he had suffered a severe hypoxic episode at delivery? (very low oxygen levels)

Q; Are you confident that any abnormal CTG tracings, obtaining and the results of the FSB or other events which occurred during 1st stage of labour that were documented, did not indicate that the possibility of an emergency caesarean section should have been discussed?

Q; Are you confident that at no time during 2nd stage were any CTG tracings, documentation of any maternal / foetal observations or any other events during this time, were not a possible indication that an assisted delivery or an emergency caesarean section should have been discussed or occurred?

Q; Can you have a copy of Dr Agarwah's notes post delivery.

Q; Can you have a copy of risk assessment form?

Q; Is there a fluid order for IV fluids administered at 03.20hrs?

RE: Joseph Lloyd Cunningham
From: **Rosamund Rhodes-Kemp**
Sent: 19 March 2007 10:57
To: Charlotte Cunningham
Cc: Claudia De Castro

Hello I went through the papers on Saturday and have dictated a reply but my secretary is off this week so may be a short delay getting it to you-I think it is worth investigating

Best Wishes until you get my detailed letter

ROSAMUND RHODES-KEMP

Specialist Compensation Claim Solicitors

BOLT BURDON KEMP

19th March 2007

Dear Mr and Mrs Cunningham

Clinical Negligence Claim

Thank you very much indeed for sending me the records that you have obtained and the photographs of Joseph.

I appreciate that words cannot really offer much comfort in these circumstances but I am dreadfully sorry about what has happened.

I am Partner and Head of the Clinical Negligence Department at Bolt Burdon Kemp. I am also a former nurse and I specialise in claims involving children either damaged children or as in this very sad case children who have died as a consequence of events during labour.

I should say at the outset that we have a number of claims against this particular Trust and there are certain common failings that seem to arise time and again.

I will not set out the facts for you partly because I have already got these in the very helpful information you provided to my colleague Claire Levene when you telephoned with the initial enquiry.

What I propose to do instead is go through the burden of proof in relation to clinical negligence claims and how these apply in this particular case and then discuss ways of taking this forward.

This case differs slightly from many because it involves the death of a child and it is therefore what is known as a Fatal Accidents Act claim and specific and even more stringent rules apply to those cases which I will also go through with you.

CLINICAL NEGLIGENCE CLAIMS GENERALLY

As you may be aware, clinical negligence cases have traditionally been difficult to prove. Fortunately the situation seems to be improving and Claimants are regularly succeeding in clinical negligence claims both in in-court and in out-of-court settlements. Nonetheless, it is important that you have an idea from the outset of the necessary components of a clinical negligence claim and various aspects of personal injuries law generally that will affect it.

In order to successfully pursue a clinical negligence claim you must be able to establish three elements, which I will deal with in turn:

1. Liability
2. Causation; and
3. Quantum

LIABILITY

The first thing to note is that the burden is always on the Claimant in a clinical negligence claim to prove that the medical care that was received fell below the standard to be expected of reasonably competent and skilful specialists in the particular field in which they were being treated.

This means that before the claim can even begin by the issue to proceedings, it is necessary for a Claimant to receive medical evidence from appropriate medical experts (and more than one report may be necessary) in the field which is under consideration advising that:-

1. The treatment actually received by the Claimant fell below the standard to be expected of a reasonably competent and skilful specialist in that field; and

2. There is no other responsible body of opinion in the field that would consider that the treatment given to the Claimant fell within acceptable boundaries.

The latter aspect takes account of the fact that there are differing fields of medical thought and provided the way in which the Claimant was treated fell within a school of thought that is regarded as reputable, it cannot be said that the treating doctor was negligent.

Hence if a medical expert advises that the treatment was not treatment which the expert would personally consider reasonable but, that nonetheless, there is another school of thought in the discipline that would consider the treatment acceptable, it would not be possible for us to proceed with the claim.

Liability in this Case

It is very helpful that you have been able to provide copies of the medical records. I think if we are going to take this further we need a continual copy of the CTG but that is no problem because the Trust would have to provide it if I requested it. It just makes it a lot easier to follow.

It would seem that there were delays in the delivery of Joseph particularly when it was realised that he was in the wrong position. I think you may have been under a mistaken view that his position could be altered by Mrs Cunningham changing her position. If a baby's head is presenting in the wrong way it needs to either move itself around, and sometimes the baby cannot, or it must be psychically moved around and finally if neither work it is usually necessary to perform a caesarean section or assisted delivery if the baby is descended too far for a caesarean section. The point about this is that usually the baby cannot change itself or struggles to do so at this late stage and I think intervention was required particularly in the presence of meconium.

Although there are lots of references to the CTG traces being reassuring I suspect that these are incorrect. I am no CTG specialist but I am afraid misinterpretation of CTG's is common. I wish really that midwives and junior doctors would air on the side of caution over the interpretation of CTG's whereas what seems to happen is that they are overly

2

confident when the CTG is saying something good when often it is trying to tell them that things are not right. There is a wide spread need for further training on CTG's in a lot of obstetric units.

Therefore I think earlier intervention should have taken place and if that had occurred then, given that Joseph probably suffered a lack of oxygen in the very last stages of the labour, he would have been intact and survived.

CAUSATION

Once we have a medical report that identifies negligence in the medical treatment, then it is necessary to show that as a result of the negligent treatment there has been some quantifiable loss or damage.

This means that where injury occurred from another cause, e.g. a non-negligent aspect of the treatment or, alternatively, the initial injury itself or illness itself, then it will not be possible to succeed in the claim.

Alternatively the expert may say that some aspect of the treatment was negligent but that the subsequent condition would have been the same in any event, regardless of any negligence in the treatment and, again, it would not be possible to pursue the claim.

Causation in this Case

As I say above I think that had earlier intervention taken place it is likely that Joseph would have been born intact and survived.

However, you would need to obtain independent medical evidence on the labour, the timings and the outcome.

The Fatal Accidents Act Claim

The rules relating to these claims are absolutely rigid and before I explain the rules I think it would be useful to explain the background to you and how the statutory provisions came into force.

There are two Acts that are relevant namely The Fatal Accidents Act 1976 and The Miscellaneous Provisions Family and Dependence Act 1934. Both of these arose to deal with industrial accidents at the beginning of the 20th century, The typical scenario would be the husband and main bread winner who worked in a factory, was fatally injured on using some of the machinery and left a widow and young dependants. The Acts were designed to give the widow and children income in the husband's absence and in the absence of a welfare state. They were also drawn up to provide compensation for funeral payments and that it is.

The legislation is totally unfit for modern family structures and fatal accidents act in the 21st century but we are stuck with them. They are harsh and cruel in situations other than the typical one that they were designed to cover and which I have described.

The Fatal Accidents Act 1976

Under this Act the financial dependants can bring a claim for compensation for the income of the child.

They are also entitled to claim a statutory bereavement award of £10,000 which is supposed to compensate for the loss of a loved one but only certain categories can make this claim mothers and fathers and children so you would qualify for £10,000.

3

The Miscellaneous Provisions Family and Dependence Act 1934

You can claim for the funeral expenses and a claim on behalf of Joseph's Estate i.e. standard issues for a claim for compensation for his pain and suffering before he died.

I note that he survived several weeks in the Special Care Baby Unit.

You would be entitled to claim for expenses associated with going back and forth to the hospital, the care of Joseph before he died and any layette that you may have purchased for him.

There is also a claim on your own behalves – possibly – for psychological harm suffered as a consequence of Joseph dying and the circumstances leading up to that death but you would need medical evidence to confirm that you have been suffering a recognised psychiatric illness such as depression not just grief. You need to prove a reaction over and above ordinary grief.

By now you will be very upset indeed I should think having read all of this and I am sorry but I think it is important that I explain to you just how technical and cold the law is in this situation.

I note from the papers that Mrs Cunningham gave up work to become a full-time mother and Mrs Cunningham has not worked since Joseph died and it may well be that you have a claim associated with loss of earnings.

QUANTUM

Compensation or damages in clinical negligence or personal injury actions are divided into two categories; General Damages and Special Damages.

As a Claimant you must prove that you are entitled to one or both.

(a)   General damages

General Damages are awarded to compensate the Claimant for pain, suffering and loss of amenity or quality of life. Unfortunately, in this country, awards of general damages are modest by comparison to some other countries. They are also by their very nature, somewhat arbitrary.

How can pain or suffering be quantified?

In fact, there are 2 main factors which are taken into account:-

➢   Duration; and
➢   Severity of the suffering.

If the case settles by agreement or goes to court then Lawyers and Judges use a system based on precedent, in other words damages awarded for cases involving similar injuries.

(b)   Special Damages

Special Damages are awarded to compensate the Claimant for any financial loss which has occurred as a result of the negligence i.e. not as a result of the original injury or illness. The financial loss must also be reasonably foreseeable. The most obvious example is loss of earnings. Other examples include travel expenses, prescription charges and care costs.

4

It is important to remember that we can only claim for those expenses that have arisen <u>as a result of the negligence</u>, not the condition which led you to seek medical advice initially, (since you would always have incurred those losses).

Your claim for Special Damages has to be proved and to do this you need to provide documentary evidence of each item claimed e.g. receipts, letters etc.

PROCEDURE

I would need to meet with you in order to obtain an up to date statement of your situation and how Joseph's death has impacted on you both. I would need to obtain the balance of the medical records from for example Great Ormond Street Hospital and possibly Queen Charlotte Hospital – I am not sure exactly where Joseph went after he became ill.

The statements and records would then be submitted to an expert for an opinion and following that opinion we would approach the Trust with a view to an early settlement.

Cases involving stillborn children settle early I am pleased to say. Famous last words because this one might be the one that breaks the mould but for the last 5 years certainly these cases have settled well before issuing proceedings and even before the Trust's solicitors become involved because there is an intermediary called the National Health Service Litigation Authority which insures the NHS Trusts' and they have in house people there and these claims are usually handled by the NHSLA.

FUNDING

You see a No Win No Fee Agreement involves you entering into a Conditional Fee Agreement with this firm. The condition is that if you lose we get nothing and if you win we are allowed to charge the other side a success fee.

However you need insurance in case you lose to cover the other side's costs and obviously a premium is payable but that is insured so you have to pay nothing. If you lose it is covered by the insurance and if you win the other side have to pay the premium.

Nonetheless taking on a case on this basis represents a risk to ourselves and the insurers and that is why often a preliminary opinion is required.

In order to get the records it will cost about £200 because there are several sources and the Trust will charge separately for the MRI imaging and the CTG copying.

To get a preliminary opinion I think would probably cost up to £300. This is not a full opinion. A full opinion from a Obstetrician will cost about £1500 and I would suggest that we get a preliminary opinion in the first instance because it may well be possible to get insurance based on that opinion and/or to settle the case.

What I would suggest is that I ask a Midwife that I use a lot to report for free and an obstetrician to report for as little as possible and certainly no more than £300.

The question is have you got sufficient funds to get this case up and running and if not have you got any Before the Event Insurance that might cover the initial cost.

I think the first step is to look for any existing insurance cover and then for us to meet to decide the best way forward.

I'd like to help you and I think I can.

5

I have not yet got the benefit of a medical opinion but it seems to me that Joseph need not have died and I would like to help you investigate this – particular in the absence of an inquest and see whether we can obtain compensation for you and report back to the Trust in the hope that they will take steps to prevent this happening to another child.

I have enclosed meanwhile three forms of authority, these are for Mrs Cunningham's GP records, for Great Ormond Street and Queen Charlotte Hospital, can you please return these in the pre-paid envelope.

I look forward to hearing from you.

Best wishes.

Kind regards.

Yours sincerely

ROSAMUND RHODES-KEMP

Date 21/03/07

Subject - RE: Joseph Lloyd Cunningham

Dear Ms Rhodes-Kemp

Many thanks for your email, we received your very detailed letter yesterday, thank you. We have made a written application today for Joseph's medical notes, and will receive them in due course. There may be a short delay due to the fact that his notes are still at Queen's Hospital and have not yet been returned to King George's (where he was born) for coding.

The staff member I spoke to will endeavour to try and expedite the notes, but in the meantime I have completed the forms of authority and have posted them today, so you should receive them very shortly. Once we receive his notes we will of course forward a copy for your attention, please advise when you would prefer to meet with us. Presumably you may wish to wait until you are in full possession of all the facts, but we are happy to fit in with your schedule.

I am not sure whether Darren mentioned that we attended a private parent-craft course ran by the National Childbirth Trust a few weeks before Joseph was born. We have built up a quite close relationship to Andrea the tutor who ran the course and we have been updating her on the sad events as they have been happening. We forwarded a copy of my medical notes to her and she together with another midwife reviewed them and has sent back a very long list of the questions that she suggests we need to be asking, which should determine whether they provided the best care for me and Joseph. I will forward her comments to you together with Joseph's notes when we receive them. I understand that you will also be contacting a midwife of your acquaintance, perhaps your colleague will think of questions that Andrea had not thought to mention.

We did not think to take out any insurance beforehand. We certainly believe that we can raise the funds necessary to get this case up and running, perhaps when we meet with you in person you can advise what insurance you would recommend us getting.

If there is anything we can be doing in the meantime, please don't hesitate to contact us.

Best wishes

Charlotte

RE: Joseph Lloyd Cunningham
From: **Rosamund Rhodes-Kemp**
Sent: 21 March 2007 15:40
To: Charlotte Cunningham

Hello

We can meet up when I have seen the notes.

I welcome any points you have got and yes our in house midwife will probably think of more.

I am just very sorry.

Mark anything for my attention-a covering note is helpful and secure everything well together

Best Wishes

Rosamund

Specialist Compensation Claim Solicitors

BOLT BURDON KEMP

26th March 2007

Dear Mr and Mrs Cunningham

Clinical Negligence Claim

Thank you for returning the forms of authority.

Unfortunately each source of medical records is going to charge at least £50 (there are 3 sources to obtain records from so far, i.e. maximum £150 charge). So I will need a cheque for copying costs as well as the initial medical opinion for £300.

Have you looked to see whether you have insurance cover, for example with your household insurance, e.g. Direct Line or your motor car insurance, e.g. the AA, that would fund a legal case? Can you please check and get back to me and also send me the money on account in respect of these disbursements. We need to decide then on how you are going to fund the case and that will depend on whether or not you have existing insurance cover.

I look forward to hearing from you.

With best wishes and kind regards,

Yours sincerely

ROSAMUND RHODES-KEMP

From: **Charlotte Cunningham**
Sent: 27 March 2007 06:13 PM
To: Rosamund Rhodes-Kemp
Subject: Joseph Lloyd Cunningham

Dear Ms Rhodes-Kemp

I just wanted to ensure that you had received the signed forms of authority that I mailed to you last week.

Whilst we are waiting for Joseph's notes if you wish us to do anything else then please just say.

With kind regards

Charlotte

RE: Joseph Lloyd Cunningham
From: **Rosamund Rhodes-Kemp**
Sent: 27 March 2007 21:27
To: Charlotte Cunningham

I did yes thank you

Rosamund

Date – 05/04/07
Subject - Joseph Lloyd Cunningham

Dear Rosamund

We would like to send a cheque to you, please can you inform me to whom it is made payable to.

Many thanks

Charlotte

Easter Time

RE: Joseph Lloyd Cunningham
From: **Rosamund Rhodes-Kemp**
Sent: 05 April 2007 12:57
To: Charlotte Cunningham

Hello it is payable to Bolt Burdon Kemp please

Rosamund

RE: Joseph Lloyd Cunningham
From: **Rosamund Rhodes-Kemp**
Sent: 05 April 2007 15:06
To: Charlotte Cunningham

Thank you and for the questions which are helpful-if you have any further documents you think will help me please do send

Happy Easter to you too

Rosamund

From: Charlotte Cunningham
Sent: 05 April 2007 03:20 PM
To: Rosamund Rhodes-Kemp
Subject: RE: Joseph Lloyd Cunningham

Hiya,

I thought so, but just wanted to make sure before I sent it.

Please expect a cheque for £450.00 to arrive probably after the Easter break now.

Hope you have a nice Easter.

Take care

Charlotte

BOLT BURDON KEMP

10th April 2007

Dear Mr and Mrs Cunningham

Clinical Negligence Claim

I write to thank you for your cheque in the sum of £450.00 which I received today.

I will now request copies of the medical records. The various hospitals and healthcare providers will have up to 40 days to provide the copies of the records I request.

I will be in touch to update you in due course.

With best wishes and kind regards,

Yours sincerely

pp J. Cu___

ROSAMUND RHODES-KEMP

Sent: 26 April 2007 08:10 AM
To: Rosamund Rhodes-Kemp
Subject: Joseph Lloyd Cunningham Case

Rosamund,

I have read that we have 6 months to file a complaint against the NHS which will come to an end on the 22nd May 2007. Is this something that you have already done on our behalf or something you plan to do in the coming weeks?

Thank you

Darren Cunningham

RE: Joseph Lloyd Cunningham Case
From: **Rosamund Rhodes-Kemp**
Sent: 26 April 2007 10:48
Sent: Charlotte Cunningham
Cc: Claudia De Castro

I shall get back to you

ROSAMUND RHODES-KEMP

From: Charlotte Cunningham
Sent: 26 April 2007 12:46 PM
Sent: Rosamund Rhodes-Kemp
Subject: RE: Joseph Lloyd Cunningham Case

Thank you Rosamund.

In the meantime I have collected today the partogram and fluid balance/drug kardex that were previously missing from my ante-natal notes.

I have forwarded them to you today.

We look forward to hearing from you in due course.

Kind regards

Charlotte

RE: Joseph Lloyd Cunningham Case
From: Rosamund Rhodes-Kemp
Sent: 26 April 2007 12:01
To: Charlotte Cunningham

Thank you

ROSAMUND RHODES-KEMP

From: Charlotte Cunningham
Sent: 26 April 2007 12:46 PM
To: Rosamund Rhodes-Kemp
Subject: RE: Joseph Lloyd Cunningham Case

Thank you Rosamund.
In the meantime I have collected today the partogram and fluid balance/drug kardex that were previously missing from my ante-natal notes.
I have forwarded them to you today.
We look forward to hearing from you in due course.
Kind regards

Charlotte

From: **Charlotte Cunningham**
Sent: 27 April 2007 01:30 PM
To: Rosamund Rhodes-Kemp
Subject: Joseph Lloyd Cunningham

Dear Rosamund

Just to let you know that today we have received Joseph's notes from King George/Queens Hospital which documents his complete care from birth up until he was transferred to GOSH.

Darren will photocopy them on Monday and will then send you a copy that same day.

Hope you have a good weekend.

Kind regards

Charlotte

From: **Charlotte Cunningham**
Sent: 01 May 2007 03:54 PM
To: Rosamund Rhodes-Kemp
Subject: JLC

Dear Rosamund,

Just to inform you that I have posted today Joseph's notes to you, all being well you should receive these tomorrow.

Kind regards

Charlotte

RE: JLC
From: **Rosamund Rhodes-Kemp**
Sent: 02 May 2007 10:36
To: Charlotte Cunningham
Cc: Claudia De Castro

Thank you

ROSAMUND RHODES-KEMP

From: **Charlotte Cunningham**
Sent: 09 May 2007 07:54 AM
To: Rosamund Rhodes-Kemp
Subject: Joseph L Cunningham

Dear Rosamund,

I mentioned earlier that the NHS expect any complaints to be made within 6 months. This I learnt from the attached web site:

http://www.nhs.uk/england/aboutTheNHS/complainCompliment.cmsx

I am not sure if this applies to us but I wanted to bring it to your attention to prevent the NHS using the lack of notification as a reason to delay or reject our case.

I am chasing the final set of notes taken for Joseph while at GOSH along with a copy of the MRI scan. When you receive the details can you have someone look at the injuries to Josephs head while he had a blood sample taken and the brain injuries he received. I want to learn if there is a connection.

Thank you

Darren Cunningham

RE: Joseph L Cunningham
From: **Rosamund Rhodes-Kemp**
Sent: 09 May 2007 08:15
To: Charlotte Cunningham
Cc: Claudia De Castro

Hi

I have written to you at weekend and asked if we can meet -perhaps you could call my secretary Claudia by end of week and make an appointment -it will probably have to be second week of June now

ROSAMUND RHODES-KEMP

Arrange to Meet

Specialist Compensation Claim Solicitors
BOLT BURDON KEMP

9th May 2007

Dear Mr and Mrs Cunningham

<u>Clinical Negligence Claim</u>

I have received the partogram and Joseph's records from Barking, Havering and Redbridge Hospitals NHS Trust and thank you for this.

I have not yet obviously seen any imaging and I am slightly concerned that the CTGs that you kindly had copied are not going to be of sufficient quality for the experts to view them. I normally get a continuous copy done from the original but nonetheless this is a really good start.

I have written to an expert asking if he would be willing to look through the papers for you and report.

In the meantime I wonder whether it would be helpful for us to meet. If so, would you be able to get to our office and could you possible call Claudia De Castro on 020 7288 4845. Unfortunately this will not be until June 2007 but we have to get the medical records sorted and off to the expert in any event.

It seems to me that there were short comings with the labour and there are a number of contributions in the notes, e.g. the levels of Meconium. It also would appear that the damage to Joseph occurred in the last 20 to 30 minutes and that if that time had been avoided he would have been born in tact and so I think it is definitely worth investigating further.

I look forward to hearing from you.

Best wishes and kind regards,

Yours sincerely

<u>ROSAMUND RHODES-KEMP</u>

From: **Charlotte Cunningham**
Sent: 10 May 2007 11:31 AM
To: Rosamund Rhodes-Kemp
Subject: RE: Joseph L Cunningham

Dear Rosamund,

Yesterday we received Joseph's notes from GOSH and Darren will copy them and send them off to you today.

We are still waiting for the CD of the MRI, but that should follow very soon.
I have given Darren the tel. number to call Claudia to make an appointment, so hopefully he will be in touch either today or tomorrow.

Kind regards

Charlotte

RE: Joseph L Cunningham
From: **Rosamund Rhodes-Kemp**
Sent: 11 May 2007 11:27
To: Charlotte Cunningham

Thanks yes he has been in touch see you soon

ROSAMUND RHODES-KEMP

Specialist Compensation Claim Solicitors

BOLT BURDON KEMP

26th June 2007

Dear Mr and Mrs Cunningham

<u>Clinical Negligence Claim</u>

It was good to meet with you.

I am enclosing a copy of the witness statement which I have prepared from the information you kindly provided. I have also used the medical records to put some timings in.

We discussed the way that these claims work and the fact that I would do everything I could to settle this by way of negotiation including an apology and some kind of learning tools to help prevent this happening again. It seems to me that it is all about natural competence, training and monitoring but some how I think we need to get into that circle in order to be able to help.

Witness statement

I have done this in the name of Mr Cunningham because I think Mrs Cunningham would have found it very distressing to go through these events and to keep going through them in order to amend the statement.

It is just a draft so please feel free to amend and I shall obtain some times from the notes once I have your comments. Please fill in the sections in square brackets.

Damage to fetal scalp

I know that Mr Cunningham in particular was very worried about this and I have written to a neuroradiologist to see whether he is able and willing to help.

Meanwhile it would be useful if you would expand on the attached statement as you both see fit about the pain and suffering you endured after Joseph was born and up until the present day.

Documentary evidence

If you could provide me with documentary evidence of any financial losses I shall be extremely grateful, even if this is simply an estimate of return mileage to any particular hospital that you would not have gone to if Joseph had been born healthy.

Funding

I explained to you about Conditional Fee Agreements and this will follow under cover of a separate letter.

You may well wish to discuss some of the issues in this case and I would feel much happier going through the CFA with one of you on the telephone before you sign anything. Could you therefore arrange a telephone appointment with my secretary Claudia, so that we can go through it? It will take about 15 minutes.

Helpful charities

You may wish to contact some of the charities – and I have set these out below for you - as it may help you both to deal with everything that has happened.

Compassionate Friends

An organisation which you may find helpful is the Compassionate Friends. This is a support group for bereaved parents and their families who have lost children of any age and through any cause. They also have a grandparents group. Their website address is www.tcf.org.uk. Their helpline number is 0845 1232 304 and it is open from 10.00am until 4.00pm and 6.30pm until 10.30pm. It is always manned by a bereaved parent who is there to listen. They also have an information number which is 0845 1203 785 this deals with membership enquiries and orders for their leaflets and publications.

SANDS

The other group that you may find helpful is SANDS (Stillbirth and Neonatal Death Society). Their website is www.uk-sands.org and their telephone number is 020 7436 5881 Monday to Thursday 10.00am to 4.00pm. SANDS also has local support groups.

BLISS

Another group that you may find helpful is BLISS. They are at 2nd and 3rd Floors, 9 Holyrood Street, London Bridge, London, SE1 2EL and can be contacted on free phone 0500 618 140.

It was a pleasure to meet with you although I wish that the circumstances had been happier.

I look forward to hearing from you.

Best wishes and kind regards,

Yours sincerely

ROSAMUND RHODES-KEMP

From: **Charlotte Cunningham**
Sent: 28 June 2007 09:50 PM
To: Rosamund Rhodes-Kemp
Subject: Witness Statement

Rosamund,

We have received your statement and read through it. We have a number
of amendments we would like to make and wonder if it's possible for you to
forward the document in word format for us to alter then return for you
to
review.

Thank you

Darren Cunningham

From: **Rosamund Rhodes-Kemp**
Sent: 29 June 2007 11:33
To: Charlotte Cunningham
Cc: Claudia De Castro
Subject: RE: Witness Statement
Importance: High

Yes indeed we can do this for you

ROSAMUND RHODES-KEMP

FW: Witness Statement
From: **Claudia De Castro**
Sent: 29 June 2007 11:06
To: Charlotte Cunningham

witness s...doc (53.2 KB)

Dear Mr Cunningham,

Please find attached the Witness Statement as requested.

Kind regards
Claudia

Specialist Compensation Claim Solicitors

BOLT BURDON KEMP

27th June 2007

Dear Mr and Mrs Cunningham

<u>Your claim on behalf of Joseph</u>

Further to previous correspondence, I enclose the following -

(a) Conditional Fee Agreement with (1) "Conditional Fee Agreements: what you need to know" and (2) my firm's Terms of Business attached;

(b) Pre CFA Explanation (Checklist and Confirmation) document;

(c) Law Assist – Clinical Negligence Checklist;

(d) Law Assist – Clinical Negligence Insurance Proposal Form for Deferred Premiums;

(e) (Law Assist Clinical Justice Plan – "After the Event" Legal Expenses Insurance Policy Summary)

May I ask you to read these documents carefully. I have not completed the insurance items until we have discussed the CFA itself.

Success Fee

After discussion with Roger Bolt, Senior Partner we have arranged a total success fee of 100% (i.e. a 100% uplift on our basic costs). The risk element of the success fee will also be 100% and we have arranged for this to be staged. This anticipates the two different stages throughout the life of the claim at which it might conclude i.e. by agreement or trial, namely:

(a)   Any time before court proceedings have been issued;
(b)   Any time after court proceedings have been issued, including before a trial or at a trial.

The total success fee will be 50% (i.e. a 50% uplift on our basic costs) if the claim concludes during period (a), rising to 100% (i.e. a 100% uplift on our basic costs) if it concludes during period (b).

1

The risk element of the success fee will be 50% if the claim concludes during period (a), rising to 100% if it concludes during period (b). The risk element reflects the risks involved in the case and they include the following:

i)   We have not yet interviewed witness or seen the Defendant's witness statements
ii)   We have not yet seen complete set of medical records
iii)   There are likely to be relevant documents in the possession of third parties that we have not yet seen.
iv)   Your opponent may be able to offer an explanation for the incident which is equally plausible and which may exonerate your opponent from liability
v)   You may struggle to show that it was circumstances of the birth that caused Joseph's condition and tragic death. Not an antenatal event/infection or some other cause.
vi)   The inherent difficulties in assessing Part 36 offers of settlement when making or receiving and added risks of the ring-fenced damages clause in the CFA
vii)   There has been no admission of liability or causation and the position of the Defendants is unknown.

It is expected that this part of the success fee, known as the risk element, or at least some of it, will be recoverable from the other side.

Disbursements

In order to proceed with your case and our investigations we shall need to pay for ongoing disbursements which are expenses such as obtaining medical records, medical reports, Court costs, experts' fees etc. **It is important you are aware that we shall need to ask you for money on account of these disbursements as the case progresses which can be quite costly.** If you win, your outlay will almost always be refunded by the Defendants in total, however if you lose then the insurance policy will cover the costs of the disbursements incurred after the Conditional Fee Agreement is signed. Some insurers will arrange a loan to cover disbursements pre-signature of the Conditional Fee Agreement.

However, as discussed we have agreed that you will be paying your disbursements as your claim proceeds.

Deductions

Please note that any deductions we make from the damages with regard to our unrecovered costs and disbursements will be capped at 10%. Therefore, you will receive at least 90% of the compensation. You have a right to have any costs we claim from you to be assessed by the court if you wish.

Pre-Conditional Fee Agreement Explanation

I am required to advise you orally and in writing in relation to the terms and conditions of the Conditional Fee Agreement **before** it is formally made. I therefore enclose a Pre CFA Explanation (Checklist and Confirmation) document, which details the relevant points which must be explained to you both orally and in writing. Please read through the Pre CFA explanation document. Then, please telephone me so that I may explain all points to you orally and give you the opportunity to ask any questions you may have before signing the document and also the Conditional Fee Agreement. Alternatively, you may wish to arrange an appointment to come into the office to discuss the Agreement with me.

2

Once you have signed the Pre CFA Explanation (Checklist and Confirmation) document and the Conditional Fee Agreement, I shall also sign the latter document and send signed and dated copies to you for your records.

Existing Insurance Cover

It is very important that **before** making the Conditional Fee Agreement and signing and dating the Pre CFA Explanation (Checklist and Confirmation) document, you check to see what, if any, existing insurance arrangements you, any member of your family or household have, which might provide you with cover for any legal costs to fund the claim and/or for which you may be liable. Existing insurance arrangements are typically provided through the following policies:

1. ~~Vehicle insurance policies~~

2. ~~Household contents insurance policies~~

3. ~~Credit card insurance policies~~

4. Any employers' insurance policies that benefit you.

5. Private healthcare insurance policies (including an employer's policy if this covers you).

6. Personal accident insurance policies

7. ~~Mortgage protection policies~~

8. ~~After the event insurance policies that may have been taken out by previous solicitors for your benefit, if you only recently transferred conduct of the claim from another firm of solicitors to BOLT BURDON KEMP~~

9. ~~Union benefits~~

If you consider that you may benefit from one or more of the above existing insurance arrangements, please notify me of this immediately and provide me with copies of any documentation you may have which relates to those insurance arrangements, for example, insurance policy schedules.

After the event insurance

Bolt Burdon Kemp is not authorised by the Financial Services Authority. However, we are included on the register maintained by the Finance Services Authority so that we can carry on insurance mediation activity, which is broadly the advising on, selling and administration of insurance contracts. This part of our business, including arrangements for complaints or redress if something goes wrong, is regulated by the Law Society. The register can be accessed via the FSA website at www.fsa.gov.uk/register.

We are not contractually obliged to conduct insurance mediation activities with any particular insurance undertaking and we have not given advice on the basis of a fair analysis of a sufficiently large number of insurance contracts available on the market to enable the firm to make a recommendation in accordance with professional criteria regarding which contract of insurance would be adequate to meet your needs. If you

3

would like further details of the policies I have selected from or why I made this selection, please let me know.

I am recommending LawAssist After the Event insurance policy to you as I believe it meets your needs as a person who enters into a conditional fee agreement with their solicitor for a clinical negligence claim and wishes to protect themselves against potential costs liabilities.

I attach a policy summary for your information.

I have taken the following steps to ensure as far as reasonable possible that my recommendation is suitable to your demands and needs:

a) considered relevant information already held;
b) obtained details of any relevant existing insurance;
c) identified your requirements and explained to you what you need to disclose.
d) assessed whether the level of cover is sufficient for the risks that you wish to insure; and
e) considered the relevance of any exclusions, excesses, limitations or conditions.

I enclose the proposal form. If you do not consider that this is a suitable insurance policy for you please contact me, failing which I will effect the insurance. We will discuss this when we discuss the overall CFA.

If there is anything you do not understand please call me to go through the documents if there is any thing that you want to discuss. In this regard, please could you contact Claudia to arrange a 15 minute appointment in order that I can go through all of this with you over the phone.

I look forward to hearing from you and working with you to make progress with the claim.

Yours sincerely

ROSAMUND RHODES-KEMP

4

From: **Charlotte Cunningham**
Sent: 03 July 2007 08:20 PM
To: Rosamund Rhodes-Kemp
Subject: CFA letter

Rosamund,

We have received your letter and have read the terms and conditions and
now have a reasonable understanding on the financial process should the case win or
not.

With respect to Existing Insurance cover, you have listed a number of
policies on page 3. When I call, to enquire, can you tell me exactly
what I should ask if the insurance policy covers please? If the answer to the
question is yes then what documentation/evidence will you require?

Thanks

Darren

RE: CFA letter
From: **Rosamund Rhodes-Kemp**
Sent: 04 July 2007 08:52
To: Charlotte Cunningham
Cc: Claudia De Castro

You need to ask if Clinical negligence claims are included in legal
cover and to send you an application form.
That should do it any problems let me know and I will call them

ROSAMUND RHODES-KEMP

From: **Charlotte Cunningham**
Sent: 09 July 2007 10:06 PM
To: Rosamund Rhodes-Kemp
Subject: Witness statement for Joseph Cunningham

Rosamund,

I have reviewed and updated the statement you sent recalling events as
best as I can remember.

Would you mind proof reading and editing any comments that you may think
is unsuitable or unnecessary. Once you're satisfied, please return a hard
copy and I will sign and return.

Thanks

Darren Cunningham

RE: Witness statement for Joseph Cunningham
From: **Rosamund Rhodes-Kemp**
From: 20 July 2007 11:32
To: Charlotte Cunningham
Cc: Claudia De Castro

Hello Mr Cunningham

I have received and dealt with yours statement and I understand we are
speaking on Monday re funding
Can I ask you please by then to have checked that you have no legal
expense insurance that would cover a clinical negligence case please?
Many Thanks

ROSAMUND RHODES-KEMP

From: **Charlotte Cunningham**
Sent 20 July 2007 02:50 PM
To: Rosamund Rhodes-Kemp
Cc: Claudia De Castro
Subject: RE: Witness statement for Joseph Cunningham

Rosamund,

I have checked as requested and can confirm that I/we don't have legal expense insurance with any other company/policy.

I have received a letter from the hospital today requesting for payment before they plan to post the MRI scans of Joseph. This will come on a CD and I will make 2 copies and post onto you.

Darren

RE: Witness statement for Joseph Cunningham
From: **Rosamund Rhodes-Kemp**
Sent: 20 July 2007 14:04
To: Charlotte Cunningham
Cc: Claudia De Castro

Thank you

ROSAMUND RHODES-KEMP

Clinical Negligence Claim
From: **Claudia De Castro**
Sent: 25 July 2007 08:10
To: Charlotte Cunningham

letter to...rtf (23.7 KB), Witness s...rtf (66.7 KB)

CLAUDIA DE CASTRO

Specialist Compensation Claim Solicitors

BOLT BURDON KEMP

26th July 2007

Dear Mr and Mrs Cunningham

Clinical Negligence Claim

Following our telephone conversation, it was good to speak to you and I am very grateful for you sparing me the time to go through the documents. If at any time there is anything that you are concerned about please do not hesitate to call me.

Meanwhile would you possibly be able to let me have a sum on account in relation to copying, because there are fees payable to the various organizations such as continuous CTG copying and GP records.

I will then need to get all the notes sorted and paginated by the medical records sorter who will charge about £235. If you would like me to look into a way of funding the disbursements by way of a loan please let me know.

The reports in this case are going to come to about £2,000 and that includes the neuroradiologist, the neonatologist and the obstetrician. It could be more but I am asking them all to limit the fees because of the circumstances. Unfortunately this is an area where high fees are charged and there are long delays in getting medical expert evidence. I am sorry because I know that you would like to see the case dealt with as swiftly as possible. I shall do my best.

You also mentioned publicity when we spoke Mr Cunningham and I have given you the benefit of my view which is that we should wait until we have got the initial expert evidence in, at least on liability, i.e. whether there was negligence because I think you will find that you have a firmer fitting then when talking to journalists about what happened. Otherwise the Trust are likely to blind the journalist with science and we are not going to have anything to bat it back with.

I wish you all the best and I am glad to hear that Charlotte is back at work.

Best wishes and kind regards,

Yours sincerely

ROSAMUND RHODES-KEMP

From: **Charlotte Cunningham**
Sent: 30 July 2007 06:33 PM
To: Rosamund Rhodes-Kemp
Subject: further funding request.

Rosamund,

I have received your letter today requesting for further funding but I would like to understand how much you are asking for as the letter says about £2,000. Is there any reason why the money is needed up front and not on completion of work?

Regards

Darren Cunningham

RE: further funding request.
From: **Rosamund Rhodes-Kemp**
Sent: 31 July 2007 11:42
To: Charlotte Cunningham

Hello it is usual to ask for this amount on account so the firm knows there will be sufficient to pay the disbursements as and when they are incurred e.g. copying medical records sorter and expert

I am happy that you pay as required if it helps. One of the other reasons is that it demonstrates commitment by the client-to what is a costly exercise-financially and emotionally. I know this does not apply in your case.

Best Wishes

ROSAMUND RHODES-KEMP

From: **Charlotte Cunningham**
Sent: 31 July 2007 10:14 PM
To: Rosamund Rhodes-Kemp
Subject: MRI Scans of Joseph L Cunningham

Rosamund,

I have run into difficulties with obtaining the complete set of MRIs
taken of Joseph.
I have received a disk from Queen's hospital that contains 11 images and
I know for fact that there are images missing simply because the images
that were used to demonstrate Joseph's injuries to me are not included. The
images are also marked with '1 of 3', '1 of 19' or '1 of 16' so if the
sequencing is true then there were at least 38 images taken. I will
forward a copy of what I have and pursue to get the missing images from GOSH since
I have received a letter from Queens Hospital claiming no more than 11 were taken.
What I have been given also comes with a statement which implies there were no
injuries to be found which is clearly not true.

Darren

RE: MRI Scans of Joseph L Cunningham
From: **Rosamund Rhodes-Kemp**
Sent: 01 August 2007 10:06
To: Charlotte Cunningham

Disappointing and frankly disturbing-if I can help let me know

ROSAMUND RHODES-KEMP

From: **Charlotte Cunningham**
Sent: 02 August 2007 07:25 PM
To: Rosamund Rhodes-Kemp
Subject: RE: further funding request.

Rosamund,

We will get a cheque in the post for £1,000 by the end of the month.

Darren

RE: further funding request.
From: **Rosamund Rhodes-Kemp**
Sent: 08 August 2007 14:02
To: Charlotte Cunningham
Cc: Claudia De Castro

Hello I have received your copy letter regarding the imaging.

Let me know if I can help

ROSAMUND RHODES-KEMP

Date - 30/08/07
Subject - Joseph Cunningham - MRI Scans

Rosamund,

I have been in constant contact with the GOSH PALS team and the family liaison team in GOSH and they have been trying to assist me to get the missing MRI scans of Joseph. I had to tell them that I had no intention of filing legal action at that time or would not have got their cooperation. The PALS team were giving me regular updates and were seen to be making progress after escalating the issue and advised me to make a formal complaint. This came to an end on Wednesday 29th August at 16:00 when I received a call from PALS to inform me that they had received a mail from you informing the NHS that I planned to take legal action. This now means that you will need to request for the missing MRI scans and any further information.

I would like to add at this point that in light that the hospital have not sent the complete set of MRI scans and confirmed that there are no further scans - which is not true simply because the scans they have given would make it impossible for the GOSH Radiologist team to have written their report.
The hospital has breached the data protection act http://www.opsi.gov.uk/acts/ acts1998/ukpga_19980029_en_1 (Part 2 Rights of Data subjects and other, paragraph 13 section 2.)   I can also honestly state that I have found this episode very stressful and worrying. The comments that come with the CD claiming there was no problem with his brain did not help matters which reads - ' 362846 28/12/2006 MRI Head
This examination shows severe artefacts due to the patient movements. There is a normal aeration of the paranasal sinuses. No pathology is seen in the orbits. The differentiation of the grey and white matter is normal and no pathological alterations in signal are present. The cortical structures and the ventricular system are normal in its configuration and width. There is no midline shift. The posterior fossa structures return a normal signal without any pathologic changes. The brain vessels, as far as they are presented, show a normal signal of flow. Conclusion Normal cranial MRI related to the patients age group.

If the hospital are adamant in their view that there are no other MRI scans then what am I to think? This would imply that the scans reviewed by GOSH and those shown to me did not belong to Joseph and that his condition was not as severe as GOSH had predicted. This also implies that I was ill advised of Joseph's condition and that taking him off the ventilator and giving him high doses of morphine where not the correct course of action. One could even go as far as to say his death certificate is incorrect and should now read morphine overdose. This might sound paranoid but what are they leading me to believe?

I've had to take time off work this week so I can get my thoughts together as I am unable to focus on my work at the moment.

On a different note, Charlotte has posted a cheque to your address for the sum of £1,000. Additional funds will follow in due course.

Regards

Darren Cunningham

Specialist Compensation Claim Solicitors

BOLT BURDON KEMP

7th September 2007

Dear Mr and Mrs Cunningham

<u>Clinical Negligence Claim</u>

It was good to speak to you although I was very sorry of the distress that you have recently suffered in relation to the images that were sent to you from Barking, Havering and Redbridge Hospitals NHS Trust.

I have pursued these images both with that Trust and Great Ormond Street and I will let you know how I get on.

Meanwhile I have written to Brian Kendall and asked him if he would be able to prepare a preliminary report on the images that we have got and evidence from Great Ormond Street.

I shall keep you closely informed and I hope that you found it helpful to at least talk to someone about what is going on so that I could reassure you that your experiences are not unusual sadly within the NHS. Records going missing or changed or tampered with are likely. It is sad but true. I have not known it to happen with images before though.

The expert that I have approached is Brian Kendall who is a world renowned expert in this field. There is no-one better and if anyone can cast some light on the situation it is Brian Kendall.

I shall do my best.

Best wishes and kind regards,

Yours sincerely

<u>ROSAMUND RHODES-KEMP</u>

Specialist Compensation Claim Solicitors

BOLT BURDON KEMP

19th September 2007

Dear Mr and Mrs Cunningham

<u>Clinical Negligence Claim</u>

I am writing to inform you that I have received a copy of the CTG trace from Barking, Havering and Redbridge Hospitals NHS Trust.

I am still waiting to hear from the Neuro Radiologist on the imaging and will be in touch as soon as I hear from him.

I hope you are feeling a bit better.

Best wishes and kind regards,

Yours sincerely

<u>ROSAMUND RHODES-KEMP</u>

Specialist Compensation Claim Solicitors

BOLT BURDON KEMP

3rd October 2007

Dear Mr and Mrs Cunningham

I am enclosing Terms of Business for your file. Please note that you do not need to action anything with regards to the Terms of Business, it is sent for your information only, however please sign and return one copy of the Terms of Business to me.

Best wishes and kind regards,

Yours sincerely

ROSAMUND RHODES-KEMP

Update request on Joseph Cunningham case.
From: **Charlotte Cunningham**
Sent: 15 December 2007 18:01
To: Rosamund Rhodes-Kemp

Rosamund,

Can you give Charlotte and I an update on your progress with our case, especially any progress on getting the full set of MRI scans please.

I'd like to share with you the news that Charlotte is now 3 months pregnant and looking forward to 2008 in the hope of starting our family.

I'd like to wish you a merry Christmas and Happy New Year and thank you for your support.

Respectfully

Mr. Darren Cunningham

RE: Update request on Joseph Cunningham case.
From: **Rosamund Rhodes-Kemp**
Sent: 17 December 2007 10:04
To: Charlotte Cunningham
Cc: Claudia De Castro

Thank you and I am delighted with your news

I have in desperation sent the images we do have and reports to Dr Kendall to see if he can advise on how best to try and get the remaining imaging and indeed if this is essential

Best Wishes and will update you once I have heard from Dr Kendall

Rosamund

RE: Update request on Joseph Cunningham case.
From: **Charlotte Cunningham**
Sent: 19 December 2007 08:09
To: Rosamund Rhodes-Kemp

Rosamund,

If by chance Dr Kendall feels there is no need for the full set of MRI scans in order to have a winning case against the NHS I would still like for you to do everything within your power to obtain the complete set of images. I Would want his opinion using the images I was shown that helped me come to the decision that taking Joseph off the Vent was the right thing to do. I also want his opinion if Joseph suffered brain damage as a result of having a blood sample taken from his head.

Respectfully

Darren

RE: Update request on Joseph Cunningham case.
From: **Rosamund Rhodes-Kemp**
Sent: 19 December 2007 09:10
To: Charlotte Cunningham

Don't worry I shall do everything I can to get these scans-everything

Rosamund

Dr Kendall's Report

Specialist Compensation Claim Solicitors

BOLT BURDON KEMP

15th January 2008

Dear Mr and Mrs Cunningham

Clinical negligence claim

I am enclosing a copy of the preliminary report of Dr Brian Kendall.

Now his reports are always couched in highly technical language but basically what he is saying is that the images that he has been shown demonstrate a prolonged period – above 10 minutes – of profound lack of oxygen at birth.

There is evidence of bleeding on the skull - you have alluded to this yourself – but it is probably related to the process of delivery rather than the application of the foetal scalpel electrode, even if the latter was botched and several applications had to be made.

I have written to Brian Kendall asking him to clarify that my understanding of his report is correct and obviously I will let you know further once I have heard from him.

I have also asked him whether any missing images are important to his opinion because frankly if they are not there is no point in chasing them. Not at this stage anyway. If they became important then obviously we will do our best to get them. In fact I am having quite a lot of trouble getting the balance of the records. There appear to be some obstetric records missing but the Trust that they have sent everything so there is an ongoing debate as it is and I have included in my further request that they provide me with any further imaging but to be honest I suspect that we would need to get quite a bit further down the line before they are going to comply.

Meanwhile I hope that Mrs Cunningham's pregnancy is going well and I think what we will do is wait to hear from Brian Kendall and then I will chase the Trust again. Once we have a complete set of records I think they should go to an obstetrician along with Brian Kendall's preliminary view. I think his preliminary view will probably be enough actually if we are talking about settlement.

Best wishes and kind regards,

Yours sincerely

ROSAMUND RHODES-KEMP

Dr Kendall replied by fax to Rosamund but the quality of the fax was so poor it has been typed out below and reads as follows:

Dr Brian Kendall
FRCR CRCP FRCS

6th January 2008

Dear Rosamund

Re: Joseph Cunningham (dob 22.12.06 deceased 29.1.07)

Thank you for your letter of 18.12.07 and for the enclosed statement of Mr Darren Cunningham and for the CDROM which contains images from a cranial MRI performed on 28.12.06. The MRI is of diagnostic quality although there is some movement artefact.
It consists of the following sections and sequences:
1.   Axial T1 and T2 weighted spin and gradient echo
2.   Coronal T2 weighted spin and gradient echo
3.   Sagittal T2 weighted.

The following abnormalities are shown:
1.   There is abnormal signal high on T1 and mixed on T2 weighted in the lateral nuclei of the thalami and posteriorly in the putamina of the lentiform nuclei.
2.   There is lack of normal low signal from the white matter of the corona radiate underlying the pre and post central gyri and in the posterior limbs of the internal capsules on the T2 weighted sections

These abnormalities indicative of brain damage are in regions of high metabolism around the time of foetal maturity. These regions are therefore vulnerable to profound circulatory insufficiency.

Mammalian experiments an clinical experience suggest that damage begun in such regions in the previously normal non acidotic foetus after 10 minutes of profound circulatory insufficiency. Continuation of the circulatory insufficiency for longer than 25 minutes often results in death or more extensive brain damage involving regions of lower metabolism.

No abnormality is shown elsewhere within the brain substance. In particular there is no evidence of damage in the border zone regions between the cortical distributions of the main cerebal arteries which occurs with partial hypoxic ischaemia.

There is no evidence of any early intrauterine brain damage.

There is no evidence of any malformation of the brain.

There is a recent interhemispheric subdural haematoma and there is also subdural haematoma in the posterior fossa, mainly around the right cerebellar hemisphere. These haematomas are not exerting significant mass effect and are not of themselves causing any brain damage.

There is also a left sided cephalo haematoma which is likely to be associated with the process of delivery rather than with the attempts of application of the foetal scalpel electrode. There is no evidence of any underlying skull fracture.

If any other imaging is available I will be pleased to assess further, but the MRI is adequate to show the mechanism of the brain damage which caused death.

I will of course await your further instructions before providing a formal report.

With best wishes for the New Year

Yours sincerely

Brian

Dr Brain Kendall

F.R.C.R. F.R.C.P. F.R.C.S.

Specialist Compensation Claim Solicitors

BOLT BURDON KEMP

30 January 2008

Dear Mr and Mrs Cunningham

<u>Clinical Negligence Claim</u>

I am enclosing Terms of Business for your file. Please note that you do not need to action anything with regards to the Terms of Business, it is sent for your information only, however please sign and return one copy of the Terms of Business to me.

Yours sincerely

<u>ROSAMUND RHODES-KEMP</u>

Specialist Compensation Claim Solicitors

BOLT BURDON KEMP

1st February 2008

Dear Mr and Mrs Cunningham

Clinical Negligence Claim

I have received the medical records back from the medical records sorter.

I have chased Brian Kendall for his report. He is the neuroradiologist. Although we thought that we had at last received everything we have just got another CD Rom from the Trust and I have asked Brian Kendall to compare this with what he has got already.

In addition though review of the records shows that there are discrepancies between the reporting of the MRI head scan take on 28 December 2006 by Queens Hospital and Great Ormond Street. The report provided by Queens claims a normal MRI scan for the age group but the report by Great Ormond Street on 18 January 2007 records subdural haemorrhages and a left cephalhaematoma as well as swelling and signal changes which are all consistent with severe Hypoxic Ischaemic Encephalopathy. This is, as you know, a condition caused solely by a lack of oxygen before birth. It was responsible for Joseph's brain damage and his death but it may have been contributed to by the neonatal care because the records from there demonstrate that Joseph had a fluid overload. It is not clear when but it would be shortly after he was born because the clinical note relating to the fluid overload is undated. The point of HEI cases is that you reduce fluids and monitor them very carefully because you do not want to exacerbate the cerebral swelling. You see the baby is born almost dead due to the lack of oxygen to the brain. As soon as the baby is born what happens is that the brain starts to swell as a consequence of the lack of oxygen and this is what causes fits. The fits are damaging in themselves so drugs are given to reduce the fits and contain the expansion or brain swelling. The last thing you want to do is to make that worse because that in turn will make the brain damage worse.

In addition to this when the overload seems to have been spotted, attempts were made to catheterise Joseph but these failed and no urine was drained because the catheter did not actually get into his bladder, it was misdirected, so in other words he carried on with the fluid overload which would have been caused in the first place but was then left to cause continuing harm because they failed to drain the fluid away having created the fluid overload in the first place.

I want to have Brian Kendall's report because we can then take a view as to whether to instruct other experts. It seems to me that a neonatologist would be helpful but these people take a long time to report and they cost a lot of money. So I have asked to the neonatologist asking if he could report more quickly and more cost effectively than for a Cerebral Palsy case, i.e. an ongoing situation and one with far more notes.

I have also written to the Trust asking them to explain some of these issues.

I shall write again as soon as possible and I hope that Charlotte's pregnancy is progressing well.

Best wishes and kind regards,

Yours sincerely

ROSAMUND RHODES-KEMP

Specialist Compensation Claim Solicitors

BOLT BURDON KEMP

11th February 2008

Dear Mr and Mrs Cunningham

Clinical Negligence Claim

I am pleased to enclose the following:

1.   Letter dated 4 February 2008 from Brian Kendall, the Consultant Neuroradiologist;

2.   Medical report prepared by Brian Kendall dated 4 February 2008.

My understanding of this report is that Joseph suffered two types of bleeding into his brain. One was a Cephalhaematoma and the other was subdural hemorrhage but neither of these were causative of any brain damage or asphyxia or instrumental in his tragic death. They were not clinically significant. The former can occur in many births, particularly a difficult delivery, and the latter I have asked Brian Kendall if it could have been caused by problems with the application of the foetal scalp electrodes.

In relation to the cause of death what Dr Kendall has said is that the imaging is conducive with an episode of profound lack of oxygen shortly before delivery and that is the most likely cause of death.

I am terribly sorry if you find all of this distressing but the report is helpful to the case. have asked Brian Kendall to clarify if my understanding is correct.

Meanwhile I have asked the Trust to send me a copy of their Adverse Incident Report and they have done so but to be honest it is so brief it is rather insulting. I am not sure if they have investigated further but if all they did was write an incident form like the one attached in relation to the death of a baby boy then no wonder that they have not learnt anything from their mistake. I have raised this with the Trust and I will get back to you.

I have also asked the Trust if they would admit responsibility, i.e. liability and they have said that they cannot do so because they have to have instructions from the National Health Service Litigation Authority to do that but that they are going to refer the matter to the NHSLA shortly.   This is a bit of a disaster because the NHSLA never answer correspondence for months on end. Nonetheless on the plus side they do have guidelines now regarding still births or cases involving the death of a baby to hurry settlement, although even that has not been 100% effective in expediting claims within that organization. They seem to be suffering from huge administrative difficulties. I thought I had better warn you now because many of my clients have been quite distressed by the lack of response from the NHSLA over the last twelve months.

If the NHSLA are not willing to admit liability then we are going to have to instruct an obstetrician to report and my advice at this stage would be to send the instructions and then press the NHSLA for a response on liability. This is so that we can threaten them with the fact that we are going to get a report and it will cost them money because ultimately we are going to win the case and they are going to have to pay the costs.

Also you waste no time waiting for the NHSLA to admit liability if the expert is already instructed and your name is on his waiting list. Otherwise you can wait 3 or 4 months for the NHSLA to tell you that they are not going to admit liability and then you have to instruct an expert. The obstetrician will cost about £1,000. I realize all of this is very expensive and I am sorry.

We can enter into a Conditional Fee Agreement with you but you would still need to pay disbursements and perhaps we can discuss that further. You would need insurance if we go ahead and issue proceedings. Personally I think that we could now enter into a CFA on the evidence available from Brian Kendall.

Perhaps you could have a think about everything that I have enclosed and get back to me.

I hope that Charlotte's pregnancy is progressing well.

Best wishes and kind regards,

Yours sincerely

ROSAMUND RHODES-KEMP

2

Dr Brian Kendall
FRCR FRCP FRCS

4th February 2008

Dear Rosamund

Re: Joseph Cunningham (deceased)

Thank you for sending the additional CD-ROMs. One of these contains only a chest x-ray. The other contains images, which are identical to those, which I have already seen.

I enclose a more formal report. The cephalhaematoma and the subdural haemorrhage about which Mr Cunningham is obviously concerned are evident on the images. A cephalhaematoma is not uncommon during delivery. It can be associated with an underlying skull fracture of which there is no evidence in Joseph but it is not of itself a dangerous condition.

The subdural haematomas are too shallow to be of clinical significance and are certainly not related to his death.

There is evidence of haemorrhagic infarction in regions, which are damaged by profound circulatory insufficiency. Although it is not evident on the imaging made so soon after birth, brain stem damage may be sufficient to make such an asphyxiated baby unviable and I presume that this is the likely cause of death.

An obstetric opinion would be necessary to determine whether there was an indication to deliver by caesarean section earlier in the labour and thus avoid the very traumatic vaginal delivery.

I am unsure whether the claim is legally aided. I enclose a provisional fee note on the assumption that it is so, which takes into account any questions you may have.

With best wishes

Yours sincerely

Brian

Dr Brian Kendall
F.R.C.R. F.R.C.P. F.R.C.S.

Medical report by

Dr Brian Kendall
Consultant Neuroradiologist

on

Joseph Cunningham

(dob 22.12.06 deceased 29.1.07)

prepared for

Messrs Bolt Burdon Kemp solicitors

dated

4th February 2008

Medical report on Joseph Cunningham (dob 22.12.06 deceased 29.1.07) prepared for the Court at the request of Messrs Bolt Burdon Kemp solicitors acting on behalf of Mr Darren Cunningham, Joseph's father by Dr Brian Kendall FRCR, FRCP, FRCS, Consultant Neuroradiologist at The Royal Free Hospital and honorary Consultant Neuroradiologist at the Hospital for Sick Children and The National Hospital for Neurology and Neurosurgery, London.

For the production of this report I was provided with the following documentation:

1. **Statement of Mr Darren Cunningham dated 25.7.07.**
2. **Letters of Instruction from Messrs Bolt Burdon Kemp, dated 26.2.07 and 18.12.07.**
3. **Neuroimaging described in the text of this report.**

It is my brief to analyse the neuroimaging in order to diagnose the pathology, which underlay Joseph Cunningham's neurological disabilities, leading up to his death.

A cranial MRI, performed on 29.12.06 is available for review imaged on two CD-ROMs. The study is of diagnostic quality though some of the images are marred by movement artefact.

The following sections and sequences are presented.

1. Axial T1 and T2 weighted spin and gradient echo.
2. Coronal T2 weighted spin and gradient echo.
3. Sagittal T1 weighted.

The following abnormalities are shown:

1.   There is abnormally high signal on T1 weighted sequences in the lateral nuclei of the thalami, the posterior parts of the putamina of the lentiform nuclei and in the cortex of the pre and post central gyri.

2.   There is abnormal low signal on the T2 weighted sequences in the lateral nuclei of the thalami and there is lack of the normal low signal in the white matter of the corona radiata underlying the pre and post central gyri and in the posterior limbs of the internal capsules. There is also a tiny haemorrhagic focus in the left paracentral white matter just below the central sulcus.

These abnormalities are indicative of brain damage in regions of high metabolism around the time of foetal maturity. Such regions are vulnerable to profound circulatory insufficiency.

Mammalian experiments and clinical experience indicate that in the previously normal, non-acidotic foetus, irreversible damage usually begins after about ten minutes of profound circulatory insufficiency in such regions. Continuation of the circulatory insufficiency for about twenty-five minutes often results in death or more extensive and severe damage involving regions of lower metabolism in survivors.

No other abnormality is shown within the brain substance. In particular there is no evidence of additional damage in the borderzone regions between the cortical distributions of the main cerebral arteries, which occurs with more prolonged peripheral perfusion failure associated with partial hypoxic ischaemia.

There is no evidence of any early intrauterine brain damage.

There is no evidence of any malformation of the brain.

There is interhemispheric subdural blood clot extending around the posterior convexities of the cerebral hemispheres, more marked on the right side. There is also subdural haematoma in the posterior fossa, mainly around the right cerebellar hemisphere. These haematomas are not exerting any significant mass effect and are not of themselves of clinical significance.

There is a left sided cephalhaematoma. There is no evidence of any underlying skull fracture or additional abnormality.

I note that Joseph was a cephalic presentation, presumably in the occipitoposterior position. The second stage of labour was prolonged and the delivery was complicated by shoulder dystocia. Mr Cunningham described the traumatic manner in which the shoulder dystocia was eventually overcome.

Joseph was born in poor condition. After resuscitation he was nursed in the special care baby unit and transferred to Great Ormond Street Hospital where unfortunately he died.

The precise cause of death is not certain but it is most likely to be due to the profound hypoxic ischaemic brain damage.

I, BRIAN KENDALL, DECLARE THAT:

1. I understand that my overriding duty is to the Court, both in preparing reports and in giving oral evidence.
2. I have set out in my report what I understand from those instructing me to be the questions in respect of which my opinion as an expert are required.
3. I have done my best, in preparing this report, to be accurate and complete. I have mentioned all matters, which I regard as relevant to the opinions I have expressed. All of the matters on which I have expressed an opinion lie within my field of expertise.
4. I have considered and drawn to the attention of the Court all material facts, of which I am aware, which might detract from my opinion.

5. Wherever I have no personal knowledge, I have indicted the source of factual information.

6. I have not included anything in this report, which has been suggested to me by anyone, including the lawyers instructing me, without forming my own independent view of the matter.

7. Where, in my view, there is a range of reasonable opinion, I have indicated the extent of that range in the report.

8. Where I have not been able to give an opinion without qualification, I have stated the qualification in the report.

9. At the time of signing the report I consider it to be complete and accurate. I will notify those instructing me if, for any reason, I subsequently consider that the report requires any correction or qualification.

10. I understand that this report will be the evidence that I will give under oath, subject to any correction or qualification I may make before swearing to its veracity.

11. I understand my duty to the court and have complied and will continue to comply with that duty.

I confirm that insofar as the facts stated in my report are within my own knowledge, I have made clear which they are and I believe them to be true, and that the opinions I have expressed represent my true and complete professional opinion.

Brian Kendall .

Dr Brian Kendall
F.R.C.R. F.R.C.P. F.R.C.S.   **4ᵗʰ February 2008**

Joseph Cunningham
From: **Charlotte Cunningham**
Sent: 12 February 2008 19:44
To: Rosamund Rhodes-Kemp

Rosamund,

Thank you for your letter regarding Joseph. I understood that you are making progress but expect the NHS will take their sweet time to come back to you. You forewarned us that this would take a while and will wait for the outcome. You mentioned a requirement for extra funding. Please let me know when and if this is necessary and we will make arrangements to find the cash.

I am still somewhat hung up on the actions taken to get a blood sample and the number of lacerations Joseph endured. Would you please send the photo I sent of Josephs head onto Brian Kendall for his opinion if the Doctor was excessive?

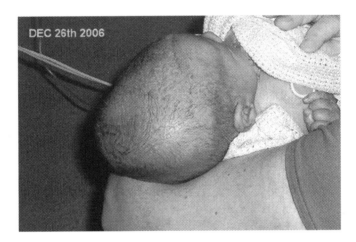

With respect to the missing MRI scans I keep going on about, let me explain the 2 significant images I was shown to learn if you have now been sent them.

The 2 images were taken in the direction from the top of the head looking down to the feet. The first image was just above eye level and the second image at eye level. What I was show in both images was the swelling on the back of Josephs head with a dark patch explained to me as a blood clot. There was also a bleed between both hemispheres of his brain near the back. The main damage was two black areas the size and shape of 2 peas 1 located in each hemisphere in the centre of his brain in line with his eyes, the same distance apart and parallel. I was told that this was the core of his Brain that led down to his spinal cord and the damage here was preventing messages from his brain to control his breathing and was irreversible and that he would not be able to control his own breathing and would die without the ventilator. I questioned this because Joseph was off a ventilator for about 8 days supporting his own breathing but I was told his was only possible because he was so heavily sedated and taking fitting suppressant drugs. I was convinced by the Doctors at this stage that letting Joseph go was the humane thing to do.

If you do have the images I would like to have copies of them for my own reference and peace of mind.

Josephs death was distressing and not without event. He was fine from 3pm - 9pm but gradually he got into a state of fighting for air and even passed out - Charlotte and I thought he had died but some 10 minutes possibly longer he awoke and was gasping for every breath. At this point it was advised to increase his dose of morphine to settle him. He did calm down but the dosage went up and up and up and on a number of occasions a manual dose was given. By 23:00 his complexion was white, the blood had drained from his skin. At 23:45 he slipped away without a sound.

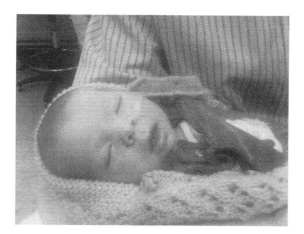

I would like to make sure Brian gets to see the 2 MRI scans that I was shown and to read his report that I made the right decision and that there was nothing else that could have been done for Joseph. It's ironic that I make decisions every day that can cost millions which down the line impact 1000's of people's lives but agreeing to take Joseph off the vent still today was the hardest decision I had to make knowing that he would die. Since the MRIs I was shown have gone missing and the Specialist Registrar claims he cannot recall the conversation he had with me I often find myself asking - did I do the right thing or should I have asked for a second opinion.

Regards

Darren Cunningham

RE: Joseph Cunningham
From: Rosamund Rhodes-Kemp
Sent: 18 February 2008 12:01
To: Charlotte Cunningham
Cc: Claudia De Castro

Thank you for this
I shall action your requests

Mr Cunningham having seen Brian Kendall's report and the extent of poor Joseph's brain damage I am
sure you did make the right decision and that it would most certainly be the hardest decision a parent
ever had to make- many years ago I read Sophie's choice and it haunts me still-making a decision that
will cause your child to die.

You did the right thing, however hard it was, Joseph's situation and his suffering would not have
improved.

I am so very sorry.

Rosamund

Specialist Compensation Claim Solicitors

BOLT BURDON KEMP

31st March 2008

Dear Mr and Mrs Cunningham

<u>Clinical Negligence Claim</u>

I am pleased to enclose the following:

1.   letter dated 22 February 2008 from Dr Brian Kendall;

2.   letter dated 20 March 2008 from Barking, Havering and Redbridge Hospitals NHS Trust enclosing the Adverse Incident Report considering the birth of Joseph.

In relation to Brian Kendall's evidence, he takes the view that in order to try and evaluate whether Joseph would have survived if the machine had not been turned off. He said that it is really impossible to say without the benefit of a neonatologist's opinion on Joseph's state at the time when the decision was made. A post-mortem is the most effective way but – often in these cases – I'm afraid no post-mortem has been done. Therefore the neonatologist has to rely on blood gases and blood test results, observations and clinical notes to try and make an assessment. I am not sure I would go down that route if I was you because the opinion will cost the best part of £2,000 and I am not sure that it would help you. You followed the advice you were given as we would all do in such a situation.

I am just very sorry.

Turning to the incident form, you will see a number of concerns have been raised and the report is damning of several people. I am not sure whether the author is a midwife for the Trust or not.

What I think we should do, subject to your views of course, is write back to the Trust indicating these criticisms and asking them to admit liability and pay compensation. The Trust will not be able to do this but if we intimate a claim they are going to have to pass the matter to the National Health Services Litigation Authority. Usually this is a disaster. Cases simply sit with the NHSLA for months on end whilst we wait for a response.

However, in cases involving the death of a baby the NHSLA are under strict time limits. I think that these follow a directive from the Chief Executive who was challenged about the amount of times sensitive cases such as a stillborn child were taking to be resolved. Following this such cases have been dealt with more promptly. I wish the same rule applied to all the cases that end up at the NHSLA. They are quite frankly the worst to deal with in terms of progressing a case.

If we were to actually issue Court proceedings then the matter would in turn be handed over to panel solicitors. There are about 20 firms who carry out work for the NHSLA. They are all experienced in defending clinical negligence cases and they will inevitably progress the matter more swiftly either through a robust defence or settlement.

Have a read of the report and then perhaps you could get back to me.

I am very sorry that I have to send you what I know is going to be further upsetting material but I think that we can work our way through the case and I am happy to support you in doing this.

I hope you are both well.

Best wishes and kind regards,

Yours sincerely

ROSAMUND RHODES-KEMP

2

Dr Brian Kendall
FRCR FRCP FRCS

22nd February 2008

Dear Rosamund

Re: Joseph Cunningham (deceased)

Thank you for your letter of 20th February and for the photograph, which shows the swelling and bruising of the scalp.

Your comments to Mr Cunningham are correct and appropriate. It is of course always a very difficult decision to decide whether a very badly damaged baby is potentially viable with prolonged intensive care. It is certainly not possible from looking at the MRI to say whether the brain stem would have resumed sufficient function for survival. That depends on clinical assessment of brain stem function.

A postmortem investigation would provide much more detailed evidence of the state of the brain stem.

If indicated, an assessment of Joseph's clinical condition at the time when the decision to turn off the ventilator was made, an expert neonatology report would be appropriate.

With best wishes

Yours sincerely

Brian

Dr Brian Kendall
F.R.C.R. F.R.C.P. F.R.C.S.

20 March 2008

Dear Sirs

Re: Joseph Cunningham

Thank you for your letter dated 11 February 2008 which was addressed to Lyon Road Store. As requested in our letter of 8 February 2008, please address all future correspondence to the writer.

The copy Incident Form which was sent to you earlier was a record of the Incident. I now attach the report on Charlotte Cunningham which was completed following investigation.

Yours faithfully,

Legal Services Manager

Ref No: **0354423**

Type of Incident. Please tick one box

Clinical Care ☑	Staffing Problems ☐	Medication Incident ☐	Infection ☐	Fire Incident ☐
Safety / Accident ☐	Equipment Problems ☐	Radiation Incident ☐	Security Incident ☐	Verbal / Physical Abuse ☐

PERSON AFFECTED   (Please tick one box)

Staff ☐   Patient ☑   Visitor ☐   Contractor ☐   Volunteer ☐

Forename: C h a r l o TT E

Surname: C u n n i n g h a m

Hospital Number (if patient): O B 9 8 2 7 5

Date Of Birth: 0 2 / 0 1 / 1 9 7 4

Gender: Male ☐ Female ☑

Address: S T R A T H F I E L D   G A R D E N S
B A R K I N G

Where Incident occurred (Please tick One Box)

Barking Hospital ☐	Barley Court Day Hospital ☐	Harold Wood Hospital ☐	King George Hospital ☑
Not on Hospital Premises ☐	Oldchurch Hospital ☐	Victoria Hospital ☐	Brentwood C.H ☐
Upney Lane Centre ☐	Fanshawe Clinic ☐		

Department/Ward where incident happened: L A B O U R   W A R D

Speciality Responsible:

Date of Incident: 2 2 / 1 2 / 2 0 0 6
Time of Incident: 0 2 : 4 1

Patient/Relative Informed? ☐ Yes   ☐ No

Outline of Incident   (Brief FACTS only)   Who By SM

presenting per vertex progressing well, caput present SR ██████ present
perineum rigid, the need for an episiotomy discussed with
Charlotte and Darren and done with consent. paediatrician called
as head advancing and mls liquor was visible in the early stages of
labour. As presenting perk delivered meconium ++ present.
presenting perk appeared large so back rest put flat, legs put into
Mc Roberts position, emergency buzzer activated at same time +
encouraged to push, still difficulty in delivering shoulders, pubic
pressure applied, then attempted to deliver posterior shoulder, then
delivered with success. Baby born in poor condition, paediatric
register called.

Immediate Action Taken / Medical Attention Given

- Cord pH taken
- paed reg called + present
- SCBU nurse called and important incubator
- Baby transferred to SCBU.

Doctor Name:

Date / Time: 02 12 06.

Darren and Charlotte read over the Adverse Incident Report and found it difficult to read. Below is what they believed they read.

Outline of Incident:

Presenting part vertex progressing well. Caput present. SR Midwifery Sister present. Perineum rigid the need, need for an episiotomy discussed with Charlotte and Darren and done with consent. Paediatrician called as head advancing and mils liquor was visible in the presenting part delivered meconium ++present. Presenting part appeared large so back rest put flat, legs put into McRoberts position, reg called, emergency buzzer activated at same time. Encouraged to push, still difficulty in delivering shoulders, pubic pressure applied, then attempted to deliver posterior shoulder tried to deliver with success. Baby born in poor condition, paediatric register contacted.

Immediate Action Taken/Medical Attention Given

- Cord PH taken

- Paed Reg called and present

- SCBU nurse called and transfer incubator

- Baby transferred to SCBU

Risk Management Midwife Report

In order to comply with the injunction placed upon the first edition of 'Josephs Life Story', the 12 paged report written by the Risk Management Midwife on behalf of the NHS as part of an internal investigation has been removed from the second edition of 'Josephs Life Story'.

From: **Charlotte Cunningham**
Sent: 06 April 2008 21:12
To: Rosamund Rhodes-Kemp

Rosamund,

Thank you for your recent letter. Interestingly enough on this occasion my wife was more emotional than I as for her it seems to raise more questions than it answered. Charlotte could not understand from the report what they did wrong as it does not pick up clearly on this other than a failure to maintain notes. She then had it in her mind again that if she could not clearly understand what the staff did wrong then maybe she did. The Risk report seemed to highlight there was a lack of reporting but did not seem to state that their actions were at fault - unless we misunderstood the comments. So if all the midwives did wrong was to fail to write up correctly and not to have notified us clearly of their actions then where is the strength in our case?

What I would like to learn is for you or the Risk Management Midwife to review the report and to state what actions/decisions were taken by the doctors and midwives on each page and what should have been done in accordance to the Midwives handbook or the nice guidelines. This would be of great help to myself and my wife to learn what was done and what should have been done and what would have been the expected outcome with each incorrect decision.

I would also like to learn is it regarded safe or an acceptable risk to try and deliver a baby that is known to have not turned as was the situation with Joseph. Is there statistics on the success rate on delivering babies who have not turned unharmed?

I am still not comfortable on the injury to the surface of his head. If I had inflicted this kind of injury to someone I would be charged with committing a serious assault. I want to learn what is regarded as an acceptable sized cut in order to take a blood sample from a new born baby. Can you help me with the above requirements please?

Thank you.

Darren Cunningham

RE: J Cunningham - Recent letter with report.
From: **Rosamund Rhodes-Kemp**
Sent: 07 April 2008 08:53
To: Charlotte Cunningham
Cc: Claudia De Castro

Hello Mr Cunningham

Leave it with me-I agree that the report does concentrate on record keeping which is not really the heart of the case.

I hope Charlotte is doing well.

Best Wishes

Rosamund

From: **Charlotte Cunningham**
Sent: 20 April 2008 13:41
To: Rosamund Rhodes-Kemp

Rosamund,

Charlotte found the following article that may be of interest.

Regards

Darren Cunningham

Attached was an article taken from the Sunday Mirror dated 6th April 2008. The headline read £800M PAID OUT FOR MATERNITY BLUNDERS. The article went onto claim that £828 million has been spent settling clinical negligence claims in childbirth cases since 1995. Also 6,447 claims were made against obstetricians or midwives on maternity wards since 1995. This equates to more than 1 claim per day from 1995 until to date.

RE: Article
From: **Rosamund Rhodes-Kemp**
Sent: 21 April 2008 11:26
To: Charlotte Cunningham

Thanks Mrs Cunningham, sad isn't it, I have dictated letters to you and the trust which should get to you shortly

Best Wishes

Rosamund

BOLT BURDON KEMP

21st April 2008

Dear Mr and Mrs Cunningham

Clinical Negligence Claim

I am yet to hear from the Trust in response to my letter of 31 March 2008 in which I asked only a couple of questions, one of which was whether ███████████, the author of the report, worked for the Trust. I think that that is important because it will no doubt influence what she has written - it is bound to.

Therefore when you say to me can either myself or the midwife who prepared the report go through each page and say what should have been done I think we ought to establish whether ██████ is the person to do this and I suspect that the answer is no it would not be for me to do it because whilst I am familiar with the role of the midwife and the guidelines I am no expert as such. I am not a qualified midwife.

I think that if you wanted to get a view on whether what happened was of an acceptable standard of care then what we should do is show this report to an expert midwife and ask her to comment but she would charge. I might be able to get a favour from someone so that we get a much cheaper report but I am afraid that I cannot see a midwife expert doing it for nothing.

It is a lot easier for the expert midwife to comment on an existing document than to prepare a report from scratch so that is one thing in your favour.

Do you want to have a think and get back to me as soon as possible as to what you would like me to do and once again I am very sorry for the distress that all of this is causing you and Charlotte.

Over and above ████████████████████████████████, there are other criticisms within the report and these are the ones that I would like to make to the Trust when I invite them to settle which I am now going to do as I have not heard back from them in relation to the other queries.

I shall let you know how I get on.

Best wishes and kind regards,

Yours sincerely

ROSAMUND RHODES-KEMP

Reply to letter sent on 21st April - Joseph Cunningham

From: **Charlotte Cunningham**
Sent: 22 April 2008 17:33
To: Rosamund Rhodes-Kemp

Rosamund,

I have to agree with your opinion in your letter on the subject of having a report comment weather what happened was of an acceptable standard of care. I see such a report would be the foundation of our case as I'm sure the trust will not deny Joseph suffered from a lack of oxygen but will stress the fact that it was either unfortunate or unavoidable. I also think we need a solid set of evidence/opinions written by credible people what would be willing to stand up in court if it came to it. Personally I hope it will go to court as I see it as the last opportunity to get down to the event in detail and will probably bring more details to the surface, as well as hear their side of the story. Let me know how much it will cost and I will sort out the finances.

Darren

RE: Reply to letter sent on 21st April - Joseph Cunningham
From: **Rosamund Rhodes-Kemp**
Sent: 23 April 2008 08:55
To: Charlotte Cunningham

Ok Mr Cunningham will get quotes and let you know

Best Wishes

Rosamund

BOLT BURDON KEMP

28th April 2008

Dear Mr and Mrs Cunningham

Clinical Negligence Claim

I note that we are holding £1,429.11 on account which you paid. There is an invoice payable to Dr Kendall for his fee in providing us with a report in the sum of £763.75 and I was writing to ask you if you could please provide me with authority to pay Dr Kendall's invoice.

I look forward to hearing from you.

Best wishes and kind regards,

Yours sincerely

ROSAMUND RHODES-KEMP

Dr Kendall's invoice

From: **Charlotte Cunningham**
Sent: 29 April 2008 17:14
To: Rosamund Rhodes-Kemp

Dear Rosamund,

many thanks for your letter received today with regards to the payment of Dr Kendall's invoice.

You have our permission to settle his invoice using the funds that are in your possession.

Kind regards

Charlotte Cunningham

RE: Dr Kendall's invoice
From: **Rosamund Rhodes-Kemp**
Sent: 30 April 2008 08:17
To: Charlotte Cunningham
Cc: Claudia De Castro

Thank you I am going to review your file on Friday and consider a strategy that will best suit to resolve this as I am tired of the slow way the trust are dealing

Rosamund

Joseph L Cunningham

From: **Charlotte Cunningham**
Sent: 12 May 2008 05:50
To: Rosamund Rhodes-Kemp

Rosamund,

Have you made any progress on locating a credible person who can make the assessment into the care Charlotte and Joseph received during labour and to comment on the actions/events on what happened vs. what should have happened? Have you been able to make a list of points that we want someone to comment on so they don't miss out on any key points of concern?

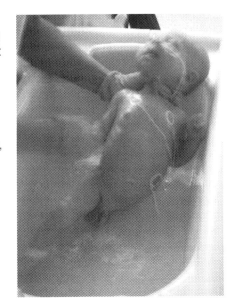

Have you done any research into the care Joseph received while in NICU that may have had a negative impact into Joseph's recovery? For example, the way he was handled during his 'first bath' was it appropriate for a child suffering from brain injury?

Was his medication also suitable or could it be deemed as excessive and aggravated the situation? Have you made a note of the occasion where Joseph nearly died in NICU (Queen's hospital) due to a trainee nurse failing to replace his feed tube correctly, the supervising nurse also ignoring the failed litmus test and then proceeding to feed Joseph? Charlotte and I checked Joseph's notes on the day when this happened and brought it to the attention of the head nurse that there was no mention in Joseph's records of the event - it was like talking to a sympathetic brick wall.

Joseph was off the ventilator and breathing unaided for many days and while on medication he seemed to be fine. Once he became fully conscious he was struggling to breathe on times as if having to take a deep breath each time (they called it strider?). He was sent to GOSH to have his throat checked out. The doctors at GOSH put him back on the vent via his nose and not his throat and as a result Joseph had the complication of fluid build up as a direct result. At this stage I am convinced GOSH had wrote Joseph off as dead. So why did the doctors opt to put Joseph back on a vent where he had managed (granted with minor oxygen assistance) to support himself without it? Joseph's medication also changed while he was at GOSH (was it appropriate), was it also appropriate to give Joseph so much morphine? I appreciate it was up to Joseph to see if he would make it on his own after

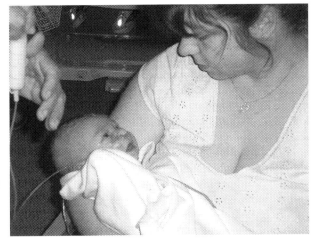

being taken off the vent but where is the line between making a child comfortable and euthanasia?

For me I want this case to be an event that brings to light ALL the failings during Joseph's care and not just to receive a letter from the NHS saying 'sorry will try harder next time' and here is a cheque goodbye. Please tell me what is your objective?

Regards

Darren

RE: Joseph L Cunningham
From: **Rosamund Rhodes-Kemp**
Sent: 12 May 2008 09:00
To: Charlotte Cunningham
Cc: Claudia De Castro

Dear Mr Cunningham,

Thanks for your letter
I have this morning written to you as I have received a letter from a midwife who will look at the liability issues raised by the Risk Management Midwife

As a midwife she can also comment on the bath incident but my view is that the damage that caused the death occurred during Labour.

I have not yet made a list of points as I must first make sure that you wish to instruct the expert and as you are aware of all your points that would be a sensible starting place so could you prepare a list of yours-I will have to go back to the expert and ask her how long she will need to spend and for a revised estimate of fees as the report will probably take much longer than she anticipated as you will wish for more detail re the care outside of the actual negligence

If you would like the NICU care looked at I can instruct a neonatalogist to look at this and obviously this will help in your understanding of what happened and why and whether it contributed to the outcome but this report will cost circa £2000 and will take about 8 months-I have to warn you that it is unlikely to affect the claim for compensation because that is constrained by the legislation governing Fatal Accidents in terms of compensation

The legal case is a rather blunt instrument I am afraid in terms of dealing with sensitive complex cases such as this-I can find out more for you but am not a neonatologist and would need evidence as would you of the care in the Special Care facilities

I have also heard from the Trust who are gathering the papers ready to authorise the National Health Service Litigation Authority (NHSLA) to act for them could you please prepare a list of all your points and I can review this and add to it and then submit all the questions to the midwife and ask her what she will charge for her report bearing in mind these points
How is Charlotte?

Best Wishes

Rosamund

BOLT BURDON KEMP

13th May 2008

Dear Mr and Mrs Cunningham

Clinical Negligence Claim

I write to update you on the position and thank you for sending me details of the cost of the negligence case regarding obstetric care.

In fact obstetrics and A&E are the highest risk areas in the National Health Service and whilst there have been significant changes in the management of A&E departments, for example 24 hour Consultant cover, these changes do not appear to have fed through to obstetrics. Partly because I think that there is a shortage of Consultant Obstetricians and probably a shortage of money to pay for them. Likewise there are fewer midwives because it is poorly paid and high risk but also there is a constant tension between midwives and obstetricians. Midwives regard themselves as an independent profession and have very strong views about the way that babies should be delivered and think that the Consultants should back off and leave them to get on with it. It is a bit of a mess.

Now, I have been informed by the Trust that following my letter setting out potential allegations of negligence as identified by ▮▮▮▮▮▮▮ in her report, that they are getting their papers together and are going to pass the matter to the National Health Services Litigation Authority. On the one hand this is bad because the papers will subsequently fall into an enormous black hole for a couple of months before re-surfacing. The good part though is that the NHSLA have a history of dealing with still birth cases very quickly at the instructions of the Chief Executive.

I have now also heard from the senior midwife who I asked to report on ▮▮▮▮▮▮▮' report if you like – so a brief report on potential allegations of negligence. This is so that we are quite sure – and have expert evidence to back – the aspects of the management that were negligence as opposed to sub-optimal. You are not compensated for sub-optimal.

Sandra Tranter, the midwife, has offered to report for £250 which is excellent value. I think you should go ahead and I would strongly recommend that you authorise me to send her the report of ▮▮▮▮▮▮▮ and the labour notes and hear what she has to say. Then we will be ready for our negotiations with the NHSLA.

I look forward to hearing from you and I hope that you are as well as can be expected.

Best wishes and kind regards,

Yours sincerely

ROSAMUND RHODES-KEMP

From: Charlotte Cunningham
Sent: 13 May 2008 07:33
To: Rosamund Rhodes-Kemp

Rosamund,

Charlotte is doing well with only 5 weeks to go and looking forward to being a mum. This is her last week in work which will be a happy/sad moment for her to take it easy but also saying goodbye to work colleagues and friends who have been good to her especially over the last few months.

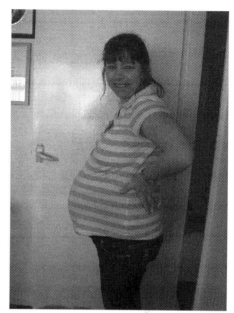

With regards to your reply I have to agree that the damage to Joseph was done during labour and the report we want from the midwife will probably be our main piece of evidence for this case.
I have thought about what you asked for questions to be raised but it's more the approach to completing the report I am interested in. What I would like to see in the report is each event broken down hour by hour listing in order what events occurred during that hour and what decisions were made and by whom - then the midwife will be expected to comment 'In her opinion' or 'as written in guide X' what was the correct action to take. Within the report I would like a minute by minute review of the 10 minutes before he was born and the 10 minutes after he was born to learn what preventative steps were taken or was the situation not handled correctly by all within the room. Once you and I are satisfied that the document covers the day end-to-end clearly I would like the midwife then to write a summary stating what led up to Joseph being injured and the key wrong decisions that were made resulting in his injury as well as the key decision that should have been taken to have prevented his injury.

In short let's leave no stone unturned for the NHS to start playing 'what if' games. I would also not want our midwife to see the report the Risk Management Midwife has written as I am sure it will influence her report until she has written and submitted the first draft. I would like for you to send the questions raised by our friend Andrea.

As for a NICU report I would like this document to carry on from the report from the midwife and in the same format but broken down on day by day. Since Joseph lived for only 38 days and some days no significant decisions were made I don't see this will be difficult to produce. I would like this report to start by questioning the actions taken from the very moment Joseph was born and in detail the first few hours. From the reports you have already sent the NICU team made errors with the first few hours of his care. Was his medical care in question, was there any event that worsened his condition, was there unethical decisions made?

With the 2 reports we will have the complete life story of Joseph in such detail the NHS will not be able to question our case. Once this is over I would like to collate the facts and (if you agree with your assistance at a cost of course) produce a single document that walks through the Josephs life and through the process of legal proceedings include e-mail exchanges and copies of letters send to capture the time it's taken. My family will then have all the facts and events to hand. Also our children will learn of their brother and what we went through to get the NHS to admit they failed us.
As for the additional cost and time this will take, I am ok with this but I have to admit Charlotte

would prefer to see this to come to an end. However I know Charlotte well and once we have the reports (with no stone unturned) she will appreciate what we are doing.

Regards

Darren

From: Charlotte Cunningham
Sent: 15 May 2008 07:36 AM
To: Rosamund Rhodes-Kemp
Subject: Regarding letter dated 13th May

Rosamund,

In regard to your letter dated 13th May and in particular to the following paragraph:
'I have now also heard from the senior midwife who I asked to report on the Risk Management Midwifes report if you like - so a brief report on potential allegations of negligence.'

Personally I don't think this is a good idea because the Risk Management Midwifes report focuses far too heavily on poor reporting and a failure to communicate with the parents. This report misdirects the reader from the real failings that occurred and as mentioned before failing to keep notes up to date didn't harm Joseph. The Risk Management Midwifes report never suggests at any point that the correct course of action is to opt for a C section which implies that the doctor's decision to carry on for a natural birth is not in question. Also the procedure they took to deliver Joseph was also not challenged; the time taken to cut the cord (some 3 minutes+) rather than help him to breath is not mentioned.

Our midwife needs to comment on the labour notes, comments made from my witness statement, the report we have from our Doctor confirming Josephs injuries sustained. If she is as good as you say then her report will complement the Risk Management Midwifes and fill in the failings the Risk Management Midwifes failed to mention. To be blunt, I'm not interested in a short report she either does a thorough report coving the whole event giving a comment on every action taken by the doctors and midwives or not at all. I appreciate this will cost more and take time but I am ok with that.

On a different note have to made any further progress on obtaining the missing MRI scans?

Regards

Darren

The offer is made

BOLT BURDON KEMP

14th May 2008

Dear Mr and Mrs Cunningham

<u>Clinical Negligence Claim</u>

Just what you did not want. On the one hand it might be.

I am attaching a copy of a letter that I have received from the NHSLA in which they have admitted liability, so that is good, they have admitted negligence.

They go on to make an offer of £20,000.

When we met I explained that in cases such as this are tragic and ghastly but they do not attract large awards for compensation.

In order to prove a high level of compensation you have to be able to show that you or your wife have suffered a psychological consequence over and above normal bereavement and financial losses such as being able to go out and work, etc. In your case you would probably not be able to do either but I would like to hear from you on both points.

Importantly Charlotte is pregnant again and the Defendants will use this to say that effectively she has got over it and she is pregnant again and all is right in the Cunningham household. I know that you will find this desperately insulting. I am terribly sorry and I apologise for the bald way in which the NHSLA have dealt with the case.

I know that this is not what you wanted at all and I told the NHSLA that I think you want a lot more detailed explanation as to how your son died.

Anyway, I have referred the offer to you and I look forward to speaking with you further about it.

Best wishes and kind regards,

Yours sincerely

ROSAMUND RHODES-KEMP

9 May 2008

Dear Ms Rhodes-Kemp,

Re; Miss Charlotte Cunningham -v- Barking, Havering and Redbridge Hospitals NHS Trust

We act on behalf of Barking, Havering and Redbridge Hospitals NHS Trust and have been provided with a copy of your previous correspondence dated 21 April 2008 which was received at the Trust on 22 April 2008.

We can confirm that liability is admitted.

In accordance with Part 36 of the Civil Procedural Rules we offer to settle your client's claim in the sum of £20,000. Your reasonable costs are, of course, payable in addition.

This offer is subject to receipt of a £nil CRU certificate. In order that we may request such a certificate we would be grateful for confirmation of your client's full address, National Insurance number and date of birth.

Should your client reject this offer but subsequently recover the amount offered or less then we reserve the right to bring this correspondence to the attention of the Court in respect of the issue of costs.

This will offer will remain open for acceptance for a period of 21 days from the date of receipt.

Finally, we would be grateful for confirmation as to how your client's claim is funded?

We await hearing from you.

Yours faithfully

Case Manager

BOLT BURDON KEMP

14th May 2008

Dear Mr and Mrs Cunningham   SECOND LETTER

<u>Clinical Negligence Claim</u>

I am writing to say that sadly I shall be leaving Bolt Burdon Kemp at the end of June 2008 and I therefore need to transfer your case to Suzanne Trask who has recently joined the firm. I shall remain in the office until 27 June 2008 and I shall therefore be able to provide an effective handover and in particular to discuss the points you have raised in your latest emails with Suzanne.

I am very sorry to be leaving you at this time and I do wish you all the very best regarding the case.

I can understand how you feel. I think of all the stillbirth cases that I have handled, and there are dozens of them now, but this one upsets me perhaps the most bar one and that is because I feel that Joseph suffered.

I wish Charlotte all the very best with her forthcoming pregnancy and that this new baby will bring some joy back into your lives.

Best wishes and kind regards,

Yours sincerely

ROSAMUND RHODES-KEMP

From:Charlotte Cunningham
Sent: 15 May 2008 08:32 PM
To: Rosamund Rhodes-Kemp
Subject: Letters received on 15th May

Rosamund,
Today Charlotte and I returned home together from work, Charlotte was tired after a long day training her replacement but pleased knowing that she only has 1 more day left in work before resigning to be a full time mum. We opened the front door and picked up the 3 letters that the postman had delivered earlier that day. The first letter was an invoice from Buckley memorials confirming they had erected Joseph's head stone. It included a picture. At £750 we agreed it was worth every penny.

The second letter we opened was to confirm that you were leaving 'Bolt Burdon Kemp' - now that was a bomb shell.

The last letter was also from you to explain that the NHSLA had admitted liability. Charlotte smiled, we hugged, we cried, the relief. Charlotte wants to accept the offer but there is still an empty hole that we are left with still wanting to know where is the explanation as to what they did wrong, what should have they done right. What were the warning signs that they failed to act on.

There is no comfort not knowing if there were any lessons learnt by those in the room that day. An explanation from the NHS before Charlotte goes into labour would be greatly received.

I want to ask you can we expect to receive an explanation from the NHS?

We talked about a press release amongst other things, are these still options we can discuss?

Many thanks for your kind words and your help with this stressful case. I hope we don't have to do business again and we wish you well in your future.

Darren

RE: Letters received on 15th May
From: **Rosamund Rhodes-Kemp**
Sent: 16 May 2008 05:16
To: Charlotte Cunningham
Cc: Claudia De Castro

Hello Mr Cunningham

What a mixture of emotions and feelings for you both

I am sorry

The Headstone is beautiful-like Joseph

I am happy to speak with you re way forward if you would feel better as am not going until end June. I agree you need answers and reassurance not a bald offer.

When would be a good time next week please?

Rosamund

From: **Charlotte Cunningham**
Sent: 20 May 2008 17:14
To: Rosamund Rhodes-Kemp

Rosamund,

Following your advice in your past letter that accompanied the NHS offer we do not plan to take the matter any further on a financial angel. Just to confirm that the sum of money offered by the NHS is not in question - Charlotte's NI number is XX99999X. However the acceptance is conditional that we receive a full explanation as to the cause of events and what should have taken place during the course of labour to have prevented Joseph's injuries.

I received a voice mail suggesting a meeting for the 18th June. Sadly this is not appropriate since Charlotte due date is on the 15th June. If you need to meet in person do you have any time on the 29th May as I am off work on this date? Alternatively we can discuss on the phone at any time that is convenient for you but ideally within the 3 weeks set by the NHS.

Darren

From: **Rosamund Rhodes-Kemp**
Sent: 22 May 2008 08:40
To: Charlotte Cunningham
Cc: Claudia De Castro

Hi I am sorry I am away next week half term
Let me put this to the NHSLA and then we can speak when I get back
I do hope all goes well

ROSAMUND RHODES-KEMP

Joseph Cunningham

From: **Charlotte Cunningham**
Sent: 17 June 2008 12:20
To: Rosamund Rhodes-Kemp

Rosamund,

I spoke with Susan a little over a week ago. I helped explain what I was expecting to receive as a means of an explanation from the NHS. She agreed to let me see her letter intended for the NHS before sending via e-mail but I have not received anything to date. I also requested for a press release which is what we agreed on when we last met once the time was right.

I would like to confirm if you still want to meet tomorrow or would you prefer to call me at home to discuss?

I would like to request for copies of all letters and e-mails you have send/received with the NHS and other parties for my records either electronically, scanned images or in hardcopy. I have kept all letters I have received from you and stored all e-mails we have exchanged.

Respectfully

Darren

RE: Joseph Cunningham
From: **Rosamund Rhodes-Kemp**
Sent: 18 June 2008 08:08
To: Charlotte Cunningham
Cc: Suzanne Trask

Hi Mr Cunningham
I have copied Suzanne so she can deal with the copies of anything you have not already got.
We are happy either way whatever suits you best

ROSAMUND RHODES-KEMP

The Handover

From this point onwards Suzanne Trask was Darren's and Charlotte's point of contact as Rosamund had decided to leave the company to work elsewhere. As it happened they had been left in good hands.

FW: Your Claim
From: **Suzanne Trask**
Sent: 18 June 2008 09:21
To: Charlotte Cunningham
Cc: Rosamund Rhodes-Kemp

Mr Cunningham,

Further to your email to Rosamund, I understand that unfortunately the below e-mail was not received. As you will see from my e-mail, I think that it would now be helpful to have a meeting with a specialist barrister to discuss the value of the claim.
I will ask my assistant to send copies of all correspondence on the file to you.
I look forward to hearing from you regarding the letter to be sent to the Trust.
Regards

Suzanne

SUZANNE TRASK

NHS Litigation Authority
DX: 169 London
Your Ref: M7CT575/029

10th June 2008
STR18513.1

Dear Sirs

<u>Joseph Cunningham (deceased)</u>

To clarify the request for further information in our previous letter dated 29th May 08, our clients require the following –

- An explanation of what failures actually caused the death of their son. Whilst errors have been noted in the Risk Assessment Report, it is still unclear how these caused Joseph's death.

- In order to fully understand the above, a clear chronological list of actions/decisions that were taken by individuals throughout the course of treatment, stating where failures occurred, and what should have taken place.

- An explanation of what clinical standards were applicable and how they were not satisfied.

The Risk Assessment Report dated 9th April 07 focuses almost entirely on failures to communicate to Mr and Mrs Cunningham, and a failure to record events properly in the medical records. They understandably believe that this is inadequate.

Our clients also seek a formal letter of apology from the Trust.

Please take instructions from the Trust on whether they will provide this information.

Yours faithfully

<u>BOLT BURDON KEMP</u>

Contact Suzanne Trask

BOLT BURDON KEMP

11th June 2008

Dear Mr and Mrs Cunningham

<u>Clinical Negligence</u>

I write to introduce myself as I have now taken over conduct of your claim from Rosamund Rhodes-Kemp. I am a Grade 4 Solicitor within the firms Terms of Business, and enclose a further copy for your information.

Yours sincerely

<u>SUZANNE TRASK</u>

25 June 2008

Dear Ms Trask,

Re; Master Joseph Cunningham (Deceased)

Thank you for your letter of 18 June 2008.

We can confirm that we have forwarded a copy of your correspondence to the Trust and we are awaiting their response as to whether they will provide the information requested. If they are, then we have suggested that they correspond with you directly in this regard.

In addition we are arranging for a Letter of Apology to be prepared and this will follow under separate cover shortly.

In the meantime we await your client's full CRU details as requested in our Letter of Response dated 9 May 2008. We would also be grateful for confirmation as to how your client's claim is funded?

Finally, we would be grateful for confirmation as to whether our Part 36 offer made on 9 May 2008, in the sum of £20,000 is accepted or alternatively if this offer is rejected, how your clients intend to proceed?

We await hearing from you.

Yours sincerely

Case Manager

From: **Melanie Whittaker**
Sent: 03 July 2008 16:01
To: Charlotte Cunningham

STR18513.1

3rd July 2008

Dear Mr Cunningham

I attach the response received from the NHS Litigation Authority. They have sent a copy of our letter to the Trust, and are waiting to see if they will provide the information requested. They are arranging to provide a letter of apology.

I will provide the information referred to in the third paragraph of their letter, which they are entitled to as part of the claim process.

Finally, they have asked whether their offer of £20,000 in full and final settlement of the claim is accepted or rejected. I am concerned that they will withdraw this offer shortly. You will note the very difficult consequences of this from my previous e-mail dated 10th June 2008. If the offer is withdrawn, it is very likely that you will become at personal risk of paying significant legal costs.

If you do not wish to accept the offer in full and final settlement of the claim, I would strongly recommend that we go ahead with the conference with the barrister as soon as possible, whilst the offer is still open for acceptance. It will be useful to discuss the value of your claim with a barrister, as they are regularly in court and will be able to give current expert advice on what a judge is likely to award.

I understand that you are being asked to make important decisions at a particularly difficult time for you and your wife. I note that your wife's due date was on 15th June 2008, and hope that everything is going well.

I look forward to hearing from you as soon as possible.

Yours sincerely

SUZANNE TRASK

From: Charlotte Cunningham
Sent: 03 July 2008 19:30
To: Melanie Whittaker
Subject RE: Joseph Cunningham

The cash offer is of little importance to us and I have no plans to contest it. As mentioned before my wife and I willing to accept this offer. However we still require a satisfactory explanation as to what actions their staff took, failed to take or should have taken so as to understand exactly what they accepting responsibility for. I would also like to learn if the offer comes with any conditions.

Regards

Darren Cunningham

FW: Joseph Cunningham
From: **Suzanne Trask**
Sent: 04 July 2008 09:52
To: Charlotte Cunningham

Mr Cunningham,

Thank you for your e-mail. Acceptance of the offer of £20,000 would be in full and final settlement of the claim, i.e. this would end the claim in its entirety and cannot be conditional that further information is provided by the Trust. If it is not accepted on this basis, it is rejected with significant costs consequences for you. I will need to know what you would like to do.

The offer is not made with any conditions only that it is in full and final settlement of the claim. I assume you are referring to a confidentiality clause? You may therefore go to the press etc after settlement, and the claim is finalised.

I look forward to hearing from you.

Regards

SUZANNE TRASK

The Barrister

Darren agreed to see a Barrister who specialised in Medical compensation claims concerning injuries to babies as advised by Suzanne. The appointment was arranged for 22nd July at 11am on Chancery Lane which is located off Fleet Street in London. Suzanne was also present to take notes and to help with providing any details. The purpose was to help explain to Darren what would be the outcome of the case should the offer be refused or withdrawn and the case continued to court.

The Barrister explained that he believed that if an emergency C-Section was performed at approximately 1 AM of the 22nd December 2006 then Joseph would have been born perfectly fine. The fact that the doctor had failed to contact the consultant on call did not go in Joseph's favour.

Darren asked regarding the cuts on Josephs head and if such injuries would have to be answered for. Apparently not in this case came the reply and it was his opinion that the cuts didn't appear to be deep enough to cause any serious injury but a post mortem would have ruled out any doubt.

It was explained to Darren that if the case went to court the evidence collected to date or any additional evidence would not have featured in the hearing, there would not be a requirement to have witnesses come to the stand nor would there be any cross examining because the NHS had already admitted liability. This would mean that the Judge would have to calculate compensation as permitted by law. The Barrister went onto explain that the expected financial outcome would be £10,000 compensation for the grief suffered by both parent for the loss of Joseph and in addition, a few additional £1,000 may be awarded for the days in which Joseph was alive. The Judge would also award money to cover the funeral expenses and mentioned a figure in the region of £3,000. Overall the sum would be less than what the NHS was currently offering to settle out of court. His final advice to Darren was simply 'Take the money'.

After the meeting was over and while Darren was returning home it was evident to him that the case was not going to yield and further information relating to Joseph. It was unlikely that the issue over the missing MRI scans would be resolved and any outstanding questions he had would go unanswered. All that the case had achieved was the NHS had admitted liability for Joseph's injuries which eventually resulted in his death. Darren had to accept this was as far as it could go with the solicitors and move on.

Your Claim
From: Suzanne Trask
Sent: 22 July 2008 12:32
To: Charlotte Cunningham

Dear Mr Cunningham,

It was good to meet with you earlier, and I am glad that you found the meeting with the Barrister helpful.

Further to your instructions, I have informed the NHSLA that the offer of £20,000 plus your legal costs is accepted in settlement of your claim. It would be useful if I could have written confirmation of your instructions for my file.

I have contacted the charity Action Against Medical Accidents with whom I work regularly, and they are looking into the various venues that you may wish to try once the claim has been concluded. They will get back to me shortly and I will pass on their advice on useful charities, forums and contacts.

Kind regards

Suzanne

SUZANNE TRASK

RE: Your Claim
From: Cunningham, Darren
Sent: 23 July 2008 11:39
To: Suzanne Trask

Thanks I have put a letter in writing confirming we accept without condition.

Darren Cunningham

Your Claim

From: **Suzanne Trask**
Sent: 04 August 2008 12:00
To: Charlotte Cunningham

Mr Cunningham,

Thank you for your letter confirming the settlement of your claim. Your file has now been passed to our costs department who will deal with the matter of finalising the claim for our legal costs from the other side, and payment of your compensation. One of my colleagues will therefore contact you shortly.

In the meantime, having contacted the charity Action against Medical Accidents (AvMA) they have discussed various charities with me, and feel that the most appropriate starting point will be the charity SANDS (http://www.uk-sands.org/Home.html) who provide services to the families of babies who die during or shortly after birth. They have also suggested that you join the AVMA support network (see http://www.avma.org.uk/) . This would mean that you were invited to various meetings, and could raise the issue with the speakers, that have previously included members of the General Medical Council, and the Health Ombudsman.

AvMA also have a discussion forum on their website, which you may wish to use to highlight the issue and ask if others who have suffered a similar experience would like to help with campaigning on the issue.

I hope that this is helpful. Best wishes to both you and your family for the future.

Kind regards

Suzanne

BOLT BURDON KEMP

8th August 2008

Dear Mr Cunningham

<u>Clinical Negligence</u>

I write further to previous correspondence.

I expect to be in receipt of a cheque in the sum of £20,000 from the Defendants within the next 28 days or so.

Further to our Terms of Business, we will be able to pay out your compensation once the legal costs are resolved.. In the first instance the money will have to be used to offset the disbursements and costs.

The majority of the costs will be payable by the Defendant Trust, but there will remain an element which the Court will not order the Trust to pay. This sum will come from the damages subject to your rights to ask the Court to decide how much you should pay. The costs team will do their best to minimise any shortfall.

Final settlement and payment of your damages will be made once the full costs contribution is paid by the Defendants.

Your file will now be passed to Susan Densham in the Costs Department to deal with the recovery of your legal fees. She will also discuss the costs consequences of acceptance of the offer with the NHSLA.

Susan Densham will contact you shortly to explain the costs process in more detail. From now on if you have any queries regarding costs, can you please contact Susan Densham or if she is unavailable, Luke Nicholls who is the Head of the Costs Department.

As always I am more than happy for you to contact me at any time.

With best wishes and kind regards.

Yours sincerely

SUZANNE TRASK

Joseph Cunningham

From: **Charlotte Cunningham**
Sent: 16 August 2008 17:46
To: Suzanne Trask

Suzanna

I have received your letter dated 8th August regarding payment.

I do have a few questions:

You mentioned there was an element that the trust will not pay can you be more descriptive as to what elements and what is the current cost of such elements?

Have you received any feedback as to where we are with learning if the Trust will come back with an explanation and a written apology?

Thank you.

Darren

RE: Joseph Cunningham
From: **Suzanne Trask**
Sent: 19 August 2008 15:41
To: Charlotte Cunningham

Mr Cunningham,

Thank you for your e-mail. I have passed on your question relating to the legal costs onto my colleague Susan Densham in the costs department, who will reply directly.

I asked the Trust to provide the apology and explanation directly to you, now that the claim has been finalised. The NHS Litigation Authority could not confirm how quickly the Trust would be able to reply, but said that our letter requesting an explanation was being considered, and that an apology would be sent.

Regards

Suzanne

SUZANNE TRASK

Legal Fees

Your claim

From: **Susan Densham**
Sent: 24 August 2008 10:33
To: Charlotte Cunningham

23rd August 2008

Dear Mr Cunningham

Clinical Negligence

I write further to Suzanne's recent correspondence.

Your file has now been passed over to me to finalise the costs issues with the defendant and release your damages to you.

Solicitor's costs are very complicated and that is why we have a specialist costs team.

I know that you have been involved in a time consuming and stressful claim and we are anxious that you should receive the maximum benefit from your damages award as soon as possible.

At this stage it is hard to know exactly what points the defendant will raise in relation to your costs so I will not know how much the possible unrecovered costs will amount to. As soon as I have a clear idea I will of course let you know.

I will attempt to negotiate our costs with the Defendants on an informal basis but if this fails I will send your file to a specialist costs draftsman who will prepare a bill in the manner set out by the Court Rules. This bill states how much we expect the defendants to pay for legal fees. If the defendants do not agree the costs then the court will decide how much should be paid and by whom. This occurs at a "detailed assessment" hearing and because of delays at the court the whole process can take as long as 6 months.

If it is necessary for us to prepare a formal bill I will send you a copy together with notes describing the "detailed assessment" process in more detail. Because your damages may be reduced by the amount of the costs not recovered from the Defendants you have an interest in the results of the detailed assessment hearing and you therefore have a right to attend. Either the solicitor involved in the case or one of the costs clerks will attend on your behalf so you do not have to attend. Most of our clients do not exercise their right to attend detailed assessment. If I do not hear from you within two weeks as to whether or not you wish to attend I shall assume that you are happy for us to represent you if we proceed to detailed assessment.

Let me assure you that I will do everything possible to make sure that the defendants pay as much of the costs as possible and that therefore you receive the maximum benefit from your damages.

As previously advised you may also be asked to pay the defendants costs from the date of their offer because their offer was accepted after it had expired. If the NHSLA submit a bill for their costs I will let you know.

I will keep you informed at all stages of the process but if you have any queries please contact me.

Yours sincerely

SUSAN DENSHAM

Clinical Negligence
From: **Susan Densham**
Sent: 14 October 2008 12:08
To: Charlotte Cunningham

14th October 2008

Dear Mr Cunningham

<u>Clinical Negligence</u>

I write further to previous correspondence.

The Defendant's costs negotiators have recently put forward an offer on costs which is considered to be far too low. The offer made was £4,351.85 against a bill totalling £16,047.26.

In the circumstances I have rejected the Defendant's offer and have now issued Part 8 proceedings. I hope that by doing this it will speed matters up and will also show the defendant that we consider that we will recover a lot more than their offer should we attend a detailed assessment hearing.

I will of course keep you updated with any progress that is made.

Kind regards

SUSAN DENSHAM

Costs Executive

FW: Clinical Negligence
From: **Darren Cunningham**
Sent: 15 October 2008 09:56
To: Susan Densham
Cc: Charlotte Cunningham

Susan,

Thank you for your e-mail but I just want to clarify.

The bill of £16,047.26 is the BBK solicitors fees that we want the NHSLA to pay and they have agreed to pay £4,351.85? - have I got this right?

I understand that the NHSLA has paid the compensation of £20,000 already - can you confirm on what date please as a matter of curiosity.

thanks

Darren Cunningham

RE: Clinical Negligence
From: **Susan Densham**
Sent: 15 October 2008 11:38
To: Darren Cunningham
Cc: Charlotte Cunningham

Dear Darren

Thanks for your email.

I can confirm that our bill of solicitors' fees totals £16,047.26 and the defendant's current offer on this bill is only £4,351.85. This offer was of course rejected.

I can also confirm that the NHSLA sent us a cheque for the compensation of £20,000.00 on 26th August 2008, which cleared in our account on 29th August 2008.

Kind regards,

SUSAN DENSHAM

Costs Executive

For the solicitor, this is where the story ends and the financial outcome is now with the costs department. The parents will now have to wait to learn if they will have to pay towards the NHS legal fees for not accepting the offer within 21 days and to learn how much of their Solicitors fees will not be paid by the NHS. All outstanding fees will be deducted from the £20,000 compensation and what's left the parents plan to put in an account for future children's education as a gift from their big brother.

The Solicitor calls for expert advice

After making a request on the 17th June to the Solicitor for copies of all letters and e-mails sent and received with the NHS and other parties, 2 days later on the 19th June Darren received far more copies of letters than he had imagined. It was evident that the Solicitors had been busy behind the scenes with the case collecting information.

Sent: 19 June 2008 14:59
To: Charlotte Cunningham

19th June 2008

Dear Mr Cunningham

Further to our telephone conversation, I enclose copies of all correspondence with the NHS LA, Trust and third parties in your claim. The content of some of the letters, particularly between Rosamund and the medical experts, consider Joseph's death in detail. I must warn you that they may be distressing to read. Rosamund has provided her own personal views on the circumstances of the claim when writing to various medical experts.

If there are any matters arising out of this correspondence that you would like to discuss, please give me a call on my direct telephone number below.

Regards,

SUZANNE TRASK

Fortunate for the parents the solicitor that had been assigned to their case (Rosamund Rhodes-Kemp) was not only experienced and passionate about her work, but also once a qualified registered general Nurse. Rosamund is also the author of a book titled 'A Remedy for Medical Complaints: A Practitioner's Guide to Complaints Procedures' and has made numerous television and radio appearances about clinical negligence issues.

Mr G. J. Jarvis

Once Rosamund had learnt the facts of the case, she wasted no time in contacting the necessary specialists needed to help make a credible case. The first person to be contacted was a consultant Obstetrician and Gynaecologist by the name of Mr G. J. Jarvis. Rosamund sent a letter on the 9th May with brief details on Joseph and requesting for his opinion, his fees and how long it would take him to complete his review. On the 22nd May Mr Jarvis replied.

9th May 2007

Dear Mr Jarvis

Joseph Cunningham (deceased)

I have been instructed by the parents of the above named.

Joseph was born at King George Hospital on 22 December 2006. he was the first pregnancy of Charlotte Cunningham who was aged 32 at the time. The pregnancy had been uneventful until labour. Interestingly she went into spontaneous labour at term plus 15 days (!).

I am attaching a summary prepared by the special registrar in paediatrics to the consultant paediatric neurologist at Great Ormond Street where Joseph was transferred shortly after he was born. He was then sent back to King George Hospital where sadly he died on 28 January 2007.

I wonder whether you would be able to look through the records that hav been obtained by mum, namely her laobur notes and Joseph's neonatal notes and prepare a preliminary opinion.

It would be helpful if we could resolve this matter with the Trust as soon as possible because I think that will help the parents come to terms with what has happened.

I look forward to hearing from you and if you are able to assist could you please give an indication of your hourly rate, your maximum fee and your waiting list period.

Best wishes and kind regards,

Yours sincerely

ROSAMUND RHODES-KEMP

MR. G. J. JARVIS

22 May 2007

Dear Ms Rhodes-Kemp

Re Joseph Cunningham (Deceased) (Your ref: RRK/18513.1)

Thank you for your letter of 9th May 2007.

I am very experienced in medico-legal work and would be happy to provide the report which you require. The possible negligence is within my area of expertise and I have no known conflict of interest.

I charge at a rate of £240.00 per hour and, whilst it is difficult to give a precise estimate without knowing the amount of work involved, most of my reports attract a fee of £960-£1680, although hopefully the fees will be in the middle portion of this range. I understand the concept of 'detailed assessment'. These fees are exclusive of VAT and this I state because I understand that VAT may have to be added in time.

I will be able to send you the finished report within about 12 weeks of receiving your instructions. I would of course produce a report on a more urgent basis than this should that be required.

I look forward to being of help if you wish to send me the appropriate papers and instructions. You may wish to send all the papers to my home (Wetherby address shown above) as things are less likely to go astray at home than when sent to a large hospital.

Kind regards.

Yours sincerely

G J JARVIS MA(OXON) FRCS FRCOG
Consultant Obstetrician & Gynaecologist

Rosamund met Darren and Charlotte and took down a statement from Darren of his accounts on what happened during labour. Since Charlotte was using gas and air as a pain relief and the discomfort of her contractions her account was hazy on times. Rosamund decided not to consent Mr Jarvis to carry out his review on Joseph but decided to use an alternative.

Dr Simon Newell

Rosamund decided to contact a Dr Simon Newell in writing on 22nd June to learn if he would be able to assist by reviewing the medial notes and sharing his professional opinion.

22nd June 2007

Dear Dr Newell

Joseph Cunningham (deceased)

I have been instructed by the parents of the above named.

Joseph was born at King George Hospital on 22 December 2006. He was the first pregnancy of Charlotte Cunningham who was aged 32 at the time. The pregnancy had been uneventful until labour. Interestingly she went into spontaneous labour at term plus 15 days (!).

I am attaching a summary prepared by the special registrar in paediatrics to the consultant paediatric neurologist at Great Ormond Street where Joseph was transferred shortly after he was born. He was then sent back to King George Hospital where sadly he died on 28 January 2007.

I wonder whether you would be able to look through the records that have been obtained by mum, namely her labour notes and Joseph's neonatal notes and prepare a preliminary opinion on causation.

It would be helpful if we could resolve this matter with the Trust as soon as possible because I think that will help the parents come to terms with what has happened.

I look forward to hearing from you and if you are able to assist could you please give an indication of your hourly rate, your maximum fee and your waiting list period.

Best wishes and kind regards,

Yours sincerely

ROSAMUND RHODES-KEMP

Unfortunately it was close to a month before Dr Newell found the time to reply.

18 July 2007

Dear Rosamund

Re: Joseph Cunningham

Thank you for your letter of instruction. I would be pleased to produce a medical report giving an independent view on this case. My fee for report work is currently £190 per hour plus 10% typing and administration. All bills from 1 May 2007 will also be subject to VAT at the standard rate of 17.5%. I would estimate that this case would take between 6-12 hours to complete. My current waiting list is 9-12 months.

I attach details of the documents I will require in order to produce a report. Having read your letter, I can see no conflict of interest. If you wish me to proceed on this basis please forward all the relevant papers at your earliest convenience.

Yours sincerely

[signature]

DR SIMON J NEWELL   MD FRCPCH FRCP
Consultant in Neonatal Medicine & Paediatrics

The required documents that Dr Newell had requested for were Obstertic notes with CTG, Neonatal clinical notes and any images, all up to date reports, Results of brain imaging (CT MRI), results of special investigations, Child's GP records, any other expert reports, Witness statements, and as an optional Mothers GP records. Although this seemed like a large list of requirements there was ample time to collect it since Dr Newell was unable to assist for at least 9 to 12 months.

Rosamund replied on the 26th June to Dr Newell requesting that she hoped that on this occasion he could complete the report quicker than 9 months. If Dr Newell did reply, a copy of his letter was not shared with the parents and no known report was produced by Dr Newell relating to Joseph.

Dr Brian Kendall – Requesting for assistance

After meeting the parents and taking a statement from Darren she decided to contact Dr Kendall who had assisted her on previous occasions and was known to be efficient in his work. The letter she wrote gave an overview of Joseph's fate and enquired if he could assist.

22nd June 2007

Dear Dr Kendall

Joseph Cunningham (deceased)

I am not sure whether you are going to be able to help with this case.

It concerns the death of a neonate. Joseph Cunningham was born on 22 December 2006 and he died on 28 January 2007.

He suffered various complications during the delivery. He was late and large. He was mum's first baby. She had Artificial Rupture of Membrane and the water that came out was stained with meconium. There was lack of progress in the first and second stage and the baby was in mal-position. When he was born he could not be delivered and an episiotomy was carried out and the baby was effectively forceably evicted from the uterus by a midwife on either side of the abdomen pushing with all their might and another midwife pulling his head out the other end.

Joseph suffered massive brain damage and died allegedly as a consequence of the mistreatment during his labour.

One of the issues that Mr Cunningham has is that the MRI scan which was interpreted at Great Ormond Street Hospital shows evidence of bleeding in the brain and multiple lacerations of the skull. Quite deep ones, as though when the doctor tried to take fetal blood for sampling he/she inadvertently cut the skull in a number of places. Mr Cunningham is extremely distressed about this an I said that I would ask whether you would be able to report on the scarring and the bleeding and discuss what a likely cause may have been.

Alternatively you may feel that this is more in the ambit of a neonatologist.

I look forward to hearing from you.

Best wishes and kind regards,

Yours sincerely

ROSAMUND RHODES-KEMP

Dr Kendall replied on the 25th June and confirmed that he could analyse the MRI images and deduce from them the type of trauma involved in their production.

27th September 2007

Dear Dr Kendall

Joseph Cunningham (deceased)

There is a mystery re the scans on this case.

Mr Cunningham has obtained 11 images from Barking, Redbridge and Havering NHS Trust. These are not in sequence and they are not from the same slice so to speak. The report that accompanies them implies that the baby is well. This is complete contrast with the repot prepared by Great Ormond Street on reviewing exactly the same scans. Mr Cunningham is also conscious of the fact that during the fetal scalp monitoring that took place during the labour it would seem that Joseph's scalp was damaged and in the scan that he originally looked at there were signs of abrasions. He believes that the images have been tampered with.

I wonder if you would be able to cast a preliminary and experienced eye over these images.

I look forward to hearing from you.

Best wishes and kind regards,

Yours sincerely

ROSAMUND RHODES-KEMP

It wasn't until 18th December when Rosamund got around to sending onto Dr Kendall the MRI images, Darren's statement and a copy of the letter Darren had written on the 1st August addressed to PALS. Once Dr Kendall had received them he began his analysis but it would be in the New Year when he would reply to Rosamund.

Dr Kendall replied by fax to Rosamund but the quality of the fax was so poor it has been typed out below and reads as follows:

Dr Brian Kendall
FRCR CRCP FRCS

6th January 2008

Dear Rosamund

Re: Joseph Cunningham (dob 22.12.06 deceased 29.1.07)

Thank you for your letter of 18.12.07 and for the enclosed statement of Mr Darren Cunningham and for the CDROM which contains images from a cranial MRI performed on 28.12.06. The MRI is of diagnostic quality although there is some movement artefact.
It consists of the following sections and sequences:
4. Axial T1 and T2 weighted spin and gradient echo
5. Coronal T2 weighted spin and gradient echo
6. Sagittal T2 weighted.

The following abnormalities are shown:
3. There is abnormal signal high on T1 and mixed on T2 weighted in the lateral nuclei of the thalami and posteriorly in the putamina of the lentiform nuclei.
4. There is lack of normal low signal from the white matter of the corona radiate underlying the pre and post central gyri and in the posterior limbs of the internal capsules on the T2 weighted sections

These abnormalities indicative of brain damage are in regions of high metabolism around the time of foetal maturity. These regions are therefore vulnerable to profound circulatory insufficiency.

Mammalian experiments an clinical experience suggest that damage begun in such regions in the previously normal non acidotic foetus after 10 minutes of profound circulatory insufficiency. Continuation of the circulatory insufficiency for longer than 25 minutes often results in death or more extensive brain damage involving regions of lower metabolism.

No abnormality is shown elsewhere within the brain substance. In particular there is no evidence of damage in the border zone regions between the cortical distributions of the main cerebal arteries which occurs with partial hypoxic ischaemia.

There is no evidence of any early intrauterine brain damage.

There is no evidence of any malformation of the brain.

There is a recent interhemispheric subdural haematoma and there is also subdural haematoma in the posterior fossa, mainly around the right cerebellar hemisphere. These haematomas are not exerting significant mass effect and are not of themselves causing any brain damage.

There is also a left sided cephalo haematoma which is likely to be associated with the process of delivery rather than with the attempts of application of the foetal scalpel electrode. There is no evidence of any underlying skull fracture.
If any other imaging is available I will be pleased to assess further, but the MRI is adequate to show the mechanism of the brain damage which caused death.

I will of course await your further instructions before providing a formal report.

With best wishes for the New Year

Yours sincerely

Dr Brain Kendall

F.R.C.R. F.R.C.P. F.R.C.S.

15th January 2008

Dear Dr Kendall

Joseph Cunningham (deceased)

Thank you for your fax dated 6 January 2008.

As you will be aware Mr Cunningham is concerned:-

a.   that certain images are missing; and

b.   that the images that are missing may well be the ones that could reveal superficial damage to the skull which he says was caused by the application of the foetal scalpel electrode.

Am I correct in thinking that what you were saying is that there is indeed evidence of superficial bleeding on the skull – you refer to it as a left sided cephalohaematoma which is more likely though in your view to be associated with the process of delivery than the attempts of application of foetal scalpel electrode.

Have I got this right?

Do you think there are missing images that we should try to obtain?

I have to be honest with you the Trust have been just about as awful as it is possible to be in relation to the medical records let alone the imaging.

I look forward to hearing from you.

Best wishes and kind regards,

Yours sincerely

ROSAMUND RHODES-KEMP

Days later, the NHS sent a copy of the MRI images which was then passed onto Dr Kendall on the 24th January, asking if he would review the CD in case it contained any additional images that the NHS had originally sent to Darren. The CD contained the same images that had also been sent to Darren previously.

Sorting out the Medical Records

The parents had contacted the NHS and received a copy of the medical notes and sent them onto Rosamund to help with the case. On receipt of the medical records from the parents, Rosamund realised that the copy of the CTG trace taken during labour was too poor to be a reliable source of information. So the task to obtain a quality copy of the CTG trace started with Rosamund requesting the NHS to provide a continuous copy of the graph in a letter on the 26th July.

Medical Records Manager
Barking, Havering and Redbridge Hospitals NHS Trust
King George Hospital
Barley Lane
Goodmayes
Essex
IG3 8YB

26th July 2007

Dear Madam

RE: Joseph Cunningham
Date of birth: 22.12.2006
Hospital number: 848366

We act on behalf of Mr and Mrs Cunningham, the parents of Joseph Cunningham (Deceased).

You have previously forwarded copies of the medical records and notes relating to Joseph Cunningham to Mrs Cunningham.

We now request that you provide us with a continuous copy of the CTG trace relating to Joseph Cunningham. In this regard, we enclose herewith a signed Form of Authority.

We look forward to hearing from you shortly.

Yours faithfully

BOLT BURDON KEMP

The NHS replied a month later on the 30th August stating that the Trust does not have the facilities to provide a continuous copy of the CTG traces but can arrange to forward the trace to 'The Times Drawing Office' upon written undertaking to meet the additional copying charges.

On the 4th September a reply was typed up and faxed back to the NHS by Rosamund accepting to pay the cost of copying the CTG by 'The Times Drawing Office'.

The NHS sent a letter dated the 5th September to Rosamund confirming that they had instructed the 'The Times Drawing Office' to copy the CTG trace and forward the copy onto Rosamund.

On the 19th September Rosamund received the CTG trace and sent a letter to the NHS to acknowledge receiving the CTG trace.

The medical notes were not indexed or in any sensible order, so Rosamund requested for the assistance of Debbie Balchin to sort the notes and have them indexed and paginated. Debbie went though the notes and soon realised that the Obstetric records were missing. Rosamund knew the missing records were important so on the 12th November a letter requesting the Obstetric records was sent to the NHS.

Medical Records Manager
Barking, Havering and Redbridge Hospitals NHS Trust
King George Hospital
Barley Lane
Goodmayes
Essex
IG3 8YB

12 November 2007

Dear Madam

RE: Joseph Cunningham
Date of birth: 22.12.2006
Hospital number: 848366

We have had the opportunity to review the records that you have provided relating to Joseph Cunningham and Mrs. Cunningham, and note that the obstetric records are missing.

Could you please provide us with a complete set of the obstetrics records as soon as possible?

We look forward to hearing from you shortly.

Yours faithfully

BOLT BURDON KEMP

After waiting over a month with no reply from the NHS for the Obstetrics records, Rosamund took the opportunity to send a second letter but also requesting for Joseph's MRI scans. On the 27th December, Rosamund received a reply from the NHS that read 'We write in reply to your letter dated the 18th December 2007. Your letter has been passed to our Maternity Department who keep the Obstetric records you require'. The letter also gave a name and telephone contact number.

On the 2nd January Rosamund received another letter from the NHS dated 24th December 2007 advising Rosamund to contact the Legal department at Queen's hospital for all further enquiries. It was now obvious the NHS were in no hurry to provide the missing documents.

24 December 2007

Dear Sirs

Re: Joseph Cunningham   dob 22.12.2006

With reference to your letter dated 18 December 2007 this has been passed to our Legal Department. All future enquiries regarding this matter should be addressed to our Legal Department at Queen's Hospital, Rom Valley Way, Romford, Essex, RM7 OAG.

Yours sincerely

Medico Legal Team Leader

Rosamund contacted the NHS by telephone to learn what was expected of her in order to obtain the records. The NHS would not release the records unless they had a completed form of authority signed by the Joseph's mother Charlotte. The form was faxed to Rosamund and arrangements were made to get Charlotte to complete the form promptly. On the 7th January 2008 the form of authority signed by Charlotte was faxed and also posted to the NHS to permit them to release the Obstetrics records and the MRI scans.

On the 24th of January Rosamund received a CD from the NHS containing the MRI scans of Joseph.

On the 25th of January Rosamund received the obstetrics records and send a letter to the NHS to confirm receipt of the records.

25th January 2008

Dear Madam

RE: Charlotte Cunningham
Date of birth: 22.01.1974

Thank you for your letter dated 14 January 2008 together with the enclosed obstetric records which we have not previously seen and so we are grateful to you for providing these.

Can you also please consider the Trust's poison on liability on this case and get back to us.

On this point, was there an adverse incident report, review, investigation, and if so can we please have documentation relating to the adverse incident report, etc?

We look forward to hearing further from you.

Yours faithfully

BOLT BURDON KEMP

The NHS on this occasion wasted no time to reply to Rosamund in writing dated the 1st February 2008 which read 'We are not in a position to confirm liability at this stage as prior authorisation is required by the NHS litigation Authority (NHSLA). We will, however, be shortly reporting this matter to the NHSLA who will revert to you in due course'. Enclosed with the letter was an Adverse Incident Report.

PLEASE PRINT USING BLACK BALL POINT PEN

Ref No: 0354423

Type of Incident. Please tick one box

Clinical Care ☑	Staffing Problems ☐	Medication Incident ☐	Infection ☐	Fire Incident ☐
Safety / Accident ☐	Equipment Problems ☐	Radiation Incident ☐	Security Incident ☐	Verbal / Physical Abuse ☐

PERSON AFFECTED   (Please tick one box)

Staff ☐   Patient ☑   Visitor ☐   Contractor ☐   Volunteer ☐

Forename: C h a r l o t t e

Surname: C u n n i n g h a m

Hospital Number (if patient): 0 B 9 8 2 7 5 1

Date Of Birth: 0 2 / 0 1 / 1 9 7 4

Gender: Male ☐ Female ☑

Address: 1 S T R A T H F I E L D G A R D E N S

B A R K I N G

Where incident occurred (Please tick One Box)

Barking Hospital ☐	Barley Court Day Hospital ☐	Harold Wood Hospital ☐	King George Hospital ☑
Not on Hospital Premises ☐	Oldchurch Hospital ☐	Victoria Hospital ☐	Brentwood C.H ☐
Upney Lane Centre ☐	Fanshawe Clinic ☐		

Department/Ward where incident happened: L A B O U R W A R D

Speciality Responsible:

Date of Incident: 2 2 / 1 2 / 2 0 0 6

Time of Incident: 0 2 : 4 1

Patient/Relative Informed? ☐ Yes ☐ No

Outline of Incident   (Brief FACTS only)   Who By: SM.

presenting peer. Vertex progressing well, Caput present. SR ▓▓▓▓ present
beeincum rigid, the need for an episiotomy discussed with
Charlotte and Durrey and done with consent. paediatrician called
as head advancing and mls liquor was visible in the early stages of
labour. As presenting peek delivered meconium ++ present.
presenting peek appeared large so bark rest phr flat, legs pur into
Mc Poberts position, emergency buzzer activated at same time +
encouraged to push, still difficulty in delivering shoulders, pubic
pressure applied, then attempted to deliver posterior shoulder, tried
to deliver with success. Baby born in poor condition, paediatric
register called.

Immediate Action Taken / Medical Attention Given

- Cord pH Taken
- pead Reg called + present
- scbu Nurse called and transport incubator
- Baby transferred to scbu.

Doctor Name:

Date / Time: 02/12/06.

210

Once Debbie had received the missing records she returned the sorted notes and replied with her findings.

D H BALCHIN RGN, BSc, MA
227 EVERING ROAD CLAPTON LONDON E5 8AL
Tel: 020 8806 5863
debbiebalchin@btinternet.com

Date:27.01.08

Dear Rosamund

<u>Your Client: Charlotte Cunningham</u>

Thank you for your instructions concerning the medical records for this client, which I now return, sorted, indexed and paginated as requested. I have e-mailed to you the word files containing this letter and the medical records index. I attach my invoice.

The GP clinical records appear to be complete up until March 2007. The GP correspondence also appears to be complete up until February 2007.

The Barking, Havering and Redbridge Hospitals NHS Trust records appear to be incomplete. There are no post natal records for Charlotte and no CTG traces. The neonatal records are incomplete as there are no EEG reports, observation charts, drug prescription charts or lab test reports.

The Great Ormond Street Hospital records appear to be complete although there are no observation charts.

There are clearly very grave concerns regarding the management of Charlotte's labour to be considered. In addition there may be issues regarding the management of Joseph's care in NICU at Queens Hospital Romford. In particular there are discrepancies between the reporting of the MRI head scan taken on 28.12.06 by Queens Hospital and Great Ormond Street hospital. The report provided by Queens claims a normal MRI scan for the age group, but the report by GOSH on 18.01.07 records subdural haemorrhages and a left cephalhaematoma as well as swelling and signal changes – all consistent with severe HIE.

There is also an undated clinical note that Joseph had fluid overload (page 128). One of the first lines of management of HIE cases is to restrict fluids to avoid exacerbating cerebral swelling. There are also records, dated 25.12.06 and 29.12.06, of Joseph's bladder being full but no urine output, a urinary catheter was inserted but was later found not to be in the bladder (pages 140 and 153).

I hope that you find the above helpful, please get back to me should you have any queries.

Yours sincerely

Debbie Balchin

Dr Brian Kendall's analysis

After Rosamund had read the letter dated 27th January 2008 from Debbie Balchin, she wrote a letter to Dr Kendall asking if he could give his opinion on Debbie's findings. Her letter to Dr Kendall also contained a copy of Debbie's letter and a copy of the MRI report by Great Ormond street written by of the country's leading experts in understanding infant MRI scans.

1st February 2008

Dear Dr Kendall

Joseph Cunningham (deceased)

I write further to my letter dated 15 January 2008 and I am attaching a copy of the records sorter's letter of 27 January 2008.

I am particularly concerned now regarding what Debbie Balchin has said about the MRI head scan taken on 28 December 2006 by Queens Hospital and the MRI report by Great Ormond Street of 18 January 2007.

The report provided by Queens claims a normal MRI scan for the age group but the report by Great Ormond Street on 18 January 2007 records sub-dural haemorrhages and a left cephalhaematoma as well as swelling and signal changes which are all, as Debbie Balchin rightly says, totally consistent with severe HIE.

She mentions the fact that Joseph also had fluid overload which of course would have damaged him further and that is a matter for a neonatologist so I will be writing to Simon Newell.

Could you possibly report now as soon as possible because I need to get back to the Cunninghams and indeed the Trust?

I look forward to hearing from you.

Best wishes and kind regards,

Yours sincerely

ROSAMUND RHODES-KEMP

Great Ormond Street Hospital for Children - Radiology Department
Great Ormond Street, London WC1N 3JH Tel: 020 7405 9200

Name	: CUNNINGHAM, JOSEPH	Hospital Number	:
Address	QUEEN'S HOSPITAL	Ward/Clinic	: Foreign Films
		Referring Consultant	: Queens Medical Centre Hospital
		Examination Date	: 17/01/2007

DOB: **22/12/2006**   Age: **0**   Sex: **Male**   Attendance Number: **1228551**

Examination(s): **Review Foreign Films-MRI neuro**

Authorised

1228551 17/01/2007 Review Foreign Films-MRI neuro
Review of exteranl MRI brain from Queens hosptial dated 28/12/06.

There are shallow right posterior fossa and interhemispheric subdural haemorrhages and a left
cephalhaematoma. There is bilateral basal ganglia and thalamic swelling with signal change within the
posterior limb of the internal capsule, thalami and putamina. Perirolandic signal change is also observed.

Appearances are of severe hypoxic ischaemic injury at term.

Page 1 of 1

Dr Brian Kendall
FRCR FRCP FRCS

4th February 2008

Dear Rosamund

Re: Joseph Cunningham (deceased)

Thank you for sending the additional CD-ROMs. One of these contains only a chest x-ray. The other contains images, which are identical to those, which I have already seen.

I enclose a more formal report. The cephalhaematoma and the subdural haemorrhage about which Mr Cunningham is obviously concerned are evident on the images. A cephalhaematoma is not uncommon during delivery. It can be associated with an underlying skull fracture of which there is no evidence in Joseph but it is not of itself a dangerous condition.

The subdural haematomas are too shallow to be of clinical significance and are certainly not related to his death.

There is evidence of haemorrhagic infarction in regions, which are damaged by profound circulatory insufficiency. Although it is not evident on the imaging made so soon after birth, brain stem damage may be sufficient to make such an asphyxiated baby unviable and I presume that this is the likely cause of death.

An obstetric opinion would be necessary to determine whether there was an indication to deliver by caesarean section earlier in the labour and thus avoid the very traumatic vaginal delivery.

I am unsure whether the claim is legally aided. I enclose a provisional fee note on the assumption that it is so, which takes into account any questions you may have.

With best wishes

Yours sincerely

Brian

Dr Brian Kendall
F.R.C.R. F.R.C.P. F.R.C.S.

Before Dr Kendall had time to reply to Rosamund's letter, She received an e-mail from Darren (see previous chapter 'Working with the Solicitor') that prompted her to write to Dr Kendall again.

11th February 2008

Dear Dr Kendall

<u>Joseph Cunningham (deceased)</u>

Thank you for your letter of 4 February 2008 and your medical report of the same day.

However, I wonder if you could just clarify for me whether quite simply what you are saying is that this baby suffered birth aspyxhia of a profound nature shortly before delivery and that that was the most likely cause of his death.

Whilst there is evidence of other bleeding in the brain, namely Cephalhaematoma and a subdural hemorrhage, these are not causative. Could you say whether or not they might have been caused by problems with the foetal scalp monitoring, which is what Mr Cunningham believes.

I look forward to hearing from you. Unfortunately this claim is not legally aided and the parents are paying privately.

I am grateful to you for your help.

Best wishes and kind regards,

Yours sincerely

<u>ROSAMUND RHODES-KEMP</u>

20th February 2008

Dear Dr Kendall

<u>Joseph Cunningham (deceased)</u>

I have received the attached, I have to say very distressing, email from Mr Cunningham and I am enclosing the colour photograph of the head scars that he refers to in that email. I have not sent you the last photograph.

Mr Cunningham is anxious to know that you have seen the two MRI scans that he describes in his email and I wonder if you could please consider this carefully and let me know. You might also mention whether you feel it was appropriate with this level of damage to take the life machine off.

I feel so sorry for Mr Cunningham because he is clearly a man tortured by the fact that he had to give his consent to Joseph's ventilator being turned off. He is not sure that it was the right thing to do because for periods of time Joseph was breathing independently and this was notwithstanding that the doctors had said that due to the area of the brain damage messages about breathing were not getting from Joseph's brain to his breathing apparatus.

What I have said to Mr Cunningham is that I am happy to put the question to you about the MRI scan but I do feel that Mr Cunningham made the right decision. This is because of the nature and extent of Joseph's brain damage. His quality of life would have been appalling if he had lived and he would have suffered because he would have had to have carried on with a lot of invasive medical treatment which is painful enough in an adult let alone a tiny neonate.

Speaking personally I can think of no worse decision in the world really that any parent could be forced to make.

I look forward to hearing from you and thank you for your assistance in this matter.

Best wishes and kind regards,

Yours sincerely

<u>ROSAMUND RHODES-KEMP</u>

Dr Brian Kendall
FRCR FRCP FRCS

22nd February 2008

Dear Rosamund

Re: Joseph Cunningham (deceased)

Thank you for your letter of 20th February and for the photograph, which shows the swelling and bruising of the scalp.

Your comments to Mr Cunningham are correct and appropriate. It is of course always a very difficult decision to decide whether a very badly damaged baby is potentially viable with prolonged intensive care. It is certainly not possible from looking at the MRI to say whether the brain stem would have resumed sufficient function for survival. That depends on clinical assessment of brain stem function.

A postmortem investigation would provide much more detailed evidence of the state of the brain stem.

If indicated, an assessment of Joseph's clinical condition at the time when the decision to turn off the ventilator was made, an expert neonatology report would be appropriate.

With best wishes

Yours sincerely

Brian

Dr Brian Kendall
F.R.C.R. F.R.C.P. F.R.C.S.

31st March 2008

Dear Dr Kendall

Joseph Cunningham (deceased)

Thank you for your letter dated 22 February 2008. I apologise for the delay in getting back to you but I have been holding fire until I had received the incident report from the Trust in which various criticisms were made of just about everyone who was handling this delivery. It really was something of a fiasco.

I have suggested to Mr and Mrs Cunningham that:

a.   it is probably not advisable to obtain the report of a neonatologist to discuss whether or not Joseph would have survived with prolonged intensive care, i.e. the machine had not been turned off. I think whether the report is going to be negative to the case or positive they will feel absolutely dreadful; and

b.   I should write to the Trust with an offer and failing that threaten legal proceedings, in which case the Trust will have to hand the matter to the NHSLA who are under directions to deal with stillborn cases swiftly.

If all else fails and we have to issue legal proceedings the matter will be handed to NHSLA panel solicitors which would mean a much quicker resolution. I often wonder why cases are not handed straight to the NHSLA panel solicitors because I think that they save an awful lot of money in the long term because cases will be dealt with in half the time.

Thank you for your help in this case. I do feel sorry for the couple.

Best wishes as always and kind regards,

Yours sincerely

ROSAMUND RHODES-KEMP

With respect to Joseph's case this was the last time Rosamund wrote to Dr Kendall to thank him for his assistance and as a matter of courtesy notifying him of her intentions.

Wanting Answers from the NHS

As a result of the letter sent to Rosamund by Debbie Belchin's dated the 27th January 2008, Rosamund wrote to the NHS in search for an explanation to some vital questions.

1st February 2008

Dear Madam

RE: Charlotte Cunningham
Date of birth: 22.01.1974

We have now reviewed the medical records in this matter and we would be grateful if you could explain or clarify the following:-

1.	The discrepancy between the reporting of the MRI head scan taken on 28 December 2006 by Queens Hospital. The report provided by Queens of this scan claims it was normal for the age group but the report of the same scan by Great Ormond Street on 18 January 2007 records subdural haemorrhages and a left cephalhaematoma as well as swelling and signal changes which are all consistent with severe HIE.

2.	There is also an undated clinical note that Joseph had fluid overload. As your clinicians will know, one of the first lines of management of HIE cases is to restrict fluid to avoid exacerbating cerebral swelling. In addition to this there would appear to be records dated 25 December 2006 and 29 December 2006 of Joseph's bladder being full, i.e. due to the fluid overload but no urinary output. A urinary catheter was inserted but was later found not to be in the bladder. We enclose copies of the relevant entries for the fluid overload.

Can you please confirm that these observations are correct and could you ask please for your clinicians to comment on these particular notes?

Yours faithfully

BOLT BURDON KEMP

A week later, the NHS replied to Rosamund's letter but sadly not to the questions put to them. The letter received from the Queen's hospital Legal Services Manager read 'I regret I am unable to ask our clinicians to comment on the points raised in your letter and respectfully suggest you direct these to your clinical experts.'

On the 11th February 2008, Rosamund wrote again to the NHS requesting for additional information and to press the Queen's Hospital legal team to pass the case onto the NHSLA to help progress the case.

11th February 2008

Dear Madam

RE: Charlotte Cunningham
Date of birth: 22.01.1974

Thank you for your letter dated 1 February 2008 and the enclosed Adverse Incident Report Form. Is there anything else at all that the Trust have in relation to this baby's death – internal memoranda, notes of meetings or training suggestions for the staff? Is there just this very brief report form regarding the death of this baby?

We should be grateful if you would send anything else please.

We note that you will shortly be referring the matter to the NSHLA and we wondered if you could please expedite that transfer because the sooner this is resolved as far as the parents are concerned the better. If you are going to transfer it to the NHSLA would you be kind enough to give us the reference so that we can correspond with the NHSLA because unfortunately we have experienced huge delays with the NHSLA over the last twelve months.

We look forward to hearing from you.

Yours faithfully

BOLT BURDON KEMP

20 March 2008

Dear Sirs

Re: Joseph Cunningham

Thank you for your letter dated 11 February 2008 which was addressed to Lyon Road Store. As requested in our letter of 8 February 2008, please address all future correspondence to the writer.

The copy Incident Form which was sent to you earlier was a record of the Incident. I now attach the report on Charlotte Cunningham which was completed following investigation.

Yours faithfully,

Legal Services Manager

Accompanying the letter from the NHS was a report written on 9th April 2007 titled 'Report on Charlotte Cunningham' written by an NHS Risk Management Midwife (see previous chapter 'Working with the Solicitor'). A copy of the report was sent onto the parents for their reference and comments.

Rosamund replied on the 31st March enquiring what the mnemonics DR C BRAVADO stood for and to learn if the Risk Management Midwife was employed by the NHS or was contracted to write the report. On the 16th April she received a reply dated 11th April 2008.

11 April 2008

Dear Sirs,

Re: Joseph Cunningham

Thank you for your letter dated 31 March 2008.

The DR C BRAVADO neumonic stands for:-

DR	-	Define the Risk
C	-	Contractions
BR	-	Baseline Rate
A	-	Acceleration
VA	-	Variability
D	-	Decelerations
O	-	Opinion

I can confirm that ▉▉▉▉▉▉▉is still employed at this Trust.

I would be grateful if all future correspondence could be address to the writer, to expedite matters.

Yours faithfully,

Legal Services Manager

After carefully reading through the report written by the Risk Management Midwife and after receiving comments about the report from Darren and Charlotte, a letter was written listing the concerns found within the report and a list of demands. The case was moving to a new stage which would invariably force the Legal team within the Queen's hospital to have no choice but to hand the case over to the National Health Service Litigation Authority (NHSLA). It would be for the NHSLA to make the decision if they wanted to take the case to court or admit liability this is what Rosamund wanted.

21st April 2008

Dear Madam

Joseph Cunningham
Date of birth: 22.December 2006
Date of death: 29 January 2007

We refer to previous correspondence.

We acknowledge receipt of your letter dated 11 April 2008 and thank you for the information provided.

You have provided a copy of the report of ██████████ which has now been reviewed by our client.

The report of Charlotte Cunningham has now been reviewed by her and we have instructed to write to you requesting an admission of liability and causation with regard to the delivery and death of baby Joseph Cunningham, who was born on 22 December 2006 and died on 29 January 2007.

Concerns raised in the report of ██████████ are as follows:-

1. ████████████████████████████
2. ████████████████████████████
3. ████████████████████████
4. ████████████████████████████████████
5. ████████████████████████████████
6. ████████████████████████████████████

7.

8.

9.

10.

11.

In the circumstances our clients would like to obtain the following:-

1. an apology for what happened

2. an explanation for how it happened

3. reassurance that steps have been taken to try and ensure that something like this does not happen again

4. compensation for their pain and suffering and the pain and suffering of their dead son.

We look forward to hearing from you as soon as possible.

Yours faithfully

BOLT BURDON KEMP

Sandra Tranter

21st April 2008

Dear Ms Tranter

<u>Clinical Negligence Claim</u>

I have an interesting but sad case involving a baby who died at Barking, Havering and Redbridge Hospitals NHS Trust and the parents initiated an investigation into the complaints process. Risk Management Midwife, ███████████, reported and I have now got a copy of the report.

██
████████████████████

██
████████████████████████████████████

██
████████████████

Anyway the parents are unhappy with this report ████████████████████████ ██████████████████████ and they have asked if it would be possible for an expert to go through the report and on each page mark what was done incorrectly and whether it amounts to poor or substandard, even negligent practice, taking into account the Midwife's Code of Contact and the NICE Guidelines. Would you be able to do this and if so what would you charge? The report from the internal enquiry is 12 pages long.

I look forward to hearing from you.

Best wishes and kind regards,

Yours sincerely

<u>ROSAMUND RHODES-KEMP</u>

7th May 2008

Dear Rosamund

Thank you for your letter of 21st April about this case of a baby who sadly died at Barking, Havering and Redbridge Hospitals NHS Trust, which I read when I returned from the BVI on Friday. I have tried to contact you by telephone to discuss this.

You have asked me to have a look through the report of the risk management Midwife, ██████████████, and comment in relation to acceptable midwifery practice. I will be happy to do so. It's difficult to estimate how long this would take although I see that the report is just 12 pages long. Would a set fee of £250 be acceptable?

I am sure that your client is aware that under the NHS Complaints procedure she is entitled to ask for an independent review of her complaint. This would take a little time to put in motion, but would be conducted by a midwife and an obstetrician from outside the Trust. I used to do these reviews when I worked for the NHS and found them to be helpful – and unbiased. Your client still has the option to proceed to a legal claim if she is unhappy with the outcome of an independent review. However, any ongoing legal action puts the complaints procedure on hold, so if she has told the Trust that she is seeking legal action they can refuse to set up an independent review.

I look forward to hearing from you again on this matter.

Yours sincerely

Sandra Tranter

13th May 2008

Dear Ms Tranter

Clinical Negligence Claim

Thank you for your letter dated 7 May 2008. I am really grateful to you for your offer of help and the amount. I am sorry I was not able to speak with you when you called. I as not aware that you had called on this matter actually but I am aware that your daughter had acknowledged receipt but I was not sure which case she was talking about!

Anyway, we are all sorted now and I am very grateful to you and I will pass on this information to Mr and Mrs Cunningham to indicate your view.

The Trust meanwhile are collecting the papers to pass to the National Health Service Litigation Authority. No doubt as usual the vast black hole will then open up and we will not hear anything for months, so we have a little time.

Once they get hold of a stillbirth case the NHSLA do tend to try and deal with it reasonably quickly although we have had a couple of false starts recently.

As always one feels desperately sorry for the parents but in this particular case I think the little lad suffered a great deal as well, which I think is terrible.

I will get back to you as soon as I have heard from the Cunninghams because I think that a report from you on events will be extremely helpful in our negotiations with the NHSLA.

Best wishes and kind regards,

Yours sincerely

ROSAMUND RHODES-KEMP

In the Hands of the NHSLA

29th April 2008

Dear Sirs,

Re: Charlotte Cunningham on behalf of Joseph Cunningham

We acknowledge receipt of your letter dated 21st April 2008 which was received by our offices on 22nd April 2008, with regard to the above named.

This Trust is a member of the Clinical Negligence Scheme for Trusts, which is managed by the National Health Service Litigation Authority (NHSLA). The NHSLA indemnifies NHS bodies in respect of both clinical negligence and non-clinical risks and manage claims and litigation under both headings. Therefore once we have collated all the relevant documentation we will be reporting this case to the NHSLA, who will contact you directly on this matter.

Yours faithfully,

Deputy Legal Services Manager

13th May 2008

Dear Madam

Joseph Cunningham
Date of birth: 22.December 2006
Date of death: 29 January 2007

Thank you for your letter dated 29 April 2008.

We note that this letter is going to be passed to the NHSLA and we should be grateful if you could let us know once you have done that and if possible to whom you have passed it because we find that a rather large black hole tends to open up when Trusts pass papers to the NHSLA and there may be no contact for several months. Obviously this will cause further distress to Mr and Mrs Cunningham.

We look forward to hearing from you.

Yours faithfully

BOLT BURDON KEMP

Rosamund received the following letter from the NHS dated the 9th May on the 16th May and much to her surprise the NHSLA had made a very quick decision not to defend against the case but to admit liability.

9 May 2008

Dear Ms Rhodes-Kemp,

Re; Miss Charlotte Cunningham -v- Barking, Havering and Redbridge Hospitals NHS Trust

We act on behalf of Barking, Havering and Redbridge Hospitals NHS Trust and have been provided with a copy of your previous correspondence dated 21 April 2008 which was received at the Trust on 22 April 2008.

We can confirm that liability is admitted.

In accordance with Part 36 of the Civil Procedural Rules we offer to settle your client's claim in the sum of £20,000. Your reasonable costs are, of course, payable in addition.

This offer is subject to receipt of a £nil CRU certificate. In order that we may request such a certificate we would be grateful for confirmation of your client's full address, National Insurance number and date of birth.

Should your client reject this offer but subsequently recover the amount offered or less then we reserve the right to bring this correspondence to the attention of the Court in respect of the issue of costs.

This will offer will remain open for acceptance for a period of 21 days from the date of receipt.

Finally, we would be grateful for confirmation as to how your client's claim is funded?

We await hearing from you.

Yours faithfully

Case Manager

14th May 2008

Dear Sirs

Miss Charlotte Cunningham v Barking, Havering and Redbridge Hospitals NHS Trust

Thank you for your letter dated 9 May 2008. Unfortunately the timing of this is extremely unfortunate because we have just had an email from Mr Cunningham saying that the last thing that he wants is an offer without any explanation of how his son died and of course that is what you have sent.

I am sure that there is a way around this but it is not a question of him simply signing on the dotted line because of the circumstances leading up to Joseph's death.

The offer does seem very low in any event.

We will get back to you as soon as we can.

Best wishes and kind regards,

Yours sincerely

ROSAMUND RHODES-KEMP

29th May 2008

Dear Madam

Joseph Cunningham
Date of birth: 22 December 2006
Date of death: 29 January 2007

We refer to previous correspondence. Our client would be willing to accept the offer of £20,000 subject to them receiving a full explanation as to –

i) the cause of the events that took place, and
ii) what should have taken place during the labour to prevent Joseph's injuries.

Our client's National Insurance number is ██████████.

We look forward to hearing from you.

Yours faithfully

BOLT BURDON KEMP

The NHS chose not to reply to the above letters and they were the last the Rosamund would write to the NHS for the case. The case was handed over to Suzanne Trask because Rosamund had plans to work for another company.

18th June 2008

Dear Sirs

Joseph Cunningham (deceased)

To clarify the request for further information in our previous letter dated 29th May 08, our clients require the following –

- An explanation of what failures actually caused the death of their son. Whilst errors have been noted in the Risk Assessment Report, it is still unclear how these caused Joseph's death.

- In order to fully understand the above, a clear chronological list of actions/decisions that were taken by individuals throughout the course of treatment, stating where failures occurred, and what should have taken place.

- An explanation of what clinical standards were applicable and how they were not satisfied.

The Risk Assessment Report dated 9th April 07 focuses almost entirely on failures to communicate to Mr and Mrs Cunningham, and a failure to record events properly in the medical records. They understandably believe that this is inadequate.

Our clients also seek a formal letter of apology from the Trust.

Please take instructions from the Trust on whether they will provide this information.

Yours faithfully

BOLT BURDON KEMP

25 June 2008

Dear Ms Trask,

Re; Master Joseph Cunningham (Deceased)

Thank you for your letter of 18 June 2008.

We can confirm that we have forwarded a copy of your correspondence to the Trust and we are awaiting their response as to whether they will provide the information requested. If they are, then we have suggested that they correspond with you directly in this regard.

In addition we are arranging for a Letter of Apology to be prepared and this will follow under separate cover shortly.

In the meantime we await your client's full CRU details as requested in our Letter of Response dated 9 May 2008. We would also be grateful for confirmation as to how your client's claim is funded?

Finally, we would be grateful for confirmation as to whether our Part 36 offer made on 9 May 2008, in the sum of £20,000 is accepted or alternatively if this offer is rejected, how your clients intend to proceed?

We await hearing from you.

Yours sincerely

Case Manager

Suzanne arranged for Darren to discuss the case with a barrister who was familiar with such cases to explain the options and possible outcomes. Darren came to the decision that he had to accept the offer without conditions even if it meant not getting answers to questions. Suzanne contacted the NHSLA by e-mail to confirm the decision on Darren and Charlotte's behalf.

Suzanne Trask

From:	Suzanne Trask
Sent:	22 July 2008 13:13
Subject:	Cunningham
Importance:	High

Dear Sirs,

We are instructed to accept your offer of £20,000 plus costs in settlement of the claim.

We understand that a written apology will also be provided, and that the request for information set out in our letter dated 18th June will continue to be considered by the Trust. Please ask the Trust to correspond directly with Mr Darren Cunningham in this regard.

We look forward to receiving payment.

Yours faithfully

BOLT BURDON KEMP

SUZANNE TRASK
Solicitor

Suzanne handed over the case to her colleague to deal with processing the legal fees.

Local MP Saves King George Hospital

The following leaflet was posted through the door sometime in July 2008 mentioning of a campaign to save King George hospital where Joseph was born.

Margaret Hodge
Labour Member of Parliament for Barking

Margaret Hodge MP

Dear Resident

Improving our health service in Barking & Dagenham - Spring 2008

I wanted to write to you about my campaign to save King George Hospital and the work I am doing to improve our health services across Barking and Dagenham. I especially want to address the problems many people are having at Queens Hospital in Romford.

King George Hospital – temporary reprieve!
Many of you will know about the threat to services at King George Hospital. The health trust has been looking at reorganising local services.

It would mean cuts or closure in Accident and Emergency services with all emergencies requiring an ambulance going to Queens at Romford or Whipps Cross in Leyton.

Because of the tremendous support my campaign received from local residents, I am glad to report that the health trust have now abandoned its plans and will look again at how our local A&E provision fits in to the London-wide picture. Whilst its great news that they have halted the original scheme to scrap A&E at King George, Dr George Alberti, who is charged with developing plans to reconfigure the NHS in London, may still recommend closure. Last year he said that King George Hospital would need major investment to retain full acute health services and that it "made sense" to have an A&E at Queens.

The people I meet when I'm knocking on doors, at my regular coffee mornings or in my advice surgeries say time and again that to travel to see a friend or relative at Queens or Whipps Cross is a real problem. I am convinced that with a growing population and 10,000 new homes planned at Barking Riverside, it will be simply irresponsible to shut the A&E at King George when local residents will obviously need that facility.

I will be seeing the health minister Ben Bradshaw MP to hand over my petition to save King George's A&E with over 30,000 signatures on it. I will argue for more not less investment in King George. We need to have proper health facilities for the people of

I was joined by 1,000 people last summer who supported me in my campaign to save the A&E at King George Hospital. We all held hands around the entrance of the Hospital. It was absolutely wonderful to see the community coming together in such a good cause.

I was delighted to support the Barking & Dagenham Recorder's campaign in support of King George Hospital. They have taken a keen interest in the future of the A&E. By working together we will achieve more.

The street meetings and coffee mornings I hold around Barking give local residents the opportunity to talk about the things that really concern them. I bring people like council officials, health practitioners and the police to these meetings so that residents get straight answers to their questions.

Barking & Dagenham.

With 14,000 more patients treated at King George A&E last year than were treated at Queens, it seems clear to me that there is a massive demand for services there. I will keep you informed and let you know when the consultation begins so that you can make your voice heard.

Sorting out Queen's Hospital

Since it opened in 2006, many of you have had to come to see me or write to me about the treatment you are receiving at Queen's Hospital in Romford. Not a week passes without people telling me about relatives having to wait for hours to be seen. People can't find their way around the hospital and too often things are going wrong with the treatment.

With any new hospital there will always be a period of 'settling-in' as staff and patients get used to the new facilities and layout, but the experience many people were having at Queens is definitely much more than a few hiccups.

So last year, to get a real feel for what was happening, I visited it several times, even going unannounced. I saw the confusing signs for myself, talked to patients who had been waiting for over 6 hours in Accident and Emergency, saw how small some of the waiting areas are and how inadequate some things remain.

The good news is that the hospital's new chief executive officer, John Goulston who has come from Barts hospital, has assured me that many of the issues that I raised are being dealt with.

I am also pleased that an extra 100 permanent nurses are being brought in to save having to use temporary agency staff. With new directors of nursing and midwifery, he feels the hospital will be able to deal with its early problems.

Mr Goulston was honest enough to admit that there should have been more consultation when the hospital was built with those who would end up using it. I am more assured that the problems we have at Queens are on their way to being solved. However I will continue my visits, both planned and unannounced to keep on top of this issue. I will also carry on with my campaign for more investment at King George Hospital. Only with two fully functional hospitals serving our community will we get the service and treatment needed.

Babies will be born in Barking again!

One of the great pieces of news that I want to tell you about is the success of my "Babies Born in Barking" campaign. Ever since the closure of the maternity unit at Barking Hospital on the Upney Lane site, mothers were having to use maternity units outside our town.

Many young mothers were concerned about the distance they, and their relatives, had to travel to the designated hospital by car, taxi or public transport.

So, thanks to the support of thousands of local people, the health authorities agreed that the land at the old Barking Hospital site could be used for a midwife led maternity unit and that the unit will open by the summer in 2009! I want to thank all those who supported the campaign and I am glad to see that, once again, babies will be born in Barking.

Improving Local Health Centres

I am really pleased with the way that drop-in centres have improved our local health services. Right across Barking and Dagenham we are seeing more modernised and new health centres like the one on Upney Lane. As well as providing blood tests it carries out x-rays and treats minor injuries including broken arms which would once have meant a trip to hospital. The centre is open every day and now has paediatricians working there so that, for the first time, children can be treated. I want to see longer opening hours and the inclusion of full-time GP services in the future.

The number of health centres carrying out blood tests is also on the increase. People no longer need to travel to one of the main hospitals but can visit any of the four centres where you can get blood tests right across Barking and Dagenham. The new Thames View Health Centre is open five days a week and this means residents no longer have to take a long bus journey for a simple blood test.

All these new improvements are due, in part, to the extra money the government has put into our local health services and now I've just been told that we will be getting an extra £14.6 million this year in Barking and Dagenham alone. We've got a bigger rise than almost any other part of the country. Rest assured I will be making sure that it is put to good use!

The need to improve GP services

Whilst ensuring our local hospitals are running effectively and dispensing the care we need, I am concerned about the GP services in Barking and Dagenham.

In 2006 alone, GP services in Barking and Dagenham were performing well below the national average when it came to giving people appointments within 48 hours. Many GP clinics are well run and offer good services to their patients, but others need to get better.

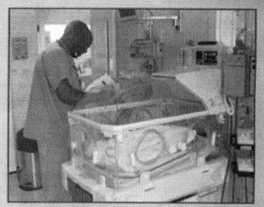

Babies will be born in Barking again! Following the campaign I waged, the old Barking Hospital site will have a brand new maternity unit opening in the summer of 2009. It's a good example of a service that should be provided locally.

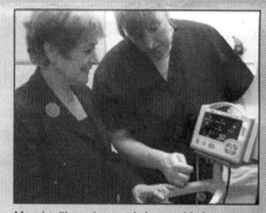

More health services are being provided on people's doorsteps. Take the newly refurbished Walk-in Centre in Upney Lane which now provides blood tests and x-rays.

Residents I meet on their doorstep tell me time and again about how difficult it is to travel to see a friend or relative at Queens or Whipps Cross. I believe it would be irresponsible to shut the A&E at King George when we have ten thousand new homes planned at Barking Reach and a growing population that will need those facilities.

Currently, the government is proposing changes to the structure of this service with the idea that we create "polyclinics" whereby local residents can access a range of services such as a GP clinic, a dentist and some x-rays from one site. As well as bringing the most used services under one roof, I also want people to be able to use these services at more convenient times like evenings and weekends.

I really want to know what your experience is on this important issue. We all see doctors from time to time, and on most occasions it's due to ill health. That's why it's vital we make this service as easy and accessible as possible. I will then be able to use this information to get the changes we need to be able to see the doctor quickly and at more convenient times. Please fill out the form below and return to: Margaret Hodge MP, Freepost LON17954, London SW1A 0YX.

With all good wishes.

Yours sincerely

Margaret Hodge MP

Charlotte and Darren had a strong urge to write to Margaret but eventually decided against it. It was evident that the MP's campaign was aimed for the greater good of the local residents and sharing their experience with her would not have made any difference. Not the kind of difference that Charlotte and Darren were interested in. That being to do whatever it took to warn the residents of what did happen, what can happen and probably what will happen again until the NHS take ownership to take necessary steps to prevent babies from being injured again due to negligence and a lack of respect for procedures.

Joseph's new Stone

On the 21st December 2007 Darren and Charlotte made their way to North Wales to spend Christmas with family and also to be close to where Joseph was now at rest. They knew it would be hard but it had to be done and they were just not strong enough to spend Christmas alone and so many miles away from Joseph. As always they were met by her brother Wayne at Rhyl station their destination and were taken to Charlotte's Father's home. The journey had been long and they retired for the night relatively early. Darren was awake early and had not slept that well. As he lay in bed knowing that it would have been his Son's first birthday today, his mind played evil tricks by recalling the events of the labour and the precious moments that he spent with his Son for what seems now as only a handful of moments. He silently wept as he looked upon Charlotte who was still sound asleep.

It was several hours later before Charlotte woke and it appeared she was more mentally prepared for the day and its significance. As if in a routine she got up got dressed, went to the bathroom and then into the kitchen to make herself a drink leaving Darren to his thoughts. Moments later she brought him in a drink and asked if he was getting up. She knew he was upset and Darren confirmed that he could not bring himself to face the world today, not today, not when it was supposed to be a happy occasion, a celebration. Darren imagined what they would have done to record his first birthday inviting friends and family perhaps, receiving cards, balloons and teddy bears. Joseph would not see any of this on his first birthday or any birthday.

It took several hours before Darren pulled himself together, got up, had a shower, got dressed and then ventured into town with Charlotte. Charlotte wanted to get Joseph some foil balloons, visit his grave, and let one go.

That afternoon on a relatively clear day in the cemetery they stood alone at his grave side looking upon his wooden cross. With great strength they wished him a happy birthday. Tied one balloon to his cross and let the second go, to be taken up into the clouds and eventually out of sight. They cried while comforted in each other's arms.

Before they left they decided while wiping away tears, that it was time to get Joseph a head stone that was fitting for their beautiful boy.

The next date of significance was the anniversary of Joseph's death 28th January 2008. For this day, Charlotte wanted to return to GOSH, not to return to the ward to visit the room where he was held in Darren's arms until he died but to visit the chapel. Within the chapel was the book of remembrance and on this date the page would be open for all to see Joseph's name along with the names of the other children who had also sadly passed away on the 28th January.

The following week was spent looking over booklets of various types of head stones. It was incredible to believe how many shapes, sizes, and colours there was to choose from. Quite quickly they agreed on what they wanted written on the stone but the hard decision was what shape to choose. It had to be suitable to represent a child but all the designs they had seen they did not seem able to connect with. Darren's Uncle Dennis suggested getting in contact with one of the local stone masons that had cleaned up the headstone of Darren's Grandparents head stone. The company traded under the name of Buckley Memorials Ltd and had just the perfect design. The order was placed on the 7th February 2008 nearly a year to the day when Joseph was buried. On the 13th May 2008 a letter arrived in the post from Buckley Memorials ltd confirming that the stone was now in place at Joseph's resting place.

It was some weeks later before Darren and Charlotte returned to North Wales due to the tragic loss of Charlotte's Father when they had the first opportunity to visit Joseph and to admire his new head stone.

The head stone with a gold inscription read:

Joseph Lloyd Cunningham
Born 22 DEC 2006
Died 28 JAN 2007
Always in our Thoughts
Forever in our
Hearts
Little Man

Does lightening strike twice?

On the 22nd May at 09:20am Darren was standing on the West Ham Jubilee Line London Underground platform waiting for a train to take him to work in Canary Wharf. A train approached, came to a stop and the doors opened. As Darren stepped onto the train his mobile rang and he noticed that it was his brother-in-laws number. Wayne never called him unless it was something serious. Darren immediately thought the worst remembering the last time Wayne had called him in the morning when Charlotte's mother had suddenly passed away just two weeks before Joseph was to be born. Reluctantly Darren answered and stepped off the train just before the train doors closed so it would not take him underground which would cut off his mobile signal. The train moved on leaving Darren standing on the platform alone. 'Darren it's Wayne, I've got some bad news, my Dad died last night'. This was the last message Darren wanted to hear as he knew how much Charlotte loved her Father and the timing could not have been any worse. After learning the details from Wayne Darren informed his manager and made his way back home to break the news to Charlotte.

By 10:00 Darren arrived home much to Charlotte's surprise and he told her about the call he had received from Wayne less than an hour ago. As expected, Charlotte was emotionally distraught and clearly in shock. She cursed and shouted and was inconsolable, she was now convinced that she was cursed and like Darren could not get over the coincidence with it being only three weeks before giving birth to her baby girl she now carried as it was when her mother died just weeks before giving birth to Joseph.

That day they made plans to travel to their home town Rhyl in North Wales in order to attend the funeral. The funeral was held on 29th May and the service went well. Although Charlotte never said, she knew that she feared the worst on how her labour would go with her little girl.

Nearly 2 weeks later on the 10th June, Darren woke at 7:00 to get up for work and saw Charlotte quietly pacing around the bedroom. He could read her body language and suspected that she was going through the initial stages of labour. Darren asked how she was and she confirmed his suspicions. By 8:00 the contractions were regular and by 9:00 they were in the hospital.

ST. ANN'S CHURCH
RHYL

IN LOVING MEMORY OF

NORMAN LLOYD WILLIAMS

WHO PASSED AWAY
22ND MAY 2008
AGED 80 YEARS

FUNERAL SERVICE ON
THURSDAY 29TH MAY 2008
AT 12 NOON

FOLLOWED BY COMMITTAL
AT BRON-Y-NANT CREMATORIUM, COLWYN BAY

Charlotte and Darren were shown to a room on the labour ward with the unfortunate ward name of 'Mary Celeste' which Darren thought was in poor taste.

The midwife assigned to Charlotte examined her and performed a sweep which helped to break her waters. The midwife recorded that she was 3 centimetres dilated and had a while to go. When Charlotte requested for gas and air to ease the discomfort of the contractions, the midwife explained that she wanted to send her back home until she had progressed further. Darren could not believe what he was hearing as it was evident that Charlotte was not coping well with the contractions and finding them very painful. Thankfully before Charlotte was moved out the consultant came to visit and decided against Charlotte leaving and was given the gas and air she had asked for. The consultant reviewed the CTG that Charlotte had been connected to earlier by the midwife. The graph reported that the baby's heart beat was dropping during a contraction. This was not a good sign and the consultant confirmed that she would be monitored closely. Every hour a consultant would come in to make an assessment on her progress. By the afternoon the pain was becoming so intense that the gas and air was no longer effective. Charlotte agreed to have an epidural.

At 2:30, Darren's mother Carolyne arrived after travelling from Rhyl on the train. The consultants were now worried that Charlotte's progress was slow which meant that the labour would be long which was not ideal for the baby.

By 17:00 matters took a turn for the worst. Even though Charlotte felt no change, she had developed a temperature. The baby was reacting to the increase in her temperature with a sharp acceleration in her heart rate from 130 beats per minute up to 200+. Charlotte was given Paracetamol which did have a positive effect, but not as sufficient as the consultant would like, so by 17:30 the decision was made to have an emergency caesarean section. At 18:11 Charlotte and Darren's healthy baby girl named Charisma Jessica Cunningham was born. When held up so Charlotte could see her baby for the first time Charisma cried which brought tears of joy because Joseph had never cried not once.

While Charlotte was being cleaned and stitched up on the operating table the main power failed not once but twice which made that day that little more eventful.

Charlotte and Charisma were kept in until the Friday 13th June before being discharged at 17:00. At 18:00, Charlotte, a proud and very happy mother stepped though the front door of her home and had brought her baby home.

The Injunction

On the 10th April, the 1st Edition of the book 'Joseph's Life Story' was finally available to the public to read about the tragic story of Joseph. This was an important moment for parents Darren and Charlotte. The book was a tribute to Joseph's memory and a gift to their friends and family to allow them to learn in detail (if they so wished) of the events in each of Joseph's days that he lived and the effort required to get the NHS to accept liability for the numerous mistakes their staff had made that cost Joseph his life.

Guided by sound advice from the book publisher, Darren contacted the local news papers (the Barking and Dagenham Record and the Yellow Advertiser) to share the story of Joseph with them and to mention the fact that he had released a book covering the loss of his son that occurred in a local hospital. The Barking and Dagenham Record and the Yellow Advertiser were both interested and willing to run a small story to cover the release of the book. Both papers independently sent their photographers to take a picture of Darren holding the book to accompany the story. The first story to be published was by the Recorder on the 8th May written by senior journalist John Philips. The story was written following a lengthy telephone interview with Darren and also after John reading a review copy of the book sent onto John courtesy of the book publisher - AuthorHouse. The story was also released on the newspapers website with the photo of Darren in colour. Just prior to the story going to press, John had contacted the NHS asking if they wanted to comment on the story but they replied – NO COMMENT.

The following week Darren had a second telephone interview with Martyn Dolton, the Barking and Dagenham reporter for the Yellow Advertiser. Martyn had also received a review copy of the book and had many questions relating to the story. After close to an hour on the phone, Martyn was satisfied that he had all the facts necessary to write the story to cover and complement the book to be published in the paper on the 14th May. Martyn had also contacted the NHS earlier in the week requesting if they would like to comment on the story and again the reply was NO COMMENT.

Early in the morning of Thursday 14th May 2009, Darren received a call from the Yellow Advertiser informing him that they would not be able to run the story in the paper this week as they had received a solicitor's letter acting on behalf of the NHS Barking, Havering and Redbridge National Health Trust placing an injunction on the paper from running the story. Although Darren asked the question why, the person from the Yellow Advertiser did not know the details at this time.

Darren was in work and busy on a conference call when solicitor Suzanne Trask called and left a voice mail message on his phone at just after 11:30 AM. Minutes later, Darren was off the phone and listened to the message from Suzanne. She requested for him to call her because solicitors instructed by the NHS had contacted her in relation to the Injunction. Darren called Suzanne and learnt that she had received a call from a solicitor representing the NHS and they had been granted an interim Injunction by a Judge to prevent the story going to press and also on the book. Suzanne could not go into any more detail because she was not aware of the terms of the injunction but mentioned that the NHS solicitors would be in touch with Darren today. She recommended that Darren should contact a media litigation specialist and gave details of a solicitors company that could help. Darren thanked her for her advice.

Soon after the call, Suzanne sent an e-mail to Darren covering what they had discussed and the contact details for the solicitor she had recommended.

The following e-mail from Suzanne Trask originally contained the name of the Solicitor dealing with the case on behalf of the NHS but has been removed from the e-mail on their request.

From: Suzanne Trask
Sent: 14 May 2009 12:32
To: Darren Cunningham
Subject: Your Book
Importance: High
Sensitivity: Confidential

Mr Cunningham,

Further to our conversation, I received a call this morning from Solicitors who has been instructed to act for the NHS Trust who provided treatment to your son. He explained that the Trust has become aware of your book, and also understands that a local newspaper, called the Yellow Advertiser, were going to write an article on the book.

The Trust instructed their Solicitors to apply for an injunction in relation to your book and the newspaper article. I am not aware of the terms of injunction, but they were granted an interim injunction at court last night. There is a court hearing on Monday when a judge will consider whether to confirm the injunction as a full injunction. The NHS Solicitors will be sending the documents to you today.

As Bolt Burdon Kemp were instructed to act for you in the clinical negligence case and this is now concluded, we cannot advise you in relation to this, which would be media litigation, a different area of law. However, we are able to recommend a media litigation specialist at Steeles Solicitors who has experience in this area, and who deals with high profile cases, called Dominic Crossley, (Head of Media Litigation) and is available on 0207 421 1720.

I hope that this is helpful.

Regards

Suzanne Trask
Solicitor

On receiving the e-mail from Suzanne, Darren dialed the contact number for Steeles Solicitors and was put through to Tim Lowles. Darren explained the situation and Tim requested for the e-mail from Suzanne to be sent onto him and said that he would look into the situation.

At 3 PM Charlotte had put her daughter Charisma down to have her afternoon sleep when the door bell rang, she answered the door and a man asked if Darren was in. Charlotte told him that Darren was in work and would not be home until the evening. The man explained who he was and that he worked for a solicitors firm who had been appointed by the NHS and that he was responsible for serving papers to Darren in person. Charlotte contacted Darren on his mobile and said that a man who worked for the solicitors representing the NHS had arrived at the house with a document that needed to be given in person to him and no one else. Darren reassured Charlotte that there was nothing to worry about and the matter was in hand and asked her to tell the man to come to his work place and he would meet him in the reception. Darren went onto say that he would call her and explain what was going on once he had read the document.

Just before 4 PM Darren received a call from the reception informing him that a visitor had arrived and would he come down to meet him. Darren made his way to the ground floor where he met the man who had earlier called at his home. Darren was given a number of letters and the man kindly suggested that he should seek legal advice concerning the matter. Darren thanked him for the documents and returned to his office.

Darren flicked through the documents and decided to call Tim to let him know what he had received. Tim asked for the documents to be faxed over and that he would take a look at them and requested to meet in his office the next day to review the situation together and to come to an agreement on the best course of action to take. Darren agreed to come into the city in the afternoon to meet up with Tim and would bring along the legal documents, a copy of the book and his passport as identification.

Recorded delivery and by hand

Date

14 May 2009

SERVICE OF ORDER

Dear Mr Cunningham

JOSEPH'S LIFE STORY (SEEKING JUSTICE) BY DARREN CUNNINGHAM

We refer to the above matter, in which we are instructed to act on behalf of Barking, Havering and Redbridge University Hospitals NHS Trust.

We were given notice of the above publication and, having read the same, note the disclosure of a number of documents provided by the Trust as part of your litigation surrounding the sad death of your son, Joseph.

All documents provided to you and your solicitors, Bolt Burden & Kemp, were provided solely for the purpose of the litigation and for nothing more. Therefore, you are not permitted disclose documentation within your book, which was provided to you and your solicitors as part of the litigation, without our client's consent or a Court Order.

We are particularly concerned to ensure our client's employees privacy and confidentiality is protected and were therefore bound to seek an interim injunction on 13.05.09. The matter was urgent because we were made aware of a local newspapers intention (The Yellow Advertiser) to publish an article about the book on 13.05.09, which we were concerned would give rise to local interest, which in turn may have jeopardised the privacy and confidentiality of Trust staff.

Our client therefore made an Application seeking a Court Order that the newspaper be restrained and prohibited from publishing or publicising the book or any part of it by any media article or description of the same until further consideration of the Application by the Court.

We also sought an Order preventing further publication and distribution of your book until references to Trust staff were removed. We also sought an Order preventing any reference to the Internal Investigation Report of ████████████, which is referred to substantially within the book.

The Judge has granted an interim injunction, a copy of which we attach by way of service.

The Order relates to the Third Respondent (The Yellow Advertiser), which is restrained and prohibited from publishing or publicising the book or any part thereof by any media article or description of the same howsoever until further consideration of the Application by the Court on Monday 18.05.09 at 10.30am.

Costs of the Application have been reserved.

Whilst the Order relates to the Third Respondent, you are referred specifically to the Notice to the proposed Defendant which indicates that any other person who knows of this Order and has anything which helps or permits the Respondent/intended Defendant to breach the terms of this Order may also be held to be in contempt of Court and maybe imprisoned, fined or have their assets ceased. You are also referred to page 3 of the Order specifically, which confirms it is a contempt of Court for any person notified of this Order knowingly to assist in or permit a breach of this Order and any person doing so maybe sent to prison, fined or have its assets ceased.

We put you on notice that the matter has been listed for further hearing, at which you are encouraged to attend to respond to the Trust's Application for a general injunction at 10.30am on Monday 18.05.09 at the Royal Courts of Justice in London. At this stage, we do not know to which Court the matter will be listed but understand the Court will notify parties on late Friday 15.05.09.

Whilst at this stage we serve a copy of the sealed Order with the Witness Statement of ████████████ dated 13.05.09 which was appended to the Application Notice, we shall be serving upon you by 15.05.09 a full Application Notice with further evidence in support of our client's Application.

We would be grateful if you would kindly acknowledge receipt of this letter and confirm whether or not you intend to attend the Application Hearing on Monday 18.05.09 to contest the Application.

You are encouraged to seek legal advice in respect of this matter.

We look forward to hearing from you.

In the High Court of Justice	
Queen's Bench Division	
Claim No	
Applicant (including ref)	**Barking, Havering & Redbridge University Hospitals NHS Trust** **(2/RBT/B613-110396 (JHS)**
Respondent(s) (including ref)	1. **Darren Cunningham** 2. **Author House UK Ltd** 3. **Yellow Advertiser (owned by or licensed to Tindle Newspapers Limited)**

ORDER FOR AN INJUNCTION

Before the Honourable Mr Justice Roderick Evans

UPON hearing counsel for the Applicant, ex parte

AND UPON reading the witness statement of ▮▮▮▮▮▮▮ dated 13.05.09

IT IS ORDERED THAT:

PENAL NOTICE

Important:-

NOTICE TO THE 3rd RESPONDENT/PROPOSED 3rd DEFENDANT:

1   This Order prohibits you from doing the acts set out in part B of this Order. You should read it carefully. You are advised to consult a solicitor as soon as possible. You have the right to ask the court to vary or discharge this Order.

2   If you disobey this order, whether by your directors, officers, servants, agents or otherwise howsoever you may be found guilty of contempt of court and you may be sent to prison or fined or your assets may be seized. In the case of a corporate defendant, it may be fined, its directors may be sent to prison or fined or its assets may be seized.

3   Any other person who knows of this Order and does anything which helps or permits the respondent/ intended defendant to breach the terms of this

Order may also be held to be in contempt of court and may be imprisoned, fined or have their assets seized.

PART B: NOTICE OF ORDERS

An application was made by telephone to the Judge on 13.05.09 by Counsel for the Applicant. The judge read the witness statement of ▮▮▮▮▮▮▮▮▮▮ dated 13.05.09 and accepted the undertakings in Schedule 1 below and considered section 12 of the Human Rights Act 1998.

IT IS ORDERED that

1   The Third Respondents be restrained and prohibited from publishing or publicising the book "Joseph's Life story (Seeking Justice)" or any part thereof by any media article or description of the same howsoever until the further consideration of this Application by the Court at 10.30 on Monday 18 May 2009.

2   Costs reserved.

PART C: GUIDANCE NOTES

NAME AND ADDRESS OF PROPOSED CLAIMANT'S SOLICITORS

The Claimant's solicitors are ▮▮▮▮▮▮▮▮, 25 Fenchurch Avenue, London, EC3M 5AD.

INTERPRETATION OF THIS ORDER

1   In this Order the words "he" "him" or "his" include "she" or "her" and "it" or "its".

2   Where there are two or more proposed Defendants then (unless the contrary appears)

     (a)   References to "the Defendant" means to both or all of them

     (b)   An order requiring "the Defendant" to do or not to do anything requires each Defendant to do or not to do it.

3   Nothing in this Order shall prevent the use of information which is already in the public domain or which comes into the public domains after the making of this order otherwise than as a result of a breach of this order.

4   Nothing in this Order shall prevent the Defendant from supplying information to his legal advisers for the purposes of taking statements from potential witnesses for the purposes of these proceedings.

THE EFFECT OF THIS ORDER

1   A Defendant who is an individual who is ordered not to do something must not do it himself or in any other way. He must not do it through others acting on his behalf or on his instructions or with his encouragement.

2   A Defendant which is a corporation and which is ordered not to do something must not do it itself or by its directors, officers, servants, employees or agents or in any other way.

VARIATION OF DISCHARGE OF THIS ORDER

The Defendant (or anyone notified of this Order) may apply to the Court at any time to vary or discharge this Order (or so much of it as affects that person, but anyone wishing to do so must first inform the Claimant's legal representatives. [For the avoidance of doubt the Defendant may apply aforesaid without the need to show any change of circumstances.]

PARTIES OTHER THAN THE APPLICANT OR THE DEFENDANTS

It is a contempt of court for any person notified of this Order knowingly to assist in or permit a breach of this Order. Any person doing so may be sent to prison, fined or have its assets seized.

COMMUNICATIONS WITH THE COURT

All communications to the Court about this order should be sent to Room WG08, Royal Courts of Justice, Strand, London, WC2A 2LL quoting the case number. The telephone number is 0207 947 6009. The offices are open between 10am and 4.30pm on Monday to Friday.

SCHEDULE 1

Undertakings given to the Court by the Applicant/Claimant

1   If the Court later finds that this Order has caused loss to the Defendant (or to any other person served with or notified of the Order) and decides that the Defendant or such other person should be compensated for that loss, the Claimant will comply with any Order the Court may make.

2   The Claimant will issue the Application Notice in respect of the application made on 13.05.09 and a Claim Form and the Claimant will serve upon the Respondents/Defendants by 4pm on 15.05.09

      (a)   Copies of the Application Notice, the Claim Form and the witness statement of ▬▬▬▬▬ dated 13.05.09; and

      (b)   A copy of this order

3   Anyone notified of this order will be given a copy of it by the Claimant's legal representatives.

4   The Claimant will abide by any order of the Court to compensate for costs incurred by any person notified of the Order by the Claimant's legal representatives.

5   If this order ceases to have effect the Claimant will immediately take all reasonable steps to inform in writing anyone to whom he has given notice of this order, or whom he has reasonable grounds for supposing may act upon this order, that it has ceased to have effect.

In the High Court of Justice		Party:	Applicant
Queen's Bench Division		Initials & surname:	
		No. of statement:	██████████
		Exhibits marked:	PM-1
		Date made:	

Claim No	
Applicant (including ref)	Barking, Havering & Redbridge University Hospitals NHS Trust (2/RBT/B613-110396 (JHS)
Respondent(s) (including ref)	1. Darren Cunningham 2. Author House UK Limited 3. Yellow Advertiser (owned by or licensed to Tindle Newspapers Limited)

WITNESS STATEMENT

FULL NAME: ████████████████████

ADDRESS: C/o Barking, Havering & Redbridge University Hospital NHS Trust Legal Department

OCCUPATION: CLINICAL GOVERNANCE DIRECTOR

POSITION IN RELATION TO THE CASE: CLINICAL GOVERNANCE DIRECTOR

1   I am the Clinical Governance Director at Barking, Havering & Redbridge University Hospitals University NHS Trust ("the Trust").

2   I make this statement in connection with an application for an injunction to prevent the publication of a book entitled "Joseph's Life Story (Seeking Justice)", written by Darren Cunningham, the First Defendant, and published by the Second Defendant and an injunction to prevent publication by the Third Defendant of any article or media reference made to that book in its current form.

3   I do not seek an injunction against the book being published in principle but merely that publication of the book in its current form be stopped and that any copies of the said book that have already been printed be withdrawn and destroyed. I exhibit "the Book" at PM-1.

4   It will be seen that the book arises out of the death of Mr and Mrs Cunningham's son, Joseph. A claim was advanced by his parents and dealt with speedily by the NHS Litigation Authority without the need for a claim form to be issued. This process complied fully with the spirit and intention of the Civil Procedure Rules.

5   Specifically, I request that the Court orders that any reference to any members of Trust staff made in the book is withdrawn and replaced with their job titles. I also request that the book removes, in its entirety, a report prepared by ████████████, Risk Management Midwife, dated 09.04.07. The report can be found from page 161 onwards but it is then referred to substantially through the book. This report was prepared as part of the Trust internal complaints procedure and was disclosed solely for the purpose of the investigation of a claim for clinical negligence brought by Mr and Mrs Cunningham against the Trust surrounding the sad death of their son, Joseph.

6   I refer this Honourable Court to the provisions of CPR 31.22(1). It is my belief that this report was a confidential internal document disclosed to the Cunninghams' solicitors purely in order to fulfil the Trust's obligations under the pre-action protocol for clinical negligence actions. I can confirm that the document has not at any time been referred to or read out in a public court hearing and that the Trust does not agree to the document, or any other document disclosed, being used for any purpose other than that for which it was disclosed.

7   In accordance with CPR 31.22(2) the Court may make an Order restricting or prohibiting the use of a document which has been disclosed, (even where the document has been read to or by the Court, or referred to, at a hearing which has been held in public, which does not apply here). I am extremely concerned as to the welfare of all Trust employees and wish to avoid any harm they may suffer by their names being published in a book such as this, particularly if any criticism is levied at them. They are members of the healthcare profession and have to carry out their day-to-day work with members of the public who must trust and respect them. Publication of any unsubstantiated report, the contents of which they may or may not accept, could potentially harm them and their reputations.

8   Further, the document itself was part of the Trust internal investigation procedure. Such procedure is designed to ascertain what, if anything, went wrong with a patient's treatment and to ensure that lessons are learnt for the future. Without the protection of the Courts, there is real concern documentation such as this report may be freely published. This will significantly impinge on the Trust's ability to carry out such investigations in the future, as participants should be encouraged to be as open and honest as possible.

9   I therefore apply for an Order that the Court restricts or prohibits the use of the report, which has been disclosed for the purpose of the proceedings only.

     I also ask the Court to order that the publisher(s) of the book anonymise all references to members of Trust staff.

10   I believe that the facts stated in my witness statement are true.

Signed ....   Dated: ...12.05.09...........

By recorded delivery and by hand

Dear Mr Cunningham

BOOK BY DARREN CUNNINGHAM

Further to our letter of 14.05.09 enclosing a copy of the Court Order, we write to ask whether or not you would be willing to consent to amending your Book? If you do consent, this will avoid the costs of the injunction hearing on Monday 18.05.09.

We ask that you remove all members of Trust staff names and replace those names with their job titles.

We also ask that you remove the internal investigation report prepared by Evette Roberts and any references to it.

As we hope you will appreciate, it is in our interest to protect employees of the Trust and we are concerned that the Trust employees' privacy and confidentiality has been breached and to avoid this continuing, we ask that the Book is changed as detailed above.

We will also ask your publishers to remove existing copies of the Book in its current form and of course ask that you do the same. Any copies of the Book that have been printed in its current form should be destroyed and we ask that you consent to this.

Please contact us to discuss this matter as soon as possible and, if possible, ahead of the hearing listed for 18.05.09.

Thank you for your assistance.

Darren checked his e-mails and found he had received an e-mail from his publisher contact which went onto say that Authorhouse had been served with a court injunction today so had to put a stop on the book until it was resolved.

Several hours later Darren had finished work for the day and made his way home. That evening he explained to Charlotte what had happened, what effect the injunction had on the sale of the book and what needed to be done for it to go on sale again.

The Media Solicitor

Darren got into the office at 8:30 AM and wrote an e-mail to his solicitor Tim Lowles.

From: Darren Cunningham
Sent: 15 May 2009 08:38
To: Tim Lowles
Subject: RE: Your Book Josephs Life Story.
Sensitivity: Confidential

Tim,

I have discussed the matter with my wife who has played a big part in the construction of the book (as you can imagine) and she is disappointed that the NHS Trust are requesting for the report written by the Risk Management midwife to be removed. I understand that we will probably need to comply with removing it from the book but I feel that we should have the right to reference its existence even if we agree to remove and not to quote any part of its content.   I have a copy of the book with me so we can discuss this today.

I want to understand if the NHS Trust is also acting on behalf of Great Ormond Street Hospital where Joseph died or can we expect for a further injunction and another list of demands.

I plan to leave Canary Waft at 13:00 sharp and hope to be in your area within the hour so if it's convenient lets agree to meet at 14:00.

Thanks

Darren Cunningham

From: Tim Lowles
Sent: 15 May 2009 09:44
To: Darren Cunningham
Subject: RE: Your Book Josephs Life Story.
Sensitivity: Confidential

Thanks Darren,

We can discuss the report when we meet; it is difficult to advise without seeing the content of the same. As we discussed yesterday whilst you need not comply with all of their demands, not doing so is likely to protract this matter further.

Best regards,

Tim Lowles
Steeles Law
for Steeles (Law) LLP

At 10AM Charlotte had received an e-mail addressed to Darren from Rosamund and forwarded into on to him. Rosamund had also been contacted by the solicitors representing the NHS.

Subject: RE: Josephs Life Story
Date: Fri, 15 May 2009 10:01
From: Rosamund Rhodes-Kemp
To: Charlotte Cunningham

Dear Mr Cunningham
I have been contacted by the solicitor for the Trust and do not intend to attend on Monday.
Do you have a good Lawyer? You need a specialist in copyright and libel I think.
Hope you are ok
Rosamund

By 1 PM as planned, Darren had left the office and was on the underground, Jubilee line heading into the city. An hour later he arrived at the Steeles Law office and waited in reception for Tim to come down and meet him. A few minutes later Tim arrived, he introduced himself and led Darren into a meeting room and offered him a drink. Darren declined, sat down and they discussed the history of events. It soon became apparent that by putting up a fight it would be a difficult case to win and would result in expensive legal fees which were something Darren was keen to avoid. In order to make the situation go away, Darren would have to take steps to destroy copies of the book he had in his possession and request his friends and family to destroy their copy. If the book was ever to be republished it would have to be without the report written by the Risk Management midwife and with all NHS staff names removed even though it meant a lot of work.

Following the meeting Tim compiled the following letter as a reply on Darren's behalf to the NHS via their elected solicitors.

Steeles Law
Solicitors

By e-mail

15 May 2009

Dear Sirs

'Joseph's Life Story' ("the Book")

We are instructed by Darren Cunningham the author of the above named book.

We have been seen copies of your letters to our client together with the Order of Mr Justice Roderick Evans against Yellow Advertiser.

Amendments

Our client has no desire to become embroiled in unnecessary proceedings anymore than he is already.

In the circumstances we confirm our client will, subject to the terms of an agreed order, consent to:

1. remove all members of Trust staff names from the Book and replace those names with their job titles;

2. remove the internal investigation report prepared by ▬▬▬▬▬▬ from the Book and not to quote any content from the same. We do not believe your client can object to our client referencing the fact that an internal investigation took place. In any event see 3 below; and

3. provide your client with a copy of the amended book for its approval prior to making it available for purchase on the Authorhouse website, subject to that approval not being unreasonably withheld.

If the above is of satisfaction to your client please provide us with a consent order for our consideration.

Publicity

We are further instructed that our client has already provided an interview, together with a photo shoot, to the Ilford Recorder. Our client has contacted the newspaper in order to request that they do not publish the interview.

Please note our client gave the interview prior to being served with the order of Mr Justice Roderick Evans and provides this information to you in the spirit of full disclosure.

We look forward to hearing from you.

Yours faithfully

Steeles Law
for Steeles (Law) LLP

Once the meeting came to an end, Darren returned home and explained what he had agreed to in the meeting and the impact it would have on the book. Much to her disappointment she watched as Darren tore up 17 copies of the book which had been intended for friends and family and place them in an orange bin sack with other rubbish to be recycled. They then made a list of who they knew who had copies of the book and spent the rest of the evening making phone calls to explain the situation and to request to destroy their copies of the book. Everyone contacted was assured that once the book had been revised they would all receive a replacement, although it would not be for quite a few months. Darren would follow up by e-mail to everyone else he could not get in touch with by phone on Monday.

On Monday the 20th May the case was heard as planned in the High court of Justice located in London. Darren and the Publisher did not attend as they had both already come to an agreement. The Yellow Advertiser newspaper challenged the Injunction and the Judge ruled in their favor and had the injunction against them printing the story revoked. This meant that the NHS had to pay their legal costs of £1,000 plus VAT.

Order

In the High Court of Justice Queen's Bench Division	
Claim No	HQ09X02062
Claimant (including ref)	Barking, Havering & Redbridge University Hospitals NHS Trust 2/RBT/B613-148799(JHS)
1st Defendant 2nd Defendant	Darren Cunningham Author House UK Limited

BEFORE THE HONOURABLE MR JUSTICE OPENSHAW sitting at the Royal Courts of Justice, Strand, London WC2 on Monday 18th May 2009.

UPON HEARING Miss Jane Tracy Forster of counsel for the Claimant, the Defendants not attending and not being represented,

AND UPON the Claimant and First and Second Defendant agreeing terms of settlement

AND BY CONSENT

AND UPON THE FIRST AND SECOND DEFENDANTS UNDERTAKING THAT if they intend to republish and reprint the Book, "Joseph's Life Story – Seeking Justice" ("the Book") they do so in an amended form as specified below:

1   All names of any of the Claimant's employees, as referred to in the Book, be removed and replaced with each individual's job title. (Such employees to include all past and present employees of the Claimant and individuals connected with the Claimant NHS Trust).

2   Any republished and reprinted version of the Book shall have the report of ▮▮▮▮▮▮▮▮▮▮, Risk Management Midwife, dated 09.04.07 or any references to that report removed, with the exception that the Book may include reference to the fact that an internal report was produced.

3   The First and Second Defendant provide the Claimant with a draft of any revised version of the Book for the Claimant's approval before publication and

257

allow the Claimant a reasonable period of time to consider the Book before responding to the First and Second Defendant.

AND UPON THE CLAIMANT UNDERTAKING THAT if provided with an updated draft version of the Book for approval, it shall not unreasonably refuse the First and Second Defendants permission to publish the Book.

IT IS ORDERED that

1   The Book be immediately withdrawn from publication and that no further copies of the Book, in its current form, be printed.

2   The First and Second Defendants use their best endeavours to retrieve and then destroy all existing copies of the Book currently in circulation.

3   There be no order as to the costs of this application.

Dated this 18th day of May 2009

Order

In the High Court of Justice Queen's Bench Division	
Claim No	HQ09X02062
Applicant (including ref)	Barking, Havering & Redbridge University Hospitals NHS Trust 2/RBT/B613-148799(JHS)
1st Respondent 2nd Respondent 3rd Respondent	Darren Cunningham Author House UK Limited Yellow Advertiser (owned by or licensed to Tindle Newspapers Ltd)

BEFORE THE HONOURABLE MR JUSTICE OPENSHAW sitting at the Royal Courts of Justice, Strand, London WC2 on Monday 18 May 2009.

UPON the Applicant and the Third Respondent agreeing terms of settlement

AND BY CONSENT

IT IS ORDERED that

1 The Injunction Order made ex parte by the Honourable Mr Justice Roderick Evans dated 13 May 2009 be revoked.

2 The Applicant shall pay the Third Respondent's costs in the agreed sum of £1,000 plus VAT thereon of £150.00, making a total payable of £1,150.00, such sum to be paid within 28 days of this Order.

3 All further proceedings in this matter against the Third Respondent be stayed save for the purpose of implementing paragraphs 1 and 2 hereof.

Dated this 18th day of May 2009.

From: Cunningham, Darren
Sent: 20 May 2009 14:01
To: Martyn - Yellow Advertiser
Subject: Re: Josephs Life Story

Martyn,

Just as a nice to know, the publisher AuthorHouse will give me their full support to make the book amendments in order to comply with the injunction and then publish the book at no cost to myself.

Once the book is ready (and this may take many weeks to make corrections then I need the NHS to review and give consent to the changes) I will contact you again with the intention to place an ad in your paper.

Regards

Darren Cunningham

From: Martyn - Yellow Advertiser
To: Darren Cunningham
Date: Wed, 20 May 2009 14:19
Subject: Re: Josephs Life Story

That's nice to hear the publisher is helping you out. Like I said yesterday I appreciate your understanding regarding our legal battle and hope that the article we are putting in this week will make up for some of the disappointment.

Regards,

Martyn Dolton
Barking and Dagenham Reporter
Yellow Advertiser

From: Cunningham, Darren
Sent: 20 May 2009 14:20
To: Martyn - Yellow Advertiser
Subject: Re: Josephs Life Story

Martyn,

In order for myself to comply with the Injunction I am writing to request that you destroy the review copy of the book titled Josephs Life Story.

Darren Cunningham

From: Martyn - Yellow Advertiser
To: Darren Cunningham
Date: Wed, 20 May 2009 14:25
Subject: Re: Josephs Life Story

Hi Darren

We will destroy the book asap.

Regards,

Martyn Dolton
Barking and Dagenham Reporter
Yellow Advertiser

In the 21st of May edition of the Yellow Advertiser, the photo of Joseph was on the front cover with the headline 'FATHER'S BATTLE TO TELL JOSEPTH'S STORY'. The paper went onto tell the story of the book and the injunction placed upon it by the NHS. The story continued on pages 4 and 5 with a further photo of Joseph and another of Darren holding a copy of the book. There was also a photo of the editor holding a copy of the injunction. The story can be read by looking on the Yellow Advertiser internet web site and searching for Cunningham.

The NHS Legal Services Manager

In order to have the book 'Joseph's Life Story' republished, Darren would have to remove all the NHS staff names and replace them with their job titles and remove the 12 page report written by the Risk Management Midwife. Removing the report would be straight forward but replacing the staff names would need assistance from the NHS to provide the correct job titles. Darren wrote to the solicitor that represented the NHS requesting for a contact and the reason.

From: Darren Cunningham
Sent: 26 May 2009 12:22
To: NHS Solicitor
Subject: Joseph's Life Story

Dear NHS Solicitor,

Would you be able to provide me with a contact within the NHS that I could request the following:

1) A list of the Job titles for the names of employees of Barking, Havering & Redbridge University Hospitals NHS Trust that feature within the book so as to make the requested corrections accurately.

2) Confirmation on who within the Barking, Havering & Redbridge University Hospitals NHS Trust I should send the revised manuscript of the book Joseph's Life Story in order to review and consent prior to republishing.

Thank you.

Darren Cunningham

The NHS solicitor replied before 2 PM the same day giving the contact details for the NHS Legal Services Manager based in Queens Hospital in Romford Essex.

Darren wrote to the Legal Services Manager asking for the same information and before the end of the day received the following reply.

From: Legal Services Manager
Sent: 26 May 2009 12:22
To: Darren Cunningham
Subject: Joseph's Life Story

Dear Mr Cunningham

Thank you for your email.

I will arrange to provide you with a list of all the job titles of Trust employees, as per point 1 below, and hope to be in a position to forward these onto you as soon as possible.

With regard to point 2, I can confirm that the revised version should be sent directly to me.

Yours sincerely

Legal Services Manager

On the 28th May a letter arrived in the post from Steeles Law, the solicitor that Darren had used to assist with the Injunction. The letter enclosed an invoice for their services to the sum of £1,026.00 plus VAT. The actions of the NHS taking legal action had cost him £1179.90 in order to have legal representation. On the 31st May, Charlotte wrote out a cheque payable to Steeles Law and posted it.

From: Legal Services Manager
Sent: 29 May 2009 12:16
To: Darren Cunningham
Subject: FW: Joseph's Life Story

Dear Mr Cunningham

I write further to my email and now duly enclose a list of all the job titles of Trust employees named within the Book.

Yours sincerely

Legal Services Manager

From: Darren Cunningham
Sent: 29 May 2009 12:24
To: Legal Services Manager
Subject: RE: Joseph's Life Story

Dear Legal Services Manager,

Thank you for your prompt reply. As requested, the NHS staff names will be changed as agreed. I will then print a copy of the manuscript and forward onto you for your review.

I would like to take this opportunity to ask if the Trust would like to consider the following:

1) Release a statement in connection with Joseph's care to feature in the book to readers hear the Trusts point of view.
2) Consider issuing a letter of apology to Charlotte Cunningham in connection with the loss of her son Joseph.
3) Provide the complete set of MRI images that were taken of Joseph on 29th December 2006 in Queens Hospital.

Regards

Darren Cunningham

From: Legal Services Manager
Sent: 01 June 2009 12:33
To: Darren Cunningham
Subject: FW: Joseph's Life Story

Dear Mr Cunningham

I write further to your email below.

As discussed with regard to point 1 : the Trust is considering this issue and I will revert back to you as soon as I have obtained senior authority.

As discussed with regard to point 2 we believed that you had received an apology letter with the action plan that was associated with the Risk Management Report, which was disclosed to your Solicitors. When I received your email below it was clear you and your wife had not received this. On reviewing the file it appears that there has been an administrative error. The intention was that the letter of apology should have been sent via your solicitors. Unfortunately there appears to have been a miscommunication between the Trust and the NHSLA for which we sincerely apologise. The NHSLA equally wish to apologise for the delay in providing this letter of apology to you both. As agreed, I attach the Letter of Apology dated 18 July, 2008 and will also ensure that a copy is forwarded to Mrs Cunningham at your home address.

With regard to point 3: I can confirm that I have obtained a complete set of Joseph's MRI images that were taken on 28 December, 2006. The images are on a CD and I will send this today along with the Letter of Apology by recorded delivery. The CD contains all the images. Out of the 11, to access for example image 4 which contains 19 slices you double click on the image and scroll down to view the complete set. Should you have any problems viewing the scans then please do not hesitate to contact me.

I note that you have requested whether the letter of apology and action plan can be included in the re-draft of the Book. I will have to obtain senior authority on this point and hope to be a position to retort back to you as soon as possible on this matter.

Kind regards

Legal Services Manager

From: Legal Services Manager
Sent: 02 June 2009 10:24
To: Darren Cunningham
Subject: FW: Joseph's Life Story

Dear Mr Cunningham

I write further to my email below and can now confirm the Trust's position on point 1 below. We feel that it would be inappropriate for the Trust to release a statement into your personal account of Joseph's Life Story. However, thank very much for offering us the opportunity.

With regard to the Letter of Apology and Action Plan I can confirm that you have Trust authority for these to be included within the book but with staff names removed.

Kind regards

Legal Services Manager

The Letter of apology finally arrives

On Wednesday the 3rd June, a letter sent by recorded delivery arrived for Charlotte. She opened it and found a copy of the letter of apology that was originally sent to her dated nearly a year ago. The letter also contained an action plan which listed the failings that were found by the Risk Management midwife who had written the 12 page incident report (that had to be removed from this book). Along with the letters was a CD of Joseph's MRI scans. Charlotte put the CD to one side for Darren to look at once he came home from work in the evening. Charlotte read the letter again as it gave her some comfort confirming that Joseph's fate was not of her doing but was the outcome in the failure of care she and Joseph had received. She could not believe that a letter of such profound importance to a grieving mother was allowed to go astray.

BY RECORDED DELIVERY

Dear Mrs Cunningham,

I write further to my conversation with your husband today and subsequent email confirming the position with regard to the Letter of Apology in connection with the loss of your son, Joseph.

As explained to your husband today the Trust believed that you had received the signed Letter of Apology from the Chief Executive together with the enclosed action plan. It was clear following your husband's email of 29 May, 2009 that in fact you had not received it. On reviewing the file there appears to have been an administrative error and the intention was that the Letter of Apology should have been sent via your solicitors. There appears to have been miscommunication between the Trust and the NHSLA for which we sincerely apologise. The NHSLA equally wish to apologise for the delay in providing this Letter of Apology to you. As requested by your husband I now duly attach the Letter of Apology dated 18 July, 2008. The Trust would wish to reiterate that the offer of a meeting as stated in the Letter of Apology still stands.

I also attach a CD containing a complete set of Joseph's MRI images that were taken on 28 December, 2006.

Yours sincerely,

Legal Services Manager

18th July 2008

Mr. & Mrs. Cunningham
c/o Bolt Burden Kemp Solicitors
Providence House
Providence Place
Islington
London
N1 0NT

Queens Hospital
Rom Valley Way
Romford
Essex
RM7 0AG

Dear Mr. & Mrs. Cunningham,

Re: Charlotte Cunningham

I write in my capacity as Chief Executive on behalf of Barking, Havering & Redbridge Hospitals NHS Trust to offer my sincere apologies for the shortcomings in care that you received from the Trust on 22nd December 2006.

Whilst I acknowledge that words cannot change what occurred at Joseph's birth, I can understand the distress that you and your family have felt since his sad death. I would therefore like to offer you and your family my sincere condolences.

As you will see from the enclosed action plan, as a result of Joseph's death, the Trust has identified training issues and equipment required to prevent such an occurrence in the future.

Although this obviously cannot change what occurred I do hope that this goes some way to assisting your family during your understandable grieving process. However, if you would find it helpful, arrangements can be made with ██████████████, Director of Midwifery for you to meet to discuss any further issues you may have.

Once again I offer my sincere condolences on behalf of the Trust.

Yours sincerely,

John Goulston
Chief Executive

When Darren arrived home from work that evening he was pleased to learn that the letter had arrived and keen to see what was on the CD. He turned on his computer and put the CD into the drive and waited for the data to load. When it finally started, he was faced with the same images that he had seen from previous CDs he had received. His initial reaction was of disappointment but he recalled the comment made by the Legal Service Manager in the email sent on the 1st June. So with the aid of his mouse he started double-clicking on the images but it would only enlarge whichever of the 11 images was selected. What Darren wanted to see was the slices as mentioned in the email. It was too late in the evening to call the Legal Services Manager so continued to play around with the MRI image viewer program in the hope to figure it out. After pressing all the keys on the keyboard he eventually stumbled across the keys that he had been looking for, the Page Up and Page Down keys were used to cycle through the slices of each image. This he regarded as a break thought as he now had access to all the MRI images taken of Joseph on the 28th December 2006. Out of curiosity Darren loaded the original CD he had received to see if they also contained all the images. It took a few minutes to load the original CD and much to his annoyance the CD was exactly the same. If only a simple user guide listing a few basic instructions and the keys required to use the image viewer had been supplied with the CD in the first place it would have saved a lot of time and frustration.

Darren reviewed all the images trying to locate the 2 images that had been shown to him to try and explain the severity of Joseph's condition. Since he could recall the images clearly in his mind and the conversation he had with the Specialist Registrar which took place on the 27th January 2007, it took no time at all to pick them out.

The first image was a top down view of Joseph's head at eye level. The Specialist Registrar pointed to the 2 black marks as shown below circled in red. The black marks was dead brain tissue due to oxygen starvation and due to their location within the brain it was the probable cause for why Joseph was having breathing difficulties as the messages from his brain were not reaching his body correctly. The Registrar commented that this amount of damage and due to its location was typical of being starved of oxygen for about 10 minutes, any longer and there would have been further significant damage. Since the brain had been damaged it would not repair itself and may even get worse and prove fatal.

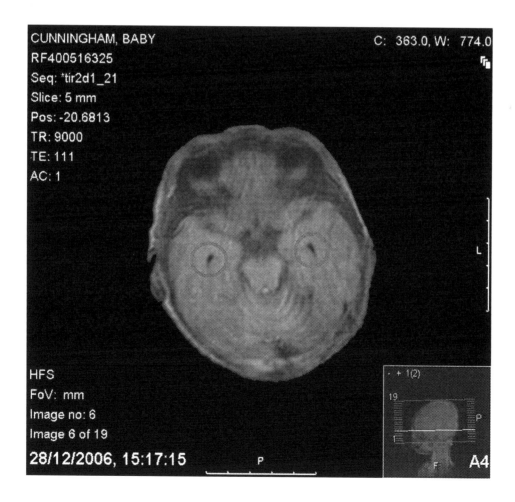

The second image to be reviewed was also a top down view of Joseph's head but higher up. The areas of the image that was brought to Darren's attention was where the two sides of brain met , there was signs of blood as shown below circled in red which was a cause for concern but again not unheard of for a traumatic delivery. Secondly the Registrar pointed to the swelling on the side of Josephs head circled in blue, he went onto say this was a result of a difficult delivery were the head had been under pressure. This in itself is not often life threatening and not usually a case of causing long term damage because a babies skull is not fused and the pressure is not to applied the brain. In such cases over time the swelling goes down.

It was the conversation with the Specialist Registrar aided with the two images that helped Darren realise that Joseph was seriously ill and was not going to get well. Switching off the ventilator was a difficult decision to make but he could not live the rest of his life on a ventilator. As much as he did not want to do it he knew it was the right thing to do.

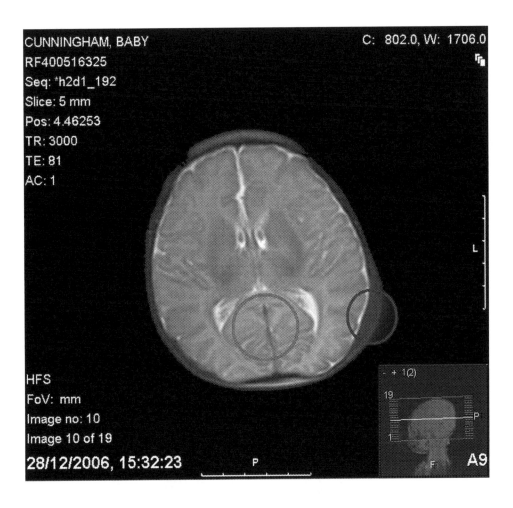

Later that evening Darren and Charlotte read the Action plan that had been set with the late letter of apology. The action plan had been written by the NHS staff following the findings of the 12 page report written by the Risk Management Midwife. Much to their surprise there was only 4 issues identified as in need of taking action which are as follows:

1) **Lack/incomplete use of tool for interpretation of cardiotocography.**

The recommendations and actions were that the maternity department was to ensure that all midwives and doctors attend weekly CTG/case reviews and yearly Drills & Skills.

- ➤ Consultant CTG sessions every Monday.

- ➤ Near Miss Meetings to conduct on CTG reviews in details.

- ➤ Weekly multi-professional CTG reviews at KGH and Queens.

- ➤ Clinical managers to allocate staff to attend session.

2) **Insufficient training on procedures. Normally applying fetal scalp electrodes.**

Staff need regular training on procedures. The maternity department is to ensure that all local inductions key procedures are incorporated. Maternity unit to ensure Drills and Skills incorporate clinical procedures.

- ➤ Midwives and doctors induction to include procedure for applying fetal scalp electrode.

- ➤ All midwives are to be trained and re-trained on venepuncture.

3) **Lack of resources: Fetal scalp electrode and accessories and fetal blood sampling kits and accessories.**

The Maternity unit is to have adequate compatible equipment on the labour ward. The maternity department is to ensure there are sufficient vital resources for the labour ward at KGH.

- ➤ Sufficient fetal blood sampling kits and accessories and a user friendly brand fetal scalp electrode and accessories to be ordered.

- ➤ Labour ward co-ordinators to devise a system for arranging and labelling equipment.

4) **Poor Standards of record keeping**

Need for raising record keeping standards. The maternity department must demonstrate that both doctors and midwives receive training in record keeping.

- ➤ All staff to undertake regular audit or records.

- ➤ Record keeping to be taught in the monthly Drills and Skills.

- ➤ Staff with a particular weakness in record keeping is to undertake the record keeping program.

- ➤ Regular record keeping sessions.

After discussing the four issues and the actions proposed, they decided that now was the time to meet with the NHS staff to discuss the incident and the issues. Darren could not believe that so many doctors and midwives that had came into the room during Charlotte's labour had all been incapable of understanding the readings from the cardiotocograph and realising Joseph was in trouble, were all incapable of escalating the situation to the consultant on-call, and none of them were capable of making the decision that a caesarean section was necessary.   Later that week, Darren sent an e-mail requesting if the invitation to meet with the Director of Midwifery was still on offer.   The reply was positive and a few days later a meeting was arranged for the date of the 18th September at 2:00pm. Darren and Charlotte spent the next few days reviewing documentation they had and making a list of questions that they wanted to cover during the meeting knowing it would likely be the only one time they would get to meet with the NHS to discuss Joseph. By the end of August a list of questions had been compiled and forwarded onto the Director of Midwifery to review and hopefully answer during the meeting.

The 18th September came around quickly. At 12:30 Darren and Charlotte left their house entrusting their daughter with her grandmother Carolyne. They took the bus and didn't speak as they travelled along the route they had taken every day to visit Joseph so many days ago. Charlotte eventually broke the silence when she came into view of the Queens Hospital entrance and commented that the last time they had visited the hospital was to see Joseph. They had arrived early so decided to get a drink and wait until 2pm. When it was time they went to reception, explained the purpose of their visit and moments later were met by the Legal Services Manager who took them into a room.   Darren and Charlotte introduced themselves to the Directory of Midwifery and the Clinical Governance Director and commenced the meeting.

The NHS Directors Meeting

Minutes of Meeting relating to the care of Joseph Cunningham

Location: Meeting Room 3, Trust Headquarters

Date: 18 September, 2009

Time: 2pm – 4pm

Present: Director of Midwifery

                    Clinical Governance Director

                    Legal Services Manager (minute taker)

                    Mr Darren Cunningham

                    Mrs Charlotte Cunningham

The meeting was opened and introductions made.

The Clinical Governance Director explained to Darren and Charlotte that the Trust was very sorry that it has taken almost 3 years for us to come to this point where we are having a meeting. She asked them to accept the Trust apologies that this has occurred. The Director of Midwifery advised that she has been Director of Midwifery since June 2007 and was therefore not in post when the incident occurred, but that she has knowledge of the case and is fully aware of the circumstances.

Darren explained the reasons behind why he had put the agenda of questions together prior to the meeting and gave a background of circumstances. In essence he advised that he and his wife had no option but to take the legal route for them to try and understand why things happened. This was due to the fact that whilst Joseph was in hospital no member of staff approached them to ask how they were doing and provide an explanation as to what had occurred surrounding the events of Joseph's birth. Darren explained that given this the only alternative and option they had was the legal route, however, even when matters progressed down this route all they received was a cheque in compensation but still no explanation. The Director of Midwifery acknowledged that the points Darren raised were very valid and that the lack of contact by the Trust was totally unacceptable. She advised that sadly in the field of Maternity one is never going to eradicate risk totally and there are times when admissions have to be made. She explained that in the last few months NHS London have changed the criteria of a Serious Untoward Incident (SUI) and when babies are born very ill. Every time that happens now this automatically triggers an investigation in order to find out what has happened. In addition there are now strict recommendations and protocols and when such an investigation is triggered the Trust would inform the parents of the same, the outcome of the investigation is shared and once completed the parents are then provided with a copy of the report.

Darren explained that he and his wife's experience was very traumatic for them. The Director of Midwifery advised that over the last 3-4 years in Maternity lessons are being learnt from such incidents and it would not be her expectation not to communicate with the parents. Darren stated that it was pleasing to know that this was now the case. However, the period of time that has elapsed has meant this information has been withheld from Charlotte, and in relation to Joseph, so she could be properly informed that the course of events that occurred were not within her control. The events were never explained to Charlotte to reassure her that there was nothing she could have done to prevent what occurred. Darren advised that they felt the members of staff looking after Joseph had already made their assessment of how he was going to turn out but unfortunately this was never disclosed to them. They were only told that Joseph was going to get better and therefore they felt let down by them as well, when this clearly was not the case.

Darren advised that he was pleased to hear that something good has come out of the case; however, The Director of Midwifery stated that whilst the Trust accepts this at the end of the day it does not bring Joseph back. Darren stated that in a way it was probably best that the meeting has been left until now as it is not so emotionally burdensome now and he and his wife have now come to terms with what occurred. He advised that the reasons for writing the book was to share the details of events with family and friends. It was also to highlight to other parents that you cannot guarantee things will go right every time, in addition to exposing how long the legal process can last. Darren explained that if anyone can learn from the book then it has paid off and those being aware of the process can save the sanity of parents. The Director of Midwifery explained that it also for staff to learn from the experience as well. Darren stated that the Trust's Risk Management report highlighted the truth of the events and it was therefore the intention to portray Joseph's story from both sides as well as to show members of the public that things have moved forward. He stated that it was therefore a shame that this had been asked to be removed in any re-draft of the book.

Turning to the Questions to be addressed the Director of Midwifery advised Darren and Charlotte that some of the answers to the questions may be similar but that each would be addressed.

1. **Given that each woman's labour is different – at what stage do you decide to forgo a natural delivery and opt for intervention? Depending on answer, ask why all the warning signs with Joseph were ignored and why a consultant wasn't informed to assess the situation and to decide if a caesarean section was appropriate.**

The Director of Midwifery explained that you can't answer this in terms of saying for example after 8-12 hours of a woman being in labour you intervene. She advised that there are guidelines as to when staff should intervene and these are 1) looking at the mother and whether the observations are normal or not, 2) the wellbeing of the baby with the monitoring of the baby's heart rate being the key issue. If there is anything out of sync with these two crucial points then that's the point in which one should intervene. So for example if a mother is 7-8cm dilated and been 12 hours in labour, progress has been ok, mother's observations and baby's heart rate are ok then you would allow this to progress, but nevertheless continue to review. However, if things begin to deviate from the normal and baby/mother become distressed the plan of care would change accordingly. The key is how people are thinking at the time, the decisions that they make, who they talk to, having a plan in place and ensuring the mother is informed of the same. The Director of Midwifery reiterated that you can't define that after 12 hours you have to intervene and at the end of the day it all comes to the condition of the baby and the mother. One has to take the whole picture into account but the Director of Midwifery acknowledged that in Charlotte's case there were clear earlier indicators when we should have bailed out and intervened. Darren accepted the variables involved and that there are not cut and dry guidelines.

The Director of Midwifery acknowledged that Charlotte's labour signs should not have been ignored and that the Trust's risk investigation had highlighted a number of problems. The Director of Midwifery explained that at the time various problems had been identified in the Maternity Department which required addressing and an external review was commissioned. The external review highlighted a number of issues which Charlotte's case depicts. Darren enquired whether this review was in the public domain and The Clinical Governance Director advised that the review had been discussed at Trust Board Level and as a result of the recommendations an action plan has been developed, which is constantly reviewed.

The Director of Midwifery explained that around December, 2006, just before the move from Harold Wood to Queens Hospital and just after the move a number of incidents occurred at the Trust that rang alarm bells. She advised that questions were asked and therefore this was why an external review was commissioned. She explained that the one of the issues highlighted in the report were around staffing levels of midwives and that the Trust became below par with anywhere else in London, coming within the bottom 3 with some other Trusts. There should be ideally 1 midwife to 28 births midwifes as a whole where as the Trust was operating on a ratio of 1 to 42. Darren advised that in Charlotte's situation they always had a midwife in attendance and they were never left unattended.

The Director of Midwifery advised that the review also highlighted a poor infrastructure on staff training. Now staff, from Consultant level down, receives yearly updates on CTG training and the Maternity Department has a robust training system in place to support staff and further increase their knowledge. The Director of Midwifery stated that in Charlotte's case protocols were not as robust as they should have been and the communication was poor. In addition, the case highlighted that staff were not up to date with their training but on the other hand they could not have been if it was not being provided. The Director of Midwifery reassured Darren and Charlotte there had been an extensive amount of work within the Trust to improve this, the ratio is now 1 to 32 for midwives, temporary staff are used as well as there being an increase in support workers to assist midwives. This in turn ensures that staff have protected training time without effecting the service. There has also been an increase in the number of hours of Consultant time on the Labour Ward and the Director of Midwifery informed Darren and Charlotte that the Trust has recently received funding for 4 more Consultant Obstetricians. This is turn ensures that junior doctors who are not as experienced are closely supervised. A training package has been devised and every month there is a protected 3 day training program, which incorporates topics such as fetal heart monitoring, record keeping. There are also skills and drills training, which is part of staff mandatory training, and regular updates are provided. In addition, there are also clinical decision workshops to ensure staff can demonstrate their training skills. The Director of Midwifery advised that this process does take time but now we currently have 80% of staff trained. The Director of Midwifery stated that it is the lack of such processes and systems that can unfortunately cause incidents to occur.

Darren enquired as to whether from 2006 to date there has been a reduction of cases similar to that of Joseph's. The Director of Midwifery stated that up until the beginning of August 2009 the Maternity Department risks had been on the Trust's Risk Register, which highlights to Executives the Trust's risks. One of those risks, she explained, where that staff were not interpreting babies' heartbeats correctly and that the outcomes of this were poor. In August this risk had been removed from the Risk Register. The Director of Midwifery advised that the level of incidents had decreased to such a level that the Risk could be removed; however, there unfortunately had been a glitch during two weeks in August which is being addressed within the Department. The Director of Midwifery advised that the Training program really established itself in 2008 and therefore the Trust is only now beginning to see the rewards in terms of the overall reduction of incidents.

The Clinical Governance Director advised that the Evening Standard newspaper are running a story of reporting of SUI's across London and that the Trust comes out second but that it is important to note this does cover all specialties as well as Maternity. The Clinical Governance Director explained that the Trust has a very open reporting culture so this is one of the reasons why our figures do look so high. The Director of Midwifery explained that the triggers for reporting an SUI to the Strategic Health Authority had until recently been such that any lady over 24 weeks and beyond whose baby dies would be classed as an SUI. The Director of Midwifery advised that it may appear that the Trust are failing when in fact most of the cases were not preventable.

The Director of Midwifery informed Darren and Charlotte that in terms of scrutiny the Healthcare Commission and Strategic Health Authority are monitoring the Trust closely and we have to report to them monthly on progress. In addition the Department of Health have monitored the Trust and its actions and we have recently been taken off their monitoring process, but nevertheless the Trust still has to provide them with regular feedback on progress. The Director of Midwifery stated that awareness has now increased within Maternity Services with the primary focus to ensure the safety of women and their babies. The Clinical Governance Director noted that sitting outside from Maternity as Clinical Governance Director she has seen that as a result of the increase in training provided staff morale and confidence has been boosted which is very positive and this impacts on the quality of care provided to patients. The Director of Midwifery advised that in the last 2 years to now be in an organisation that is receiving the investment required is good progress and the top priority targets for Maternity relate to safety and outcomes for mothers and their babies.

2. **The midwife who eventually delivered Joseph mentioned during labour that the hospitals Trust prides itself on its low caesarean section rate – surely that is the wrong attitude if it puts babies and mothers lives in danger. Surely what the Trust should be more concerned about is delivering healthy babies, not its league tables.**

The Director of Midwifery explained that she could understand why the midwife's statement may have appeared to come across wrong, but that the Trust does have a low caesarean section rate, however, this is not at the cost of the health of a mother and her baby. She explained the figures do vary across the months. The key points the Trust reviews is; 1) Whether the caesarean section was appropriate; 2) Whether there were women that should have had caesarean sections that did not. The Director of Midwifery explained that the Consultants now review every morning, looking back at caesarean sections performed over the previous 24 hours and address whether it was the correct decision, whether the correct people were involved and whether there were cases e.g. instrumental, ventouse deliveries where one should have performed a caesarean section. Darren advised he and his wife got the impression that the Trust would do anything possible to avoid performing a caesarean section. The Director of Midwifery stated that points 1 and 2 interlink and that if there is any risk to the mother and her baby then the Trust would perform a caesarean section. She described that back in the 70s and 80s there was a high caesarean section rate as at that time if a woman had not delivered by a certain time then a caesarean section would be performed. Now, one has to strike a balance between a natural delivery and when one needs to intervene. It was accepted in Charlotte's case that a caesarean section should have been performed.

3. **I would like to know if possible the percentage of full term babies born at King George in a mal condition. It is obvious from hearing about a baby born in King George by the name of Ammar who also suffered from oxygen starvation in 2005 that the Trust has not learnt from that experience otherwise Josephs outcome would have been a lot different.**

The Director of Midwifery advised that she could not confirm an exact percentage as the criteria has changed for babies delivered at King George Hospital. Women at the lower end of the risk spectrum would deliver at King George Hospital where as women with previous caesarean section, diabetes and medical problems would be considered high risk and deliver at Queens. The Director of Midwifery also stated that Consultant staff rotates within the Units, but that Queens is more intense in terms of workload when compared with KGH. Darren explained that he would like figures for 1) babies who have died 2) babies born severely disabled/brain damaged and for him and his wife to see that the figures have come down since Joseph's birth. The Director of Midwifery confirmed that she could obtain the figures for the Trust as a whole, but that the numbers have come down. Darren stated that this was a comforting factor in that something good has come out of Joseph's case and that the events have not been in vain. The case of Ammar could not be discussed for Data Protection reasons, Darren accepted this.

ACTION: The Director of Midwifery to provide figures requested above.

4. **What changes if any has the Trust made to ensure that other families do not have to suffer the loss of their baby?**

Addressed at point 1 above. Training and improvement of guidelines discussed. The Director of Midwifery stated that the Risk Management Report prepared was very good, however, there is now a very structured way of undertaking investigations and staff follow a template. The recommendations are logged and monitored. The Clinical Governance Director also advised that the investigations now highlight both good and bad practices. The Director of Midwifery informed Darren and Charlotte that the Department also has a Message of the Week circulation which is read out before every staff shift begins. This ensures lessons learnt can be disseminated effectively and also good practice highlighted. This has been very successful, in terms of good communication and ensuring feedback to staff. The Trust also has weekly meetings of Consultants and midwives, who review cases and incidents in the previous week and whether further investigation is required. The Director of Midwifery advised that even where there are no care management problems per se the Trust would still carry out an investigation if there are lessons that can be learnt. The meeting also identifies good practice as well.

5. **According to NICE guidelines 2001 the fetal heart is to be checked every 15 minutes with a Pinnards or hand held sonic aid during the first stage of labour. Why was this not done?**

The Director of Midwifery acknowledged that NICE guidelines were not followed and/or adhered too in Charlotte's case, which again emphasizes the lack of training provided to staff at that time.

6. **Why was the consultant obstetric registrar not contacted to inform them of slow progress?**

The Director of Midwifery explained that this depends on a individuals ability to be able to recognise the warning signs in the first place to alert them to the fact that senior advice should be sought, but that in order for this to occur the Department must have in place training and support to ensure that staff feel they have the ability to ask their seniors for assistance. At the time of Charlotte's case appropriate training was not in place for staff members. Darren explained that he and his wife got the impression that as it was near to Christmas (22 Dec) and staff did not want to disturb the on-call doctors. The Director of Midwifery advised that a written communication has been distributed to all staff from the Consultants that if they are unsure or unhappy no matter what level they are, they should call them directly. The Consultants, the Director of Midwifery explained, have taken ownership of this previous problem. The guidance has changed and now stipulates which cases they should be informed of and if this does not occur, the relevant staff member is questioned. Darren described that in their case when the Registrar walked in the midwife would turn into, 'air hostesses' and would take a step back but when the Registrar left the midwives would, 'switch on' again. He felt there was a sense of military authority and they got the impression the midwife would feel uncomfortable questioning a doctor. The Director of Midwifery stated that it is Registrars to understand that at the end of the day we are all here for the woman and her baby but that attitudes and perceptions have changed and now any level of staff can call the Consultant and/or Midwifery Manager on-call.

7. **When I had my waters broken there was signs Grade 1 to 2 meconium present and blood clots, why wasn't this a cause for concern and even after twenty minutes it was still seen to be draining?**

The Director of Midwifery explained that there are different levels of meconium, which dictates when intervention is required. So for example if this is coupled with deterioration in the baby's heartbeat then intervention is required. Darren explained that the midwives brought into the room the resusitaire, which Charlotte only thought was for a precautionary measure. The Director of Midwifery advised that if meconium is present in the water then a baby may aspirate and therefore the resusitaire is there to try and prevent that once the baby is delivered.

8. **A number of entries are illegible, have the members of staff who were involved in my care since reviewed their handwriting and deciphered what they wrote and can we have that missing information.**

The Director of Midwifery acknowledged that some of the handwriting was ambiguous and appalling, and that if Darren and Charlotte required any section to be translated she would be happy to arrange this. Darren confirmed that he would review the notes and come back to the Director of Midwifery with the relevant sections. The use of electronic records were discussed and the Director of Midwifery confirmed that the Trust was halfway there in terms of electronic records in respect to plans of care, however, maternity requires intensive documentation by midwives and at present if a midwife documented all the notes on a computer then this will take them away from and impact on the care provided to a mother and her baby.

9. **At 19.25 it was noted there was difficulty in locating a fetal heart rate, a small amount of fresh blood was seen vaginally with clots. Although the Obstetric Registrar carried out an examination and failed to document her findings why wasn't this cause for concern and a caesarean section considered?**

The Director of Midwifery advised that this comes down to the knowledge of the doctor, whether they have put together the picture as a whole and can recognise the severity. The Director of Midwifery explained that she could not answer why an individual did not do what was required but that if there was difficultly in locating the heart rate, coupled with the blood loss she would have expected the Consultant to have been called. She would expect the doctor to have had a conversation with the Consultant to either decide on whether there should have been a review in 2 hours time or whether a caesarean section should have been performed at that time. Darren advised that Charlotte's notes have been shown to numerous professionals who have all advised that Joseph should have been delivered before 2.30am. The Director of Midwifery stated that she agreed and that the Registrar should have been thinking about performing a caesarean section well before this time.

10. **When an FBS was carried out even against the parent's wishes this left Joseph with at least six one inch+ long lacerations on his scalp. This is believed to be excessive is there an explanation for this?**

The Director of Midwifery accepted that the 6 lacerations to Josephs' head was totally unacceptable and that either the person was not skilled in performing the FBS and/or they may have had poor visibility.

The Director of Midwifery advised that there is a light source that is attached to the tube, which is usually plastic. Darren advised that he recalled a steel tube was inserted but he could not recall a light being used. Darren explained that he did not expect there to have been six attempts, the Director of Midwifery agreed and advised this comes down to poor training and lighting. Darren stated that when he tried to explain his concerns to staff neither he nor Charlotte was offered any explanation. They did not know whether this had contributed to his current heath, which they later learnt that it did not, but they were not aware of this at the time. The Clinical Governance Director and the Director of Midwifery accepted this statement and the anxiety caused. Darren asked whether the insertion of the tube is meant to be as painful as it was for Charlotte. The Director of Midwifery advised that this depends from woman to woman as they all have different pain thresholds. The body's ability to cope is obviously lowered when a woman is in labour and the process can be uncomfortable. The Director of Midwifery said that it often helps if staff talk woman through the process. Darren stated that 3 attempts were made to insert the tube over a period of 10 minutes which he thought was excessive. The Director of Midwifery stated that a woman should be placed in stirrups from the outset to ensure easier access; however, Darren confirmed that Charlotte was not placed in the stirrups until the 3rd attempt. It was acknowledged that this could explain why the process was so painful for Charlotte.

11. **From 19.30 up until the time of his birth his heart rate was dangerously up and down on numerous occasions. Again why was there no consideration for a caesarean section?**

The Director of Midwifery explained that if the heart rate is tachycardic (too high) and there are differences and changes then this is a pre- warning. If there are then decelerations then you have to act quickly. Darren advised that he recalled asking the midwife managing the ward at the time to explain what was an acceptable heart rate and being informed between 110-150. Darren explained that he had these figures in his mind throughout Charlotte's labour and therefore when he saw the figures going up and down and alerted staff to this fact no one paid any attention to this. The Director of Midwifery confirmed that she would have expected action to have been taken by the Midwife and Registrar. Darren asked whether the staff involved with the labour are still employed the Trust and have received any training. The Director of Midwifery confirmed that the midwives are still employed and have received all the training. The doctor involved has since left the Trust as they would have been on rotation. The Director of Midwifery advised that there has been a real change in the way doctors are managed now; each doctor has their own supervisor who regularly reviews their competence. If there is any question as to a doctors' competence then they will receive increased monitoring and they will be taken off shifts, i.e. Night shifts where there are less senior staff present.

12. **At approximately 01.30am the Specialist Registrar examined Charlotte and stated to Darren and the Midwifery sister (who eventually delivered Joseph) that Joseph had not turned, but gave no explanation as to the risks that this placed on Joseph or if the situation was normal or not. Her decision was for Charlotte to start pushing and that she would return in an hour's time to re-examine Charlotte. Why was this not cause for concern and a caesarean section considered? It was apparent to the staff that Charlotte was set to experience a difficult delivery as the Midwifery sister had acknowledged that her colleagues were on standby and that she intended to press the emergency button once Joseph's head began to crown.**

The Director of Midwifery explained the occipito-posterior position, i.e. Baby on its back against mother's back with face looking up, **which** is an uncomfortable position. The Director of Midwifery explained that the pressure created by contractions usually causes the baby head to rotate against the cervix; however, if the application is uneven then the process can be laborious. The Director of Midwifery informed Darren and Charlotte that her labour was not plotted well. Darren recalled that Joseph was born with his face up, Charlotte had a long labour and Joseph's shoulders were difficult to deliver. The Director of Midwifery confirmed that the occipito-posterior position of the baby is not a reason for performing a caesarean section alone so long as the mother and baby are doing well. She advised that it can cause a longer labour but that if the baby stays in that position, there has been a prolonged labour with poor progress and augmentation then you would consider a caesarean section. The Director of Midwifery confirmed that Charlotte had other combining factors that warranted earlier intervention.

Charlotte advised that they knew Joseph was a big baby as she had had a private scan which she did insert into her maternity notes. The Director of Midwifery stated that most shoulder dystocia cases are unpredictable but they can be managed as there are a certain set of manoeuvres staff go through to release the baby's shoulders when they impact behind the pelvic bone. This is covered in the Skills, Drills training provided to staff and if for example a woman has had a difficult delivery in the past then an appropriate plan is considered. The Director of Midwifery noted that staff did in Charlotte's case undertake the appropriate manoeuvres. Darren advised that he got the impression from the staff reactions that it was not planned and he recalled hoards of people coming into the room. He specifically recalled that the midwife pulled on Joseph's neck very hard and that he felt that Joseph's head was in danger, Charlotte was then flattened down on the bed and her stomach was pushed, which then released Joseph. The Director of Midwifery confirmed that this was a resuscitative manoeuvre as it is an emergency procedure and that in 90% of cases these manoeuvres are successful.

13. **At 02.30am the emergency buzzer was pressed and no less than five people rushed into the room to assist. If the situation was that grave, why was this not avoided by performing a caesarean section?**

see 12 above

14. **Once Joseph had been delivered he was suspended while the midwife cut the cut before handing him over to her colleagues at the resuscitation trolley even though he was not breathing. Why was it so important to cut him from the cord which took several minutes rather than attend to his breathing difficulty as a priority to avoid further oxygen starvation?**

Darren explained that he felt that Joseph's body was held aloft for some time whilst the cord was being cut. The Director of Midwifery stated that one has to cut the cord to separate mum from baby but that this should only have been for a couple of seconds at most, not minutes. The cord is clamped and cut and the baby taken to the resusitaire. The Director of Midwifery noted that Joseph would have been taken to resusitaire and the staff go through various motions in order to stimulate the baby. Sometimes the warmth and stimulation alone is enough to rouse the baby, or extending the head and if these stages do not work then one proceeds to bag and oxygen. Darren advised that he recalled there being a man and woman and that the man appeared to be more concerned with the heating and dials on the resusitaire. The woman, he recalls, was checking Joseph's reflexes and that when he did start breathing it was erratic. He stated that it bewildered him why no effort was made to get Joseph breathing by then. He and his wife have learnt that there are a number of indicators in Joseph's case which indicates to them that if an experienced person had been involved then the outcome would have been so different. The Director of Midwifery said this was a fair judgement, she could not comment for certain whether the outcome would have been different. Darren stated that if the care had been optimum after Joseph's delivery he may have lived and he did think there was room for improvement in the care provided after delivery.

15. **Once Joseph was handed over to the resuscitation trolley it was noted by the father that little effort was being made in order to assist Joseph with his breathing for the first five minutes.**

During this time they were testing his responses and reflexes for example by lifting his arm and letting it fall to his side. It was evident from his colour that being blue, that he was in need of oxygen. Eventually after 5 minutes they inserted a tube into his airway; unfortunately this was too late for Joseph. What is the correct procedure to assist a child under Joseph's circumstances to avoid oxygen starvation?

See 14 above.

16. **One of the first lines of HIE cases is to restrict fluids to avoid exacerbating cerebral swelling. There are records dated the 25th and the 29th December of Joseph's bladder being full but with no urinary output, a catheter was inserted but was later not found to be correctly sited in the bladder. In light of Joseph's severity, why was this overlooked, placing Joseph in further danger?**

The Director of Midwifery reviewed Joseph's medical notes in relation to his bladder. She noted that his bladder was distended and a scan was therefore performed. Joseph was catheterised but that on a subsequent scan the catheter was identified as not being correctly sited. On compression, however, a flow of urine was passed and therefore the management plan was for intermittent bladder decompression rather then re-catheterising Joseph. The Director of Midwifery advised that this was the plan according to the notes. Darren stated that staff failed to pick up that the catheter was not in the right place for some time and that this could also have had a significant effect on his health. He and his wife were so aware of Joseph's personal circumstances and the care after his birth, and thus do question whether if it was primary then this may have affected the outcome. The Director of Midwifery explained that the Risk Investigation concentrated on the Labour not the ITU care however, we are learning as indeed the Trust now undertake combined investigations looking at both the labour and neonatal care. The Director of Midwifery advised she is not a neonatal expert but that reviewing the notes if a baby is distended and catheterised and the levels of urine output are still inadequate then you would escalate this rather than leaving it. You would look at whether there is some form of checking process / check list in place to ensure that it had been correctly sited. Darren stated that there were a number of examples of such incidents and described one occasion where a tube had been incorrectly sited into Joseph's lung and he was fed milk. Immediately his heart rate fell and when the milk was stopped his heart rate increased again. The Director of Midwifery advised that should they require a Consultant to answer questions on either the labour or neonatal side she would be very happy to arrange this.

Additional notes:

Darren thanked the Director of Midwifery and the Clinical Governance Director for taking the time of going through the questions with him and his wife. He explained that he takes comfort that Joseph should have been a caesarean section, which is what he and his wife have thought all along. The Director of Midwifery explained that we can never eradicate errors 100% but it is about reducing the levels to as low as we can and monitoring Maternity services more robustly than they have been in the past. Darren confirmed that he would clarify the illegible notes and query with the records. The Clinical Governance Director explained that if Darren and Charlotte want to come back for a further meeting, i.e. with a consultant then they are very welcome too and that this can be arranged.

Darren advised that the Letter of Apology from the Chief Executive explained what had occurred, together with the action plan, and if that had been received when it was dated then it would have taken a considerable amount of pressure away from Charlotte in terms of knowing that the circumstances were not within her control. The Clinical Governance Director explained that when the Legal Services

File was reviewed the Letter of Apology had been sent to the NHSLA for onwards transmission to Darren and Charlotte via the Solicitors but that this did not occur. Darren enquired as to whether in the future the Trust could request an acknowledgement from the Claimant's Solicitors that the Letter of Apology has been received. The Clinical Governance Director stated this could be followed up.

Darren stated that it was just a shame the unanswered questions have taken so long to be answered and that the conversation today did not occur earlier. He stated that if he and his wife had been communicated with and offered a meeting from the outset it would have made a massive difference. They would have accepted the invite had it been offered at that time.

The meeting concluded and it was agreed that the minutes would be prepared and forwarded to Darren and Charlotte. A copy of the minutes as above was sent in the post dated the 14th October. Although there was action items as a result of the meeting the NHS did not provide the promised information at a later date.

To summarize - the reason given by the Director of Midwifery for Josephs fate was due to the qualified midwives and doctors for not having the necessary training to deal with the events that occurred. The reason the midwives had not attended the necessary training was explained as due to a lack of midwives available to allow any of them to be released to attend training courses.

With the minutes of the meeting from the discussion with the NHS Directors entered as the final chapter, it brings the story of Joseph to an end once again.

This book is dedicated to the memory of Joseph and his loving mother Charlotte.

APPENDIX A:
Friends and Family – Who's who

Family

Below are some of the family members who have been mentioned in Joseph's life story and how they are related to Joseph's parents (Darren and Charlotte).

Name of Family Member		How they are related to the parents
Heather	Conde	Darren's sister
Janine	Cunningham	Darren's sister
Daniel	Cunningham	Darren's son from a previous relationship
Carolyne	Cunningham	Darren's mother, also known as Nanny Boo.
John	Cunningham	Darren's father
James	Conde	Married to Heather, Darren's brother-in-law
Lauren	Conde	Heather and James's daughter, Darren's niece
Rachael	Blackborow	Darren's daughter from a previous relationship
Susie	Williams	Darren's Auntie, Darren's father's sister – no blood relation to Charlotte
Norman	Williams	Charlotte's Father
June	Williams	Charlotte's Mother
Wayne	Williams	Charlotte's Brother
Louisa	Penlington	Charlotte's Sister
Gareth	Penlington	Charlotte's Brother-in-law
Teresa	McKenna	Charlotte's auntie, Charlotte's Mother's Sister.
Leon	McKenna	Charlotte's cousin
Dennis	Oldfield	Darren's Uncle, Darren's father's brother-in-law
Jacqueline	Oldfield	Darren's cousin

Friends

The friends who were close to Joseph's parents and their relationship are listed below:

Name of Friend	How they are known to the parents
Sandra and David Burns	Neighbours
Linda and Monica Hartwell	Linda was Charlotte's Manageress while Charlotte worked for the Antony Nolan Trust. Monica is Linda's sister.
Andrea Mcfadden	Darren and Charlotte attended a training course for expecting parents and Andrea was the midwife who ran the course they attended.

APPENDIX B:
The Family Tree

The ancestor diagram below features the relations to Joseph and his parents of which many have been mentioned in Joseph's life story.

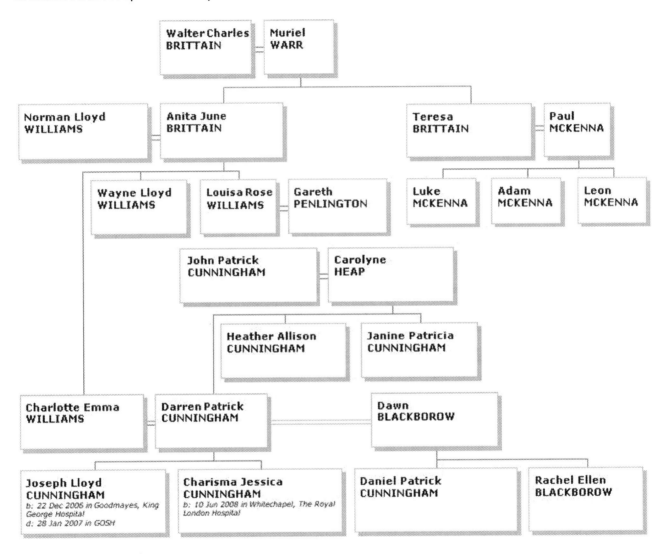

The diagram is only a fraction of the known family as Darren was inspired to learn of his family history after hearing tragic family stories of babies dying soon after birth. To date Darren has recorded over 470 individuals covering his own and Charlotte's ancestors, 111 marriages, recorded over 100 different surnames, and traced ancestors as far back as 1652.